# National Parliaments as Cornerstones of European Integration

**EUROPEAN MONOGRAPHS**

*Editor-in-Chief Prof. Dr. K.J.M. Mortelmans*

1. Lammy Betten (ed.), *The Future of European Social Policy* (second and revised edition, 1991).
2. J.M.E. Loman, K.J.M. Mortelmans, H.H.G. Post, J.S. Watson, *Culture and Community Law; Before and after Maastricht* (1992).
3. Prof. Dr. J.A.E. Vervaele, *Fraud Against and Community: The Need for European Fraud Legislation* (1992).
4. P. Raworth, *The Legislative Process in the European Community* (1993).
5. J. Stuyck, *Financial and Monetary Integration in the European Economic Community* (1993).
6. J.H.V. Stuyck, A.J. Vossestein (eds.), *State Entrepreneurship, National Monopolies and European Community Law* (1993).
7. J. Stuyck, A. Looijestijn-Clearie (eds.), *The European Economic Area EC–EFTA* (1994).
8. R.B. Bouterse, *Competition and Integration—What Goals Count?* (1994).
9. R. Barents, *The Agricultural Law of the EC* (1994).
10. Nicholas Emiliou, *The Principle of Proportionality in European Law* (1996).
11. Eivind Smith, *National Parliaments as Cornerstones of European Integration* (1996).
12. Jan H. Jans, *European Environmental Law* (1995).

# National Parliaments as Cornerstones of European Integration

Edited by

Eivind Smith

KLUWER LAW INTERNATIONAL
LONDON THE HAGUE BOSTON

Published by Kluwer Law International
Sterling House
66 Wilton Road
London SW1V 1DE
United Kingdom

Sold and distributed in the USA and Canada
by Kluwer Law International
675 Massachusetts Avenue
Cambridge MA 02139
USA

Kluwer Law International incorporates
the publishing programmes of
Graham & Trotman Ltd,
Kluwer Law & Taxation Publishers
and Martinus Nijhoff Publishers

In all other countries, sold and distributed
by Kluwer Law International
P.O. Box 85889
2508 CN The Hague
The Netherlands


First published in 1996

ISBN 90 411 0898 X

British Library Cataloguing in Publication Data and Library of Congress
Cataloging-in-Publication Data is available



Typeset by BookEns Ltd, Royston, Herts.
Printed and bound in Great Britain by Athenaeum Press.

# Contents

# Preface

In June 1995 I had the pleasure of organising a conference at the Faculty of Law of the University of Oslo on 'National Parliaments as Cornerstones of European Integration'. It was organised as part of the LOS research programme of the Norwegian Research Council in collaboration with the Department of Constitutional Law at the University of Oslo and the COST A7 (Evolution of Rules for a European Single Market) Management Committee.

The conference originated from my own research in the field of constitutional and extra-legal norms regulating parliamentary action, as well as from my interest in the role of *popular sovereignty* in a European context where so-called *national sovereignty* appears to be fading.

Since Norway did *not* become a member of the European Union from 1995, it may seem strange – at this time and in this country – to study the role of national parliaments in the perspective of European integration. But the conditions for discussions on fundamental questions of a general character are often better well away from noisy electoral campaigns – like that which took place in Norway prior to the November 1994 referendum – than in the middle of them. And there are a number of reasons for not regarding the outcome of the referendum as fatal in this respect.

If the role of Parliaments is vital for the future of democracy in Europe, even the subject of this book is vital for the future of a large number of well established systems of representative government. Different forms of international cooperation more or less strongly influence the faculties of national parliaments to fulfil the tasks traditionally conferred upon them within their own national borders. Moreover, supranational cooperation, as developed in Western Europe over the last decades, has given rise to growing concern about the conditions for democracy even at supranational level. This concern quite obviously deserves attention within not only what is called the European Union, but also in the surrounding world – including the European Economic Area, of which Norway is after all a member. In the absence of genuine 'democracy' at European level, to what extent can the concern be properly met through reference to national parliaments as democratic cornerstones of European integration?

The volume has been compiled from papers that scholars in public law and political science delivered at the conference and afterwards revised. I thank them all for interesting written as well as oral contributions. Thanks also to the Members of Parliament who contributed to the discussions in such a lively manner and to Mr Patrick N Chaffey for his efforts regarding the English form of texts delivered by authors whom English is not the natural language.

I am most indebted to the institutions and persons whose support made the conference possible.

*Eivind Smith*

# Notes on Contributors

**Frank Burmeister** is Academic Assistant at the Department for Public and Community Law, University of Hamburg.

**Louis Dubouis** is Jean Monnet Professor at the Faculty of Law and Political Science, University of Aix-Marseille (Aix-Marseille III). On European law, he has published in *Revue trimestrielle de droit européen, Revue française de droit administratif* and *Revue de droit sanitaire et social.*

**Sverker Gustavsson** is Associate Professor at the Department of Government, Uppsala University. His publications include works on research policy, welfare state theory and European integration. He is currently working on a book on supranationalism and democratic accountability in the European Union.

**Meinhard Hilf** is Professor at the Department for Public and Community Law, University of Hamburg. He is a former Member of the Max-Planck-Institute for Foreign Public and International Law (Heidelberg) and of the Legal Service of the EC-Commission (Brussels) and he is Legal Advisor to the Institutional Committee of the European Parliament. Professor Hilf is the author of multiple publications on EC-law as well as on Public International Law.

**Jørgen Albæk Jensen** is Associate Professor at the Department of Public and International Law of Aarhus University. His publications include *Parlamentarismens statsretlige betydning* [*Parliamentarism and Constitutional Law*] (1989) and *Politiske partier i amerikansk forfatningsret* [*Political Parties in American Constitutional Law*] (1991).

**Colin R Munro** is Professor of Constitutional Law at the University of Edinburgh, where he has taught public law since 1990, following appointments at the Universities of Birmingham, Durham, Essex and Manchester. His publications include *Studies in Constitutional Law* (1987).

**Philip Norton** is Professor of Government, and Director of the Centre for Legislative Studies, University of Hull. He is also President of the Politics Association in the UK. His publications include 20 books, among them *The British Polity* (now in its 3rd edition), *The Constitution in Flux, Legislatures, Does Parliament Matter?* and *The Commons in Perspective.*

**Joël Rideau** is Jean Monnet Professor at the University of Nice-Sophia Antipolis and member of the Institut universitaire de France. His publications include: *Droit institutionnel des Communautés européennes* (1994), *Code de procédures Communautaires* (1995) and *Droit des communautés européennes* (1995).

**Fredrik Sejersted** is Research Fellow at the Centre for European Law, University of Oslo. His publications include *Vedtaksprosessen i EF's konkurranserett* (1994) and *EØS-rett* (1995, in collaboration).

**Eivind Smith** is Professor of Public Law at the University of Oslo and Director of Research (Norwegian Research Council) at the Institute of Social Sciences (Oslo). His publications in the field of domestic and comparative public law include *Les droits de l'homme dans le droit national en France et en Norvège* (ed.) (1990) and *Høyesterett og folkestyret* (The Supreme Court and Democracy) (1993).

**Öyvind Österud** is Professor of International Conflict Studies and Head of the Department of Political Science, University of Oslo. His publications include a comprehensive textbook in political science and a monograph on nationalism.

# Part I

# Introduction

# Introduction: 'Sovereignty' – National and Popular*

*Eivind Smith*

## 'Union'

The European Union was created by the treaty signed in Maastricht (Netherlands) on 7 February 1992. It is based upon the pre-existing (and still existing) European Communities. Together with the 1957 Treaty of Rome and other instruments, the Treaty on European Union confers wide powers upon the Union's organs. But those powers have quite heterogeneous effects on the sovereignty of the member states.

A certain number of them are of a traditional, inter-governmental type; this is so for instance with respect to the Union's tasks regarding police and foreign affairs. Others are supranational in the sense of limiting the national sovereignty of the parties. Most of the latter powers exist within the framework of the European Communities. The Economic and Monetary Union which, according to the Maastricht treaty, shall be established by the end of the century, would no doubt represent a considerable step further in that same direction. But it is still the case that important aspects of the powers conferred by the Treaty on European Union are not of a genuinely supranational character.

* An abridged version of this text has been published in *Harvard International Review*, Vol. XVII, No. 3, 1995 on sovereignty, at pp. 12–14 and 71–72.

Like human beings, states that – in good faith – engage in close and long-lasting, treaty-based cooperation will have to realise, however, that their ability to act in a really independent manner, at home as well as internationally, will be closely affected by such relations. Their sovereignty *de facto* will be affected to the same extent. In this respect, the European Union is exceptional only as far as it may be said to be more ambitious or far-reaching than any other set of contemporary instruments of international cooperation.

As a matter of fact, it is easy to mention other examples of far-reaching international engagements with more or less similar effects on the political or financial freedom of action of governments (WTO, UN, NATO, the European Economic Space, and so on). Even for its own, at present 15 member states, the European Union just carries one set among hundreds of treaty-based, international, regional or bilateral fetters on their freedom of action. But it nevertheless remains exceptional in the way just mentioned.

## 'National Sovereignty'

In order fully to understand the specificity of the cooperation within the EU, therefore, we should not content ourselves with highlighting effects on governmental action that a close formal and personal relationship between governments and national representatives at many levels is always likely to have. Neither should we stop at pointing out the circle of mutual dependence to which any system – including this one – is likely to lead. We will also have to recall some fundamentals regarding the inherited notion of national sovereignty.

By tradition, a state is 'sovereign' as far as it is sole master of its own affairs, at home as well as with respect to which engagements to accept *vis à vis* other states. Of course, the faculty of engaging in international agreements has no sense unless it is used to limit the freedom of action – at home or internationally – of the contracting parties. But they are free to decide which obligations to take upon themselves. They are also free to decide to withdraw, according, of course, to the limits to that freedom which may be established by each particular treaty (notification a certain time before withdrawal, and so on). In this respect, the sovereignty of the contracting parties is safe.

It is safe at least formally, for a state to feel *more or less free* to stay away from binding engagements with neighbours or at multinational level. And even more it would often – politically, economically or otherwise – be difficult for a country to withdraw from a given treaty before arrangements to that effect had been duly negotiated between the contracting parties. The *salonfähigkeit* of a country might suffer severely, for instance, from that country's withdrawal from the Council of Europe Human Rights instruments in order to protest against judgments of the European Court of Human Rights. And unilateral withdrawal from membership of the European Union might easily turn out to be destructive for the economy of a state (and, politically, for the institutional set-up as a whole).

It has been argued, by the way, that in the long run severe constraints upon the parties may have counter-productive effects on the stability and internal peace of the Union as a whole. The basic idea is close to the commonsense observation that anybody who has the feeling of having lost personal freedom may be tempted to break out – if necessary by dramatic action. We thus see that the relationship between freedom and obligation in European affairs is closely related to the degree of popular acceptance of European integration to which I will soon return.

## 'Supranationality'

For reasons that will have emerged, the importance of formal sovereignty should not be overestimated in a world of manifold political and financial constraints upon most countries. But the recourse to genuinely *supranational* means of decision-making nevertheless remains one of the most distinctive features of the EU. Few would deny that this part of European integration goes directly into the core of the inherited notion of *national sovereignty*.

We meet the supranational character of this part of European integration, first, in the fact that important parts of EC market regulations apply directly in the domestic law of the member states without having to be accepted by competent, national authorities. *A fortiori,* we meet it in the pretension of EC law of having priority over every norm within the domestic legal order of each member state. This pretension flows primarily from the jurisprudence of the EC Court of Justice, by which it is constantly reinforced. And it has never been invalidated by political decisions with binding effect upon the Court of Justice (ie by formally amending the 'constitution', see below).

The supranational character of the EU will be strongly reinforced when – or if – the Economic and Monetary Union as prescribed by the Maastricht treaty comes into force. As pointed out by the French constitutional council (the *Conseil constitutionnel*) on 9 April 1992, the monopoly of 'making money' is one of the main attributes of sovereignty: the decision describes the coming into force of the 'third phase' of the Maastricht treaty as a loss of parts of the essential conditions for the exercise of sovereignty (*'les conditions essentielles d'exercice de la souveraine nationale'*).

From a legal point of view, the very core of the supranational character of European integration lies in the aspects of the EU system just mentioned. This is so already with regard to the power of international organs to adopt binding measures with respect to the member states without their prior consent in each case, as needed according to the inherited system of decision-making by mutual consent (ie by treaty).

Even more is it so when it comes to the obligation of national authorities – of which the judiciary is no exception – to obey community 'legislation' even in cases where this is in conflict with domestic legal norms. As we have seen, one of the basic criteria of national sovereignty is the privilege of each government to have the last word regarding norms to be applied within its own jurisdiction.

The opposition between 'sovereignty' and 'integration' becomes vital when the doctrine of priority for EC law is to be applied against national legal norms of a *constitutional* rank. For obvious reasons, this part of the doctrine is controversial already when it comes to the sovereignty of Parliament as the fundamental norm within the British 'constitutional' system. Is it really possible, without giving it up – and thus entering into some form of revolution – to combine the doctrine of Parliament's formally unfettered freedom of action with a legal hierarchy of the present EC type?

In none of the other member states do we find a pretension of full sovereignty for Parliament similar to that of the British 'constitution'. As a matter of fact, the other constitutional systems of the EU countries are formally based upon written texts that make Parliament a *constituted* power with freedom of action only within the limits actually set out by constitutional provisions. The majority of them even live under constitutions where one system or another of judicial review of the constitutionality of statutory enactments effectively operates.[1]

In such situations, the introduction of EC law as part of the domestic legal order does not give rise to problems similar to those met by the British legal system; at least, their written constitutions may be amended in order to enable EC law to operate as part of the domestic legal and political system. But even the latter countries will invariably have to reconcile their hierarchical legal order with the priority EC law pretends to have.

As far as the priority doctrine applies only to domestic legal norms of infra-constitutional rank, no problem arises, at least

[1] With the United Kingdom, Finland and the Netherlands offer examples where this is not the case.

formally. As we have seen, each constitution-making power may consent to the introduction of such elements. Each constitution may also be amended in order to *re*-confer power to adopt norms superior to EC law to domestic state organs. In the two cases, the last word remains with the national constituent power itself.

On the other hand, the priority doctrine applies in principle, as it currently stands, to every part of the domestic hierarchy of legal norms. It also seems evident that the possibility of effective integration might be severely affected if each of the member states were free to block the applicability of (parts of) EC law simply by amending its own constitution. But even the sovereignty problem quite evidently remains: If the national constitutions – be they written or not – could be violated (or even formally amended) by the EC 'law-maker' without the consent of the relevant constitution-making powers, could the member states really claim to be sovereign any more? A negative answer seems unavoidable.

No surprise, therefore, to find more or less explicit provisions in national constitutions that seek to block the transfer of powers to adopt constitutional amendment to the EU.[2] No surprise either that constitutional judges in some of the member states have found opportunities to express themselves along similar lines. The decision of 12 October 1993 by the Federal Constitutional Court of Germany (the *Bundesverfassungsgericht*) on German membership in the Treaty on European Union is just one of those decisions (but certainly the most famous one).

The relative infrequency of such decisions may seem more surprising than the mere fact that they have appeared. Among the reasons we may briefly enumerate are first, that the *institutional* set-up of the EU has generally been constitutionalised in each member state at the time of its joining the different instruments; second, the Court of Justice of the Community has developed a system of *principes généraux de droit* that is likely to avoid most conflicts with provisions concerning *fundamental rights* in each of the national constitutions. This system, that *petit à petit* has become a part of the famous *acquis communautaire*, is likely to reduce the possibility of conflicts in the future.

Practical problems may nevertheless occur. At least, we may certainly expect that from time to time national representatives will take advantage of alleged constitutional barriers when negotiating possible steps towards closer integration. And as a matter of principle, the task of reconciling the doctrine of priority of EC law with the superiority of national constitutions as the final test of

2 See for instance Art. 20 of the Danish Constitution and Art. 93 of the Constitution of Norway.

national sovereignty remains: to what extent could effective integration be secured without violating the sovereignty of each national constitution? And if it could not: to what extent could the latter principle be abandoned without violating supraconstitutional principles of national independence?

The supranational character of European integration through the EU is reinforced further by the existence of institutions where national representatives in the literal sense are simply *not* admitted. The European Commission is certainly the best known example of this type. But when it comes to national sovereignty, the Court of Justice – with its long-lasting 'judicial politics' in favour of integration, its pretension of ensuring superiority of EC law over national legislation and its power to state the law with binding effect even for the supreme judges of each of the member states – is at least as important. And what about the European Central Bank, which – according to the Maastricht treaty – shall enjoy independence *vis à vis* political authorities of the Union and of the member states to an extent at least equal to that of any of the present national monetary institutions?

It is of course true that the Union has no police or armed forces that it might display against rebellious member states. But fair enough, this absence provides no important argument, in present-day Western Europe, against the qualification of important elements of the Union as 'supranational'.

## Continuation: Decision-Making by Unanimity or by Majority?

The supranational character of integration through the EU is also affirmed by the recourse to majority decisions, according to the treaties and increasingly even in institutional practice. Consequently, national representatives may have to submit to decisions by a majority of representatives from other countries even in cases where they express strong opposition. Concern for democracy at European level is even more easy to discern when the qualified majority principle of EC law is compared to the fact that ordinary inter-governmental decisions will only acquire binding force on states by which they have been explicitly accepted.

Somewhat paradoxically, however, it should be noted that the need for consent from all the contracting parties under the unanimity principle makes choices by judges, as well as political choices adopted by majorities, more difficult to correct than decisions that are subject to amendment by majorities. At national level, the constituent power of each country has the possibility of correcting, in the last resort, controversial choices through constitutional amendment. I believe that this possibility should be regarded as one of the critical conditions for the democratic *legitimacy* of judicial review of legislation within national legal systems.[3]

However more or less accessible, formally or *de facto*, the possibility of constitutional amendment is always open in national legal systems, whereas it is easily closed when it comes to the 'constitutional' treaties on which EC law is based: those treaties may only be amended with the consent of *all* the contracting parties. This is so in a system of which an increasing bulk of legal constraints upon the member states, established through decisions by judicial as well as political bodies, is one of the distinctive features. Is it wise to forget about this – in a certain sense – undemocratic character of the unanimity principle when it comes to European integration?

The unanimity principle in public international law is frequently regarded as a precondition for the sovereignty of nations and – thus – for the superiority of national democratic systems even in Europe. But as we have seen, it may be argued that the very same principle may constitute a barrier to the possibility for democratically accountable organs to correct controversial choices by judges or politicians within the EU system by treaty-amendment.[4]

## Popular Scepticism

The emergence of the European Communities must be understood in the light of World War II, which to a large extent originated from and took place in Europe and certainly was not the first example of devastating wars between neighbours on the Old Continent.

On behalf of two of the main opponents throughout the centuries, French and German leaders thus took up a stand to fight further wars by peacefully establishing economic interdependence in order to render armed conflicts the more and more

[3] See further E. Smith, 'The legitimacy of judicial review of legislation – a comparative approach', in E. Smith (ed.): *Constitutional Justice under Old Constitutions* (The Hague: Kluwer, 1995) pp. 363 ff.

[4] The same is true, by the way, to the extent that similar decisions of inferior rank are more difficult to adopt – and thus to amend – under EC law than under national law. In this sense, the extensive need for *qualified* majorities under EC law at points where simple majorities are sufficient under national constitutions may be regarded as anti-democratic (not to speak of the anti-democratic elements embodied in EC law when it comes to the far stronger numerical representation for small than for large populations).

inconceivable. Measures progressively adopted include rules for a common market and supranational powers as far as deemed necessary for ensuring equal competition and control over market operations.

To the initial post-war aims should be added the need for extending the 'internal' market in search of more competitive production in a Europe facing international (including American and Japanese) financial actors and, hence, for ensuring a minimum of public control over trans-frontier market operations. It has also become an aim to fortify the interests of the Old Continent in cultural, agricultural and other fields.

As one might expect, EU performances have not always been spectacular. For instance, unemployment remains high, and the Bosnian war has shown that history should not easily be forgotten, even when it comes to traditional 'shares of influence' between the most powerful nations of Western Europe. But after all, why should the European Union be more successful in many respects than most governments of far less heterogenous polities?

Notwithstanding the problems, few would actually deny that the EU has become a most important actor on the international as well as on the European stage. But still there seems to be widespread popular scepticism regarding the Union as a means of European cooperation.

This state of minds appears *inter alia* in a series of national referenda. With the notable exceptions of Austria and Ireland, the normal score in favour of one aspect or another of European integration over the last years has proved to be more or less close to 50%: Denmark 56.2% (1986), 49.3% (1992) and 56.7% (1993), France 50.9% (1992), Finland 56.9% (1994), Sweden 52.3% (1994). In Norway, the scores have been very similar (53.5% in 1972, 52.2% in 1994), were it not for the fact that the Norwegian majorities voted *against* membership of the EEC or EU respectively.

We thus see that the electorate in many countries, when asked to express itself in this solemn manner, has had a tendency to vote according to a 1:1 figure. This is striking even if the outcome of most direct consultations like this could not reasonably be interpreted in the light of just one aspect of popular concern.[5]

The level of participation in direct elections to the European Parliament (59.4% in 1984, 58.5% in 1989, 56.2% in 1994) may equally be cited as a sign of scepticism (or of indifference). In a European context, this overall level – which of course hides

[5] Exceptions may of course occur, for instance when it comes to questions perceived as vital for national independence, as in Norway in 1905 or, more recently, in the post-communist world.

considerable variations among the different electorates – is relatively feeble (and even decreasing).

It has been said that some sort of *EU-phory* has often been apparent, during Jacques Delors' period at the head of the European Commission, among leading politicians in most EU countries. It may even be argued that the Maastricht treaty itself is one of the most prominent outcomes of a *hybris* that seems to contrast with widespread popular scepticism. How may this apparent gap be explained?

Of course the reasons are far too numerous to be discussed here. Moreover, a certain number of them are rather local (concern over fisheries in Norway, over the Deutschemark in Germany, and so on). Not unfrequently, people even seem to adopt attitudes towards European integration similar to those frequently adopted towards one's own national political and administrative elites: you complain, but that doesn't mean that you seriously plan to emigrate!

One of the reasons that seems to be of a more general character should nevertheless be examined more carefully here: in different versions, a *concern for democracy* in European integration is regularly met in political debates throughout Europe, including in much campaigning prior to the above-mentioned referenda.

The basic *question* may be formulated as follows: it may well be that most states in Europe are too small to oppose the anarchy of international movements of capital or to ensure vital environmental needs – pollution doesn't respect national frontiers, and so on. It may also well be that supranational decision-making is needed to cope with such challenges.[6] But how do you know that supranational bodies – be they regional or global – will really deal with such questions in the best possible manner? How do you know that the accompanying loss of national sovereignty – be it more or less formal – will really be compensated by better decisions at crucial points?

The only honest answer to such questions is probably: *you cannot know*. What we may suppose is, of course, that good supranational decisions are more likely to reach their aims than excellent, but more or less isolated decisions at national level. But this is unlikely to give entire satisfaction to scepticism along the above-mentioned lines.

As a matter of fact, it has become frequent to look for a better answer along lines developed throughout the last centuries concerning *democracy* at national level: of course we don't know the outcome of each decision to be taken by bodies that are more or

6 I leave aside whether cooperation only within (parts of) Europe is really sufficient.

less democratically elected. Even less have we any certainty of satisfaction regarding the substance of individual decisions or regarding the sum of such decisions. But still most of us are willing to encounter such risks, provided that – and as far as – our governments are exposed to public criticism and may be defeated through succeeding elections.

Most of us would even ask for a minimum of *Rechtsstaat,* namely in respect of human rights and access to independent courts. It is certainly not by chance that 'democracy' and the 'rule of law' have become twin standards for governments to acquire international legitimacy. It is true that the exact meaning of the 'rule of law' requirement is not easy to discern, nor is its relationship with the notion of democracy. But such questions must be left apart on this occasion.

## Democracy Through the European Parliament?

At least formally, the unanimity-based inter-governmental parts of the EU system do not give rise to particular problems with respect to democracy. This is so at least insofar as we forget about the arguments that tend to explain why the unanimity principle makes corrections at 'constitutional' level even more difficult to achieve than constitutional amendments within each of the nation-states.[7]

As we have seen, the situation is different when it comes to supranational parts of European integration. To what exent is the quest for democracy actually met – and to what extent *could* it possibly be met – without giving up the principle of cooperation between sovereign states?

Two main answers seem conceivable. The one which has probably prevailed in current debates, emphasises democratic elements within the EU structure as such, including the present system of direct elections to the European Parliament. Reflections of such an attitude are frequently exposed, quite recently for example in Commission President Jacques Santer's inaugural speech to the European Parliament on 17 January 1995.

For several reasons, this line of argument is not entirely convincing. First, the European Parliament is still far from having powers of initiative, legislation and control over the 'executive'

[7] On this occasion, I thus leave aside the problems with respect to democratic accountability that are nevertheless linked even to the running of the inter-governmental 'pillars' in the fields of foreign affairs, etc.

similar to those enjoyed by most national parliaments.[8] Second, and even more important, no 'parliament' could properly act as the cornerstone in a democratic system of government if isolated from a social and political context that deserves the qualification of 'democratic'. But the 'people' that the Parliament in Strasbourg is supposed to serve, is far bigger and far more heterogeneous when it comes to numerous cultural parameters (language, and so on) than any of the parliaments of the EU member states.

It is hardly surprising not to discern convincing signs of a genuine, common sphere for public debate at EU level. This means leaving it wide open to what extent a credible context for a parliamentary democracy could really be established in the absence of such *öffentligkeit* in the Union's Europe.

We may nevertheless assume, of course, that the preceding observations give no decisive argument against conferring a role similar to that of most national parliaments upon the European one. But then politically 'heavy' arguments against such a development most certainly would pop up: establishing a European Parliament with prerogatives up to common constitutional standards of democratic states would easily mean transforming the Union into a genuinely *federal* system. For the time being, it seems highly unlikely that such a development would be acceptable to all the member states.

Of course, the preceding remarks give no sufficient ground for completely ruling out the possibility of establishing some sort of a genuine democracy at European level. But it may, at least, be concluded that the prospects for such a development, during the first couple of decades, are sufficiently unconvincing for us to turn to the other possible main answer to the quest for democracy.

## Democracy Through National Parliaments?

The purpose of the present volume is to explore the possible links between democracy at national and at European level: to what extent may a satisfactory degree of legitimacy[9] of the European Union *vis-à-vis* common standards of democracy be established

8 Incidentally, this may be said to give the electorate some reasons for *not* taking part in elections to the European Parliament in massive numbers.

9 Whereas the preceding remarks on 'popular scepticism' focus upon 'legitimacy' in what may be called a sociological sense, I am now turning to what I call 'normative legitimacy', ie the 'Anerkennungswürdigkeit' of the level of democracy in the EU when compared to common standards of democracy at national level. See further my remarks in E. Smith (ed.): *Constitutional Justice under Old Constitutions*, op. cit. at pp. 369 ff.

through insisting on the possible role of national parliaments as cornerstones of European integration?

National parliaments *are* actually cornerstones of European integration in the sense of being, in most cases, mandatory fora for decisions regarding membership of the EU (or of the EEA) and amendments in the treaties on which the cooperation is based. In other words, they are the *Herren der Verträg*, as they are bound to remain so, according to the aforementioned 1993 decision of the *Bundesverfassungsgericht*.

But even in this role the national parliaments are not necessarily free – politically speaking – to refuse to accept treaties established as the outcome of more or less difficult negotiations. And even if this role – as assigned to them by the constitution of each state – is fundamental in itself, it clearly does not suffice, in the long run, for ensuring a minimum of democracy at European level.

Even when it comes to the current operation of the supranational parts of European integration as established by the EU, however, there is still a possibility of qualifying the parliaments of the member state as cornerstones: the most important parts of the decision-making power within the Union remain with organs in which representatives of each member state sit together (such as the European Council and the Council of Ministers). Ministers are responsible to the representative assembly of their countries, as other representatives are responsible to 'their' ministers. In this way, the national representatives even become responsible – at least indirectly – to the national electorate as such.

Why should we not be satisfied with the democratic character of such an arrangement, and, thus, with the democratic legitimacy of European integration?

First, the representativity chain of arguments should of course be tempered by pointing out that important powers within the EU are conferred upon institutions where proper representatives of the member states are *not* admitted (such as the Commission and the Court of Justice). But this observation may here be left aside.

Further, we meet a number of problems regarding the possibility for national parliaments really to influence Community decision-making before decisions have actually been taken, *de facto* if not *de jure*. In this respect, some parliaments have been more performant than others – the role of the standing commission for European affairs in the Danish Folketing is often cited as the most prominent example. But such experiences give rise to a number of problems of their own: how may the creation of separate mini-assemblies with the effect of excluding the bulk of MP's from real participation in European affairs be avoided? How may the parliament's pressing need for information on current EU affairs – in time for really being able to influence the decision-making processes *and* in a form that makes it informative – be met? And how can the minister be bound by the majority will within 'his' parliament without excluding him from active participation in such bargaining which often takes place in order to reach compromises?

To this should be added the problems ineluctably met by a parliament trying to exercise retrospective control over ministerial action in European bodies where decisions are most often based upon compromises reached throughout complex bargaining before ministers ever meet (or upon successive, more or less informal contacts). And who should you charge in an instance where your own minister, in a case submitted to decisions by qualified majorities, actually voted against a controversial decision by which you are bound anyhow?

Further downstream, subsequent legislation at national level is far from always being required for making community norms effective within each of the member states. But even to the extent that such enactments are needed, the margin of appreciation enjoyed by the national legislator is reduced to an extent that makes it doubtful whether the dignity of parliaments is really well served by the need for bringing such matters before them.

The EEA Agreement offers a salient paradox at this point: formally, the decisive role of the national parliaments of the member states has been conserved to a considerably higher extent than in the EU countries themselves. But in the real world, it is more than doubtful whether this system has anything else to give than underlining the weakness of the EFTA parliaments.

Let it finally be mentioned that even relative success in the efforts to ensure effective upstream participation of national parliaments in community decision-making through national representatives may create separate problems. The possibility of efficient decision-making at supranational level is not necessarily hampered in a serious way as far as such efforts are actually conducted in a small number of member states only. But could the same be said if numerous national parliaments move in the same direction? To what extent should efficiency at EU level be allowed to suffer from such more or less consensus-blocking or delaying effects that might easily stem from the active participation of a number of parliaments, acting more or less openly on behalf of particular interests of their own states, in a decision-making process supposed to be common?

We thus see that the 'national parliaments as cornerstones' response to the widespread concern for democracy – even if it is found convincing – has to be confronted with the problem of cost: what is a reasonable price to pay when exchanging a higher degree of democracy for possibly less effective fulfilment of the aims for which the supranational decision-making mechanisms within the EU have been adopted?

## National Parliaments as Cornerstones of European Integration?

Most fundamentally, 'democracy' means 'rule by the people'. In other words (and with evident links to constitutional theory of the most classical vein), we may talk about sovereignty of the people – or *popular* sovereignty.

Few would deny that this programme is seldom – if ever – met fully in the every-day life of nations. But if you take away the *pretension* of a given state to realising popular sovereignty in one way or another, you take away one of the most fundamental parts of the legitimacy of that state.

There are solid grounds for assuming that so far, reasonable degrees of democracy are *only* realised – if ever – at national level. Correspondingly, we may assume that the seemingly widespread concern for democracy within the EU is perfectly legitimate. It may also be assumed that transfer of national sovereignty to supranational institutions is likely to entail a corresponding decline in popular sovereignty. If proper remedies are not found, European integration faces a real problem regarding its democratic legitimacy.

This is the field that has been selected for this volume. Its title – '*National Parliaments as Cornerstones of European Integration*' – is deliberately provocative: as a matter of fact, the contributors are *not* necessarily of the opinion that the parliaments of the member states of the European Union (and of the EEA) are suitable means for assuming a proper degree of democracy in European integration. But on the other hand, the volume is actually based upon the assumption that the widespread concern for democracy in the EU as we know it today cannot be met without exploring the possible role of democracy at national level in the struggle for filling up the *democratic deficit* at European level.

In this way, the role that national parliaments do actually play as cornerstones of European integration becomes vital. So does the role that they *may* possibly be assigned in the future.

The principal aim of the present volume is to explore some of the general questions to which this theme gives rise. The main aspects of this character have been gathered in Parts I and III of the book. First, the question of national parliaments as 'cornerstones' of European integration cannot reasonably be discussed without taking into account the present-day role of parliaments at *national* level (see the paper by Philip Norton). We also have to take into account the possibilities of answering the quest for democracy through different forms of cooperation between the national parliaments and the European one (see Joël Rideau's contribution in Part III). And finally, vital parameters for democracies – such as *size* and *national*

***community*** – are summed up in Öyvind Österud's 'concise exposition' on democracy between national government and supranationality.

In the present context, it gives little meaning, however, to discuss general questions in complete abstraction from practical experiences. For this reason, selected ***national models for parliamentary influence on EU affairs*** are discussed in Part II of the book. And the interdependence between the more general parts of the volume and the contributions in Part II is intimate also the other way round. As a matter of fact, the authors to whom the task of discussing particular national experiences has been assigned, do not content themselves with more or less technical presentations of their own 'models'. On the contrary, they often contribute to the more general discussion in stimulating and – sometimes – frankly provocative ways, for example, by discussing whether we had better *preserve* the democratic deficit (Sverker Gustafsson).

Different criteria have determined the selection of national experiences to be discussed, including the need for having small as well as large nations represented and for considering some of the most distinctive approaches to the task of ensuring a prominent role of national parliaments. Only five of the EU member states are explicitly covered (in Part II), and of course we do not pretend to cover every question discussed and every problem met by the others. But the selection has been governed by a concern to include a range of national experiences sufficient to serve as a background for the more global approaches to the problem of the democratic deficit in European integration reflected most directly in Parts I and III of the book.

In this perspective, Denmark has been selected as being probably the first one to have dealt with the problem of safeguarding a minimum of influence of the national assembly in European affairs through the system of prior parliamentary consent to Danish EU policies (Jörgen Albæk Jensen). France and Germany have found it necessary to proceed, during the last few years, to constitutional reform in order to meet the challenge of European integration to the role of national parliaments in presumably better ways than before (see the contributions of Louis Dubouis, on the French Parliament, and of Meinhard Hilf and Frank Burmeister, on the German one). Moreover, the latter countries – unlike Denmark (and Sweden) – are governed by different versions of bicameral systems; Germany even offers a prominent example of how the need for reconciling federalism and supranationalism has been handled.

While the latter countries have been leading powers in the development of European integration, the United Kingdom is interesting *inter alia* due to the rather oppositional role it has played during the more than 20 years since it joined the communities. Westminster deserves interest in our perspective also for a number of other reasons, including the particular problems created by the absence of a written constitution (see further Colin Munro's contribution).

Finally, one of the newcomers into the EU (Sweden) is included in order to see how the opportunity – at least theoretically – for learning from more experienced member states has been handled (see Sverker Gustavsson's chapter).

To the discussion of national experiences of some of the member states of the EU, a text on the role of national parliaments in 'medium-speed Europe' has beed added. Dealing with the possibilities of the Norwegian parliament to influence decision-making and implementation under the European Economic Area (EEA) Agreement, Fredrik Sejersted's contribution even offers comparative reflections on the possible role of national parliaments under the 'supranational' and 'inter-governmental' models of European integration.

• • •

It is far from evident whether concern for the so-called 'democratic deficit' at European level in itself gives sufficient grounds for a state to stay outside the EU, or for leaving it. In a world of competition and war, this series of arguments can certainly not be said to be the only one deserving interest. But Europe is the last continent that should feel free to forget about the intimate relationship between national and popular sovereignty.

This is precisely why the present-day struggle for integration and peace in Europe is facing a real dilemma, where satisfactory compromises may be uneasy to find. The concern for democracy in European integration thus ought to be regarded as one of the major challenges to the inter-governmental treaty conference of 1996. But it will most certainly remain one even after the end of this conference.

# National Parliaments in Western Europe

*Philip Norton*

Legislatures – be they titled parliaments, congresses or assemblies – are features of most political systems. Almost nine out of every ten countries have one. They are well entrenched in Western Europe. The nineteenth century was the high point of parliamentarianism, but the attachment to legislatures remains strong.[1] Though the 'decline' of legislatures has been variously trumpetted, that decline has – though real – been in one particular function, that of making the law. Parliaments continue to have a number of important consequences for their respective political systems.

All fulfil the defining role of a legislature – the giving of assent on behalf of citizens to measures that are to have binding applicability – and a number of other tasks that derive from the fact that they are parliaments.[2] In terms of public policy, the parliaments in Western Europe have had some modest impact on the content of legislation. I have elsewhere distinguished three types of legislature[3] (see

1 The findings in this paper derive from a cross-national study of national parliaments and the European Union, funded by the Nuffield Foundation [Grant Soc/100 235] and due for publication, as a special issue of The Journal of Legislative Studies, in November 1995. Sections of this paper draw heavily, and in some cases exclusively, on my concluding chapter for that volume. See also P. Norton, 'Parliaments: A Framework for Analysis', in P. Norton (ed.), ***Parliaments in Western Europe*** (London: Frank Cass, 1990) p. 2.

2 See P. Norton, 'Introduction', in P. Norton (ed.), ***Legislatures*** (Oxford: Oxford University Press, 1990) pp. 1–2.

3 P. Norton, 'Parliament and Policy in Britain: The House of Commons as a Policy Influencer', ***Teaching Politics***, 13(2), 1984, p. 201.

**Figure 1. Types of legislature**

*Policy-making legislature*
Can modify or reject policy brought forward by the executive, and can formulate and substitute policy of its own.

*Policy-influencing legislature*
Can modify or reject policy brought forward by the executive, but cannot formulate and substitute policy of its own.

*Legislature with little or no policy affect*
Can neither modify nor reject policy brought forward by the executive, nor formulate and substitute policy of its own.

Figure 1). West European legislatures occupy the increasingly crowded category of policy-influencing legislatures. Their ranking within that category varies. Some, notably the Italian, Swedish and Dutch, have formed particularly strong legislatures of this type, the Italian coming close to occupying the category of a policy-making legislature.[4] The French and Irish parliaments are weak policy-influencing legislatures.[5] None, though, occupies the category of a legislature with little or no policy affect.

Parliaments have consequences other than those identified by Packenham as decisional.[6] The parliament fulfils important tasks of legitimation. It gives the seal of approval to measures that are to have binding applicability. The assent of parliament is necessary for all or most measures if they are to be the law of the land and be enforced by the courts. In most cases it is not sufficient. The assent of the head of state is also required. In some cases, it is not necessary. The executive may be vested with powers under the constitution to issue orders that have the force of law. Such exceptions do not invalidate the statement that parliaments are an intrinsic part of the national law-effecting process.

4 See P. Furlong, 'Parliament in Italian Politics', in P. Norton (ed.), *Parliaments in Western Europe* (London: Frank Cass, 1990) pp. 52–67, and, in the same volume, D. Arter, 'The Swedish Riksdag: The Case of a Strong Policy-Influencing Assembly', pp. 120–42 and K. Gladdish, 'Parliamentary Activism and Legitimacy in the Netherlands', pp. 103–19.

5 See the chapters by Frears and Arkins in Norton, *Parliaments in Western Europe*, and P Norton, 'The Legislative Powers of Parliament', in C. Flinterman, A. W. Heringa and L. Waddington (eds.), *The Evolving Role of Parliaments in Europe* (Antwerp: MAKLU, 1994) pp. 15–32.

6 R. Packenham, 'Legislatures and Political Development', in A. Kornberg and L. D. Musolf (eds.), *Legislatures in Developmental Perspective* (Durham NC: Duke University Press, 1970).

The parliaments also serve as important means of maintaining consent for the political system.[7] They can act as safety valves – another legitimising function noted by Packenham – and allow different views in society to find an authoritative public outlet. They can serve as safety valves for individuals as well as groups: in some parliaments, pursuing the grievances of individual citizens is an important and sometimes time-consuming occupation. They can serve as channels through which interests are articulated and represented to government. In western parliaments, these tasks appear to be increasing rather than decreasing in importance, with parliamentary lobbying by pressure groups and demands for action by constituents increasing in volume.[8]

Packenham also identified recruitment, socialising and training functions. These are especially important in Western Europe, where political systems are almost wholly parliamentary as opposed to presidential. Election determines not only who will serve in the parliament but also, wholly or (in the case of France) in part, the composition of the government. When electors go to the polls to elect members of parliament they are, in effect, voting for the party they wish to be in government. Where ministers are drawn from the parliament, then they have some appreciation already of parliamentary needs and nuances. Where they remain within the legislature, they mix with and are answerable to other members (though just how answerable depends on the system). There is, presumptively at least, less likelihood of them being able to avoid parliamentary scrutiny than in a presidential system.

Parliaments are thus important – indeed, inextricable – elements of the national political systems in Western Europe. How they are perceived by citizens can and does vary. Some are less well regarded than others – as shown by Eurobarometer data – but levels of turnout in parliamentary elections remain high and extra-parliamentary activity is, in most countries, limited and sometimes close to non-existent.

Given the place of parliaments in national political systems, then one would expect the establishment of a supranational rule-making process to have significant implications for the parliaments of the nations involved. The creation of the European Community, now the European Union, had and continues to have profound implications for national parliaments of the Member States. This paper addresses two basic questions, one descriptive and one normative. The first, the descriptive, is: what role have national parliaments played in the

7 See Norton (ed), *Parliaments in Western Europe*.

8 For the example of the UK, see P. Norton, *Does Parliament Matter?* (Hemel Hempstead: Harvester Wheatsheaf, 1994).

moves toward greater European integration? The second, the normative, is: what role should they play?

## What Role Have National Parliaments Played?

Under the treaties establishing the original European Communities, national parliaments were accorded no formal role. They received no mention in the treaties. They were not required to be consulted, let alone to give assent to measures enacted by the Community. Where deemed to form part of the national authorities, parliaments could play a role in determining how directives were to be implemented, but they were not empowered to negate them. Nor were the parliaments involved directly in legitimising the Community law-making process. Ministers were the representatives of the national governments, and the national governments derived their popular legitimacy from elections to the national parliament. But the real driving body behind the formulation of EC law – the Commission – was not elected. And there was no direct link between national parliaments and the law-making process. Each national parliament could seek to influence, even determine, the stance taken by the minister in the Council of Ministers and seek, through its members in the European Assembly, to influence the content of EC measures, but each ultimately lacked any formal power to approve or reject measures enacted by the institutions of the EC under the provisions of Community treaties.

Central actors in the national law-making processes, national parliaments thus found themselves playing no role – certainly no direct role – in the new supranational law-making process. They thus faced a choice between accepting that status – and confining themselves to their work in the national arena – or seeking to change it by institutional reform and even by treaty amendment. An analysis of the institutional response of national parliaments to EC membership reveals two basic stages. The first is one essentially of opting for the first option. This spanned the period from the creation of the European Communities through to the mid-1980s. The second period is one of institutional change. This dates from the mid-1980s and the challenge posed by the single market and, in treaty terms, the Single European Act.

### *The first period: staying out*

Most chambers of the legislatures of the original six Member States did not change their structures or procedures in response to the moves towards European integration. Not only were the parliaments accorded no formal role in the process of supranational law making, they also showed little inclination to seek such a role. Opinion within each country was strongly supportive of moves towards greater integration. The task of achieving that integration was seen as properly belonging to the new institutions created by the treaties. That view permeated the political elites within each country. National parliaments were content to leave European rule making to the supranational institutions set up for the purpose. National interests were articulated and defended by governments and they remained answerable to their national parliaments. 'European' issues were treated as falling within the domain of foreign policy – usually an executive prerogative – and not as having great import for domestic politics. There thus seemed little reason for national parliaments to concern themselves.

The period from the 1950s to the mid-1980s thus saw little interest in EC affairs in national parliaments and certainly little institutional change in order to take account of the new situation. A committee to consider European affairs was established in only one lower chamber – the Belgian House of Representatives in 1962. It achieved little and was abolished in 1979.[9] Committees were established in three upper houses – in Holland, Italy and Germany – but again had little impact. The majority of legislative chambers lacked a dedicated European committee and, overall, the interest and involvement in Community law making may fairly be described as minimal.

## *The second period: responding to the Single European Act*

The second period – from the mid-1980s through to the enactment of the Treaty on European Union in 1993 – saw a marked change in the stance of most national parliaments. During this period, we see notable institutional change. The principal, but not exclusive, changes came in response to the Commission's White Paper on the Single Market and the implementation of the Single European Act (SEA) in 1987.

I say 'not exclusive' because some changes occurred before the mid-1980s, principally in the case of the three countries that became members of the Community on 1 January 1973. The United

9 L. De Winter and T. Laurent, 'The Belgian Parliament and European Integration', *The Journal of Legislative Studies*, vol. 1(3), 1995.

Kingdom and Denmark were sensitive to the implications of membership for their existing constitutional arrangements. Both had parliaments that were jealous of their status within the national law-making process. The Danish *Folketing* established an advisory committee in advance of membership and the two Houses of the British Parliament established committees consequent to the UK's accession. The Irish parliament also went through the motions of establishing a committee (of both Houses), albeit a committee – operating within a weak policy-influencing parliament and a national mood strongly supportive of membership – that achieved little, if anything.[10]

The Commission White Paper, 'Completing the Internal Market', identified a timetable and the measures needed in order to complete a single market by 1 January 1993. The Paper was approved by heads of state and government at the Milan European Council in 1985. The completion of the internal market was then embodied in the SEA. Ratification of the SEA created the means by which that market could be realised.

The SEA incorporated a number of policy areas not included in the existing EEC treaty, including the environment, health and safety, and economic and social cohesion.[11] It also brought into being a new legislative procedure – the co-operation procedure. Through the introduction of this procedure, the Act effected a shift in the power relationship ***between*** the national institutions of the Member States and the institutions of the Community, the latter being given much greater power. It also effected a shift in the relationship ***between*** the institutions of the Community, with the European Parliament acquiring a somewhat greater role and, for the first time, a positive role in the legislative process.[12]

The White Paper and the SEA ensured that the reach of EC institutions extended into sectors that were previously the exclusive domain of national governments. More regulations and directives flowed from Brussels. To cope with the changed conditions, national governments adapted their procedures for dealing with EC affairs. So too did most of the national parliaments. There was a realisation not only that the policy competence of the EC was being extended but that a shift in the decision-making process was also taking place. Policy-making power was flowing

[10] E. O'Halpin, 'Irish Parliamentary Culture and the European Union: Formalities to be Observed', *The Journal of Legislative Studies*, vol. 1(3), 1995.

[11] See J. Lodge, 'The European Parliament', in J. Lodge (ed.), *The European Community and the Challenge of the Future* (London: Pinter, 1989) pp. 68–9.

[12] See P. Norton, 'Introduction: Adapting to European Integration', *The Journal of Legislative Studies*, vol. 1(3), 1995.

upwards to the supranational level and with a directly-elected Parliament having a greater opportunity than before to be involved at that level.

For national parliaments, there was the problem of how to respond to the changed conditions. They could not rely solely on the European Parliament to scrutinise EC documents and hold the Commission and Council of Ministers to account. The EP was accorded a greater role to play than before, but it was still not a fully-fledged legislature. There was a need for national parliaments to get involved.

The result has been that, in the field of EC affairs, national parliaments have exhibited, from the mid-1980s onwards, three distinct characteristics: (i) specialisation; (ii) greater activity; and (iii) some attempts to integrate MEPs into their activities.

*(i) Specialisation.* The specialisation is to be found in the creation of committees devoted to European affairs. The 1980s became the decade of EC Committees, especially in lower chambers. The Belgian House of Representatives established an Advice Committee in charge of European Affairs in 1985. It was followed by six other parliaments, including the two new Iberian Member States (though Portugal had established a committee prior to accession). In 1990, the Belgian Senate established an Advice Committee. In 1991, the German Bundestag appointed a Standing Committee on European Community Affairs, superseding the sub-committee of the Foreign Affairs Committee.[13] By the 1990s, EC committees were the norm. Each national parliament had one or more committee dealing with European affairs.

*(ii) Greater activity.* National parliaments began devoting more and more time to scrutinising documents to be submitted to the Council and/or the implementation of directives. Some of the burden has been carried by parliaments in plenary session. In the case of the Dutch parliament, for example, there has been a marked increase in the number of times a European item has been considered in plenary session and in committee and in the number of new European themes put on the parliament's agenda.[14] More noticeably, the burden has fallen on committees, the responsibility being shouldered by the European Affairs Committee or being shared between committees. In some parliaments – such as the German

[13] See T. Saalfeld, 'The German Houses of Parliament and European Legislation', *The Journal of Legislative Studies*, vol. 1(3), 1995.

[14] M. P. C. M. Van Schendelen, 'The Netherlands: From Founding Father to Mounding Baby', *The Journal of Legislative Studies*, vol. 1(3), 1995.

and the British – additional committees have been formed to supplement the established committees. In 1988 the German Bundesrat set up a second committee, giving it specific responsibility for EC Documents. In 1991 the British House of Commons established two European Standing Committees to consider EC Documents recommended for debate.

*(iii) Integration of MEPs.* Until direct elections in 1979, members of the European Parliament (MEPs) were drawn from the parliaments of the Member States. After direct elections, some countries permitted a dual mandate (a member of the national parliament being permitted to seek election also to the EP), but such mandates became a notable exception rather than the norm. Links between the national parliaments and the EP withered rather than grew. The greater role of the EP in the legislative process from 1987, and the greater volume of legislation, provided a spur to try to include MEPs more in the work of national parliaments.

Various attempts have been made to integrate MEPs. These have taken different forms. In Ireland, Belgium, Greece and Germany, it has involved MEPs serving as full or advisory members of parliamentary committees.[15] A number of other chambers allow MEPs to attend committee meetings, either as of right or by invitation. In other cases, the relationship has developed – or is intended to be developed – through meetings between members of the national parliament and the country's MEPs, as in the case of Spain and Portugal, or through inviting MEPs on occasion to provide information or give evidence to committees, as in the case of the committees of the UK House of Lords and the Dutch Eerste Kamer. Some links may also be established through the medium of parties, allowing MEPs to attend party meetings and giving them a place on party bodies.

There have also been further changes in response to the debate over, and the implementation of, the Treaty on European Union. Some countries have strengthened the position of their parliaments in determining whether treaty provisions should be implemented (Germany, for example, and the Netherlands). Article 88 of the French Constitution was amended in June 1992 to allow the

[15] Irish MEPs were included as members of the Joint Committee of the Oireachtas when it was established in 1973. The Advice Committee of the Belgian House of Representatives has ten MEPs and ten MPs as members. The German Commission on European Affairs, in existence between 1983 and 1986, had eleven MEPs and eleven MPs as members. Eleven MEPs are given 'observer' status in the new German Standing Committee on European Affairs, though without the right to vote.

National Assembly the right to intervene – through the submission of resolutions – in the conduct of European policy, previously treated as falling within the domain of foreign policy.[16] Some countries, such as Portugal, have also extended the competence of their European affairs committees.[17] Some parliamentary committees have also made some efforts to meet on occasion with their equivalent committees in the EP.

So much for what national parliaments have done individually. There is also growing cooperation between parliaments. The most regular and institutionalised contact is through the Conference of European Affairs Committees (known by the French initials as COSAC), comprising representatives of the committees dealing with European affairs in the national parliaments. The Conference meets twice a year to review structures of cooperation. There is also a longer-established Conference of Presidents, comprising the presiding officers of parliamentary chambers. A larger body of cooperation, but one which has so far met only once, is the Conference of Parliaments.[18] The Conference, or *assises,* met in Rome in 1990. It involved more than 300 members of national parliaments and of the EP (in a ratio of roughly three to one). Members sat in party groups and not by national delegation. The Conference endorsed the position of the EP on European union and declared its support for enhanced cooperation between national parliaments and the EP, as well as for more meetings of such conferences.

National parliaments, individually and to some extent collectively, have thus developed their institutional arrangements in response to moves towards greater Euopean integration. Taken together, the changes constitute a significant advance on what existed before. Yet the changes may be seen as constituting attempts to keep abreast of developments which do not permit of such treatment. National parliaments remain marginal actors in the European law-making process. The explanations for this marginality are significant also in the context of the normative debate.

16 F. Rizzuto, 'The French Parliament and the EU', *The Journal of Legislative Studies*, vol. 1 (3), 1995.

17 J. M. Magone, 'The Portuguese Assembleia Da República: Discovering Europe', *The Journal of Legislative Studies*, vol. 1 (3), 1995.

18 See M. Westlake, 'The View from Brussels', *The Journal of Legislative Studies*, vol. 1 (3), 1995.

## What Role Should They Play?

The 'democratic deficit' has been subject to different definitions,[19] but may be said to derive from the limited input into the law-making processes of the EC by directly-elected representatives of the people. The European Parliament was not initially elected nor even formally styled a parliament. The original treaties provided no role for national parliaments.

Though there appears to be widespread recognition, both at the national and supranational level, of the need to tackle this perceived deficit, there are conflicting interpretations of how it should be tackled. On the face of it, there is general agreement that national parliaments should play a more active role. The view that they should be more actively involved found expression in two declarations appended to the Maastricht Treaty. It also finds expression in the proposals being prepared for the 1996 Inter-Governmental Conference. The British Government, the Commission, and the European Parliament each take the view that national parliaments should be more actively involved in EU affairs.

There, though, the agreement ends. There are different views as to the form such increased involvement should take. One view, taken by the European Parliament, is that the involvement should be by parliaments individually at the national level. This would involve national parliaments exerting more rigorous scrutiny of draft legislation and of the stance taken by government, ministers being accountable to and more involved in the activity of the national parliament and its committees. The other view, taken for example by the British Government and expressed by the Conference of Parliaments in 1990, is that the involvement should be collective and at the Union level. This would involve, according to some proponents of this view, regular meetings of the Conference of Parliaments. Some politicians have also called for collective influence to be exerted through the creation of a new chamber in the European Parliament, or a Committee of Parliaments, each comprising members drawn from national parliaments.[20] From a somewhat different perspective, the German *Länder* advocate a Regional Chamber of the EU with significant powers.

Each view found expression in declarations appended to the

[19] See K. Neunreither, 'The Democratic Deficit of the European Union: Towards Closer Cooperation between the European Parliament and the National Parliaments', *Government and Opposition*, vol. 29 (3), 1994, pp. 299–300.

[20] See M. Heseltine, *The Challenge of Europe* (London: Weidenfeld & Nicolson, 1989) p. 35, and L. Brittan, *Europe: The Europe We Need* (London: Hamish Hamilton, 1994) p. 226.

Treaty on European Union. The declaration on the role of national parliaments envisaged that national parliaments should receive Commission proposals in good time for examination and that there should be a greater exchange of information and reciprocal facilities between the national parliaments and the EP. This, in effect, gave voice to the first view. The declaration on the Conference of the Parliaments – establishing the Conference and stipulating that it should be consulted on the main features of the European Union – gave expression to the second view.

The problem with the two approaches is not that they are logically incompatible. Both could be achieved if the political will existed. Rather, the problem is to be found in the absence of the political will. The European Parliament believes that the way to meet the democratic deficit is to increase its own powers – thus strengthening it in relation to the Commission and Council of Ministers – and to strengthen national parliaments at the national level – that is, in relation to their own governments. In the words of the leader of the European Parliamentary Labour Party, Wayne David, 'rather than seeing the European Parliament and the House of Commons as competitors, we ought to see both institutions as partners in the process of creating a more democratic Europe'.[21]

However, this partnership does not extend to according national parliaments a collective role. The EP supports the first view, but not the second. Allowing national parliaments a collective role is seen as usurping the role of the EP itself. It takes the view that it represents electors at the supranational level. National parliaments represent voters at the national level and can feed in their views through the Council of Ministers and through contact with MEPs. The EP has therefore been an opponent of a second chamber and has taken a critical view of the Conference of the Parliaments. An additional chamber or regular meetings of the Conference would, according to EP President Klaus Hänsch, 'lead to confusion'.[22] When the EP found it could not prevent the meeting of the Conference of the Parliaments in Rome, it manoeuvred instead to ensure that it controlled the administration of it. Given that there is little incentive for national parliaments to press for it to meet regularly – it lacks powers, a fixed timetable and institutional leadership independent of the EP – the omens are not good for it to develop as a body of collective influence.

Some supporters of the second view – wanting a collective role

[21] W. David, 'Foundations for an Open Union', *The House Magazine*, 24 April 1995, p. 6.

[22] K. Hänsch, 'Europe's Parallel Parliaments', *The House Magazine*, 22 May 1995, p. 19.

for national parliaments – are also opponents of any extension of the powers of the European Parliament. They tend to view parliamentary power as a zero-sum game: any extension of power to the EP takes power away from national parliaments. Furthermore, any extension of the EP's powers would not, in their view, address the democratic deficit. The EP has not yet engaged the interest and enthusiasm of voters throughout Europe. Hence the emphasis on national parliaments and the potential for them to act collectively.

The problem with making progress on the first view is the stance taken by many if not most national governments. This view involves national parliaments having some impact on EU affairs through national governments. Hence they serve as potential constraints on national governments. Even the British Government, keen to see some role for national parliaments as potential brakes on the activities of EU institutions, is less keen to see British parliamentary committees act as brakes on *its* activities in relation to the EU. It has thus refused, for example, to approve a widening of the terms of reference of the EC Committee in the House of Commons.[23]

Though the idea of national parliaments playing a more active role in the EU attracts considerable support, perceptions of what that role should be clearly differ. That is the political problem. Even if agreement were to be reached on the role national parliaments should play, there are practical problems. National parliaments have been unable and, in many respects, unwilling to play a significant role in European law making. The inability to play a significant role is constitutional and, to a lesser extent, procedural. The unwillingness is essentially ideological and cultural.

As to the *constitutional* limitations of the parliaments, the original treaties accorded no formal role to national parliaments in EC law making. The declarations appended to the Maastricht Treaty still accord them no formal role in that process, and the declarations themselves pale into insignificance alongside the power shifts effected by the Single European Act and the Treaty on European Union. The extension of qualified majority voting in the Council of Ministers limits the capacity for national parliaments to affect outcomes. Even if the role of national parliaments is strengthened in relation to national governments, national governments are themselves limited now in their capacity to prevent undesired outcomes.

The disparate institutional response of national parliaments to moves toward European integration has also been affected significantly by the different provisions and norms of national constitutions. Some have clearly facilitated the integration of the

[23] See J. Garrett, *Westminster: Does Parliament Work?* (London: Victor Gollancz, 1992) p. 220.

state into supranational processes, others – such as those of the United Kingdom and Germany – have created some difficulties, the UK from the time of accession and the German Basic Law more recently in relation to the position of the *Länder*.

***Procedural*** limitations derive from the existing structures, procedures and workloads of national parliaments, from the jealousies of parliamentarians, and from the fact that these features vary considerably from one parliament to another.

In some parliaments, responsibility for consideration of EC documents lies with subject-specific committees, the European Affairs Committee acting as a coordinating body rather than as the lead committee for discussing such documents. This is the case, for example, in Ireland and the Netherlands. Some operate through sub-committees, as in the British House of Lords and the *Comisión Mixta* of the Spanish Cortes. Some are vested with considerable powers, notably the European Affairs committee of the Danish *Folketing* and the committees of the Italian House, but most are not. The size and competence of the committees vary considerably.[24]

These procedural differences mean that there is no standard 'European Affairs Committee' in the parliaments of the Member States. In some cases, as in the German Bundestag, there is some conflict between committees over responsibility for EU affairs. The specific arrangements can limit the impact of the committee that has the 'European' designation. The failure in some cases to create an effective committee structure has led to calls for further change, such calls in the case of Ireland and the Netherlands actually calling into question the continued existence of the 'European' committees. Taken together, these differences limit the capacity for collective action and influence. To talk of European Affairs committees is to convey an impression of a uniformity that does not exist.

There is also a problem deriving from the workload of legislatures. Again, there is variation from parliament to parliament. However, dealing with an increasing volume of European documents places great pressures on the institutional capacity of a national parliament to deal with it. The workload of national parliaments and increasingly of the European Parliament also

[24] This is sometimes apparent within two chambers of the same parliament. The British House of Lords, for example, is a very active committee, operating through sub-committees. The House of Commons has one committee on European legislation, with more restricted terms of reference than its House of Lords counterpart, and making no use of sub-committees. Documents recommended for debate by the Commons committee stand referred to a European Standing Committee. Documents recommended for debate in the House of Lords are debated in the chamber.

impinges on attempts to develop links between national parliaments and the EP. Even if parliamentarians are keen to maintain links with MEPs, there is the problem of finding the time to build those links. It is often not easy for MEPs to spend time visiting national parliaments. Even where MEPs serve as full or advisory members of committees of the national parliament, as in the case of Greece and Ireland, they are noted more for their failure to turn up than for assiduous attendance. Similarly, for members of national parliaments to spend time in Brussels and Strasbourg requires a commitment of time that may be difficult to achieve. In the words of a member of the British House of Lords, a former MEP, 'you cannot be in two places at the same time'.

These practical problems have limited the capacity of national legislatures to give the time and attention to European affairs to the extent that they may wish and, in so far as national parliaments address European issues, have produced a disparate response. The existing workload of some parliaments means that it will be difficult for them to be more involved in EU affairs. The lack of uniformity among EC committees means that it will be difficult to co-ordinate a collective response in the future. This is apparent from meetings already of COSAC and the Conference of Presidents: in the case of the former, there is the problem of selecting members who are representative of their committee and parliament, and in the case of the latter impartial presiding officers (notably those of the two Houses of the British Parliament) are thrown together with political figures who occupy leadership roles.

Constitutional and procedural variables combine, then, to limit the capacity of national parliaments to have a significant impact on EU affairs. There are then the variables that render some parliaments unwilling to be centrally involved.

The *ideological* constraint refers to the position taken on the issue of European integration. In the case of many parliaments, there is a commitment to the principle of European integration and hence a recognition that the supranational level is the appropriate one for the formulation, debate and enactment of European law. The commitment was apparent in the stance taken by the original Member States. That commitment remains strong in countries such as the Netherlands. It is a view shared by some of the more recent recruits to the EU, not least Spain and Portugal.

In some other countries, the ideological commitment is weak. Both Britain and Denmark – the former at government and mass level and the latter at mass rather than governmental level – have taken a more critical view, regarding membership as instrumental. With many politicians in Britain, in so far as there is an ideological commitment, the commitment is to a single market and not to full European integration.

The absence of a uniform ideology militates against reaching agreement among Member States of the role of national parliaments. It would seem logical to assert that the greater the commitment to European integration, the greater the emphasis on the European Parliament; the more sceptical the view of European integration, the greater the emphasis on the role of national parliaments, especially at the level of collective influence.

*Political culture* also has a bearing, not least the fact that the culture is not uniform throughout the Member States. In some countries, the culture emphasises the role of the national parliament. The United Kingdom, with an unbroken parliamentary tradition spanning several centuries, is the prime example. Others, with a broken history or – in the case of Germany – no strong tradition of parliamentarianism, are less committed to protecting the role of the national parliament. There may also be a culture of parliamentary quiescence. In Ireland, this culture is well established. There, the absence of a strong tradition of scrutiny and challenge of the domestic executive lends itself to a distinctly casual and unquestioning attitude towards European institutions.

However, by culture I refer also to what may be termed a culture of mistrust between national parliaments and the EP. Even though there may be a commitment at the ideological level to European integration, there may be a more specific hesitancy about the role to be played by the EP and by MEPs. Members of national parliaments have variously displayed a territorial instinct in their dealing with the EP and with MEPs. A survey of 72 out of 81 German MEPs in 1987-1988 found that almost half of them felt that Bundestag MPs had very little interest in maintaining contact with them. Three-quarters of the MEPs believed that their relationship with national MPs was strained by feelings of rivalry on the part of the Bundestag MPs.[25]

This culture of mistrust may also be inferred from the unwillingness of national parliaments to integrate MEPs fully into their procedures. Even the most integrationist are generally unwilling or unable (by virtue of their rules) to go beyond conferring limited powers to attend and speak. Others accord MEPs no formal role at all in parliamentary deliberations. And, though the number of meetings between committees of national parliaments and the EP Parliament has increased in number, the number remains small in absolute terms and few committees of national parliaments

[25] Survey by Hrbek and Schweitzer, cited in T. Saalfeld, 'Previous Research on the Bundestag and its Links with the EC', note prepared for the Research Group on National Parliaments and the European Union (Centre for Legislative Studies, University of Hull, 1993).

have shown much enthusiasm for regular or institutionalised contact.

The resentment is not one-sided. 'National MPs generally resent their European counterparts' lifestyles and posturing, and MEPs resent not being taken seriously by their national counterparts'.[26]

## Conclusions

National parliaments have an important role in their respective political systems. That role is intrinsic and extensive. They have some policy influence and they fulfil tasks that serve to bolster support for the political system.

This is in sharp contrast to their position in the European Union. They are accorded no direct part in the formal process of rule making. What role they can play is indirect and derives from the provisions of their domestic constitutions. In terms of EU policy making, they are best described as peripheral actors. They have not served as agents of regime support. Attempts to develop the means of exerting indirect influence – or even direct influence through links with the EP – have been limited, bearing relatively little reward for the effort expended. Many European committees have had difficulty coping with the burden of EC documents and some have fallen foul of demarcation disputes between committees.

There has been a major shift of political power upwards to the institutions of the European Union. That shift has not been matched by a shift in democratic accountability, either at the level of the EP or through national parliaments. The EP has increased its powers enormously, but could be described as still only on the edge of constituting a legislature. Furthermore, it is still not clear that popular perceptions of its role accord with the increase in power. Despite a commitment to the principle of integration, there is a perception of 'Brussels' as distant, with little popular involvement in elections to the European Parliament. In terms of voter turnout, national parliaments can still claim a greater popular mandate.

Until popular perceptions change and the EP acquires the status it seeks, the democratic deficit not only will remain but may, given the events surrounding and subsequent to debate on the Treaty on European Union, become more – rather than less – pronounced. If national parliaments are to contribute to remedying the deficit – and, for reasons already discussed, that remains a very big and much contested if – then it is far from clear what they can do in order to

[26] D. Dinan, *Ever Closer Union*? (London: Macmillan, 1994) p. 290.

achieve that. They lack any formal role in the process and there is no obvious means by which they can achieve that role, even if they want to. Both the EP and national parliaments recognise the need to co-operate with one another, but remain wary of the motives of the other.

A prerequisite for change is the political will for that change to occur. The deliberations leading up to the 1996 Inter-Governmental Conference confirm that there is a conflict rather than a merging of wills. For many engaged in the debate on the future of the EU, national parliaments may constitute an answer. Unfortunately, they are not asking the same question.

# Part II

# National Models for Parliamentary Influence

# Prior Parliamentary Consent to Danish EU Policies

*Jørgen Albæk Jensen*

One of the basic features of Danish constitutional life is the parliamentary principle, according to which (in the Danish version) a government cannot be formed or continue to sit if a majority in the Folketing (the Danish parliament) passes a vote of no confidence – so-called negative parliamentarism. Thus, there is no requirement for a positive majority in the Folketing for a government, and in fact most Danish governments are minority ones.

The parliamentary principle plays an extraordinary role in Denmark because of the historical experience leading to the recognition of the principle. For more than a quarter of a century (from 1870 to 1901) a majority in the Folketing fought for a parliamentary government while the King kept appointing governments from the minority party. This led to a constitutional crisis where the majority for extended periods blocked important legislation, and where the government answered back by issuing provisionary acts, thus in effect ruling by decree. Finally, in 1901, the parliamentary principle was recognized in practice, as a government in accordance with the Folketing was appointed. However, the Constitution was not altered accordingly, not even in 1915 when the Constitution underwent a major revision. Another major crisis concerning the parliamentary principle occurred in 1920 when the King dismissed a parliamentary government against its will. The outcome of the crisis, however, strengthened parliamentarism, as in the end the King had to give in to the majority in the Folketing. Since then, the parliamentary principle has never been in doubt – not even during the German occupation (1940-1945), and finally in 1953 the principle was established in the text of the Constitution itself (section 15).

This is probably the background for the fact that Danish politicians and the Danish public have been especially sensible to the challenges posed to parliamentary influence by the EU membership.

## The Problem

The policies of the European Union play an increasing role in the creation of national rules in the member states. Regulations are directly applicable in the member states, and directives in almost every policy area have to be implemented into national law and thus limit the sovereignty of the national legislative bodies (ie in practice the national parliaments).

As all member states of the EU adhere to a parliamentary form of democracy (in various forms, however), these facts pose a problem because the decision-making process of the EU changes the normal (national) balance between the legislative and executive powers. In a parliamentary democracy Parliament has the final say in relation to new legislation; in the EU, however, the ministers of the member states (in the Council) can pass regulations which are binding – also for the national parliaments. At least in theory this could lead to a situation where the minister of a member state participates in carrying through new regulations without any guarantee that a majority in the national parliament supports the measure and will be willing to pass the necessary implementing legislation.

This places the national parliament in an unacceptable dilemma: either to pass legislation that would not otherwise have commanded a majority or to break the international obligations connected with membership of the EU. Consequently, national procedures to avoid this situation should be found.

Turning to Denmark more specifically, the possibility of a conflict of viewpoints between the relevant minister and the parliamentary majority in EU questions is not only a theoretical, but also a practical possibility, because most Danish governments – as mentioned – are minority governments.[1] Thus, there is no guarantee that the

1 For the last 50 years there have only been majority governments for 12 years (1957–1964, 1968–1971, and 1993–1994).

government in every policy question can command a majority in Parliament, even though the parliamentary principle in itself of course assures that the government is in accordance with Parliament in its overall policies.[2]

With regard to foreign policy questions in general, the Danish Constitution has acknowledged this problem in section 19. This provision states that foreign policy is conducted by the government as a so-called 'royal prerogative'. However, this principle is greatly modified, as the consent of the Folketing is necessary *before* any obligation is entered into by the Danish government if the obligation requires new legislation in Denmark or in any other way requires the participation of the Folketing (e.g. by requiring new appropriations). In this way the Folketing can never be placed in the dilemma described above in relation to foreign policy in general.

However, it is generally assumed that section 19 does not apply to the actions of Danish ministers in the EU decision-making bodies. Here the ministers do not act 'on behalf of Denmark' (as section 19 requires), but as members of the authorities established by the EU treaties. Consequently, there is no constitutional requirement that the government secures a majority in the Folketing for the Danish point of view before accepting new EU legislation. The considerations leading to the modifications of section 19, however, are even more relevant in relation to the EU as at least some EU regulations become Danish law directly, whereas ordinary obligations according to international law must be transformed into Danish law before having any legal effect in Denmark.[3]

## The EEC Accession Act of 1972

To a certain extent it was realized as early as 1972 when Denmark became a member of the community that the relationship between the government and the Folketing in relation to EEC questions could not be handled in a satisfactory way within the existing Danish rules. Thus, the Accession Act section 6, para. 2 stated that the government was obliged to *inform* a committee of the Folketing

2 In countries where majority governments are the rule, this problem is less relevant. However, party discipline can be broken on specific matters (eg this has been the case in the UK), and from a democratic point of view it seems natural that Parliament takes part in the formulation of policy in any case.

3 Denmark adheres to the so-called principle of dualism with regard to the relationship between international and Danish law. This means that international treaties etc entered into by the Danish government – even with the acceptance of the Folketing – have no direct legal effect in Denmark.

of Council decisions that were directly applicable in Denmark (regulations) or required the action of the Danish Folketing (directives). As indicated, this requirement was only a duty to inform, however, and not to demand the acceptance of the committee. Thus, it could still be possible that the relevant Danish minister did not have the support of a majority in the Folketing for the point of view that he presented in the EEC Council.

A Committee for Common Market Affairs had been established in connection with the negotiations leading to Danish accession to the EEC, and this committee has since then been the committee that received the information required by the Accession Act. The committee – since 1994 called the EU Committee – consists of 17 members elected proportionally by the parties of the Folketing. As party discipline is very strong in the Danish Folketing, and as the parties generally choose some of the more influential members to sit on this committee, it means that the proposals which are acceptable to the committee can also be expected to be accepted by the whole Folketing.

## Developments Since 1972 Concerning the Formulation of Danish EEC Policies

After a couple of instances in the first year of EEC membership where a parliamentary majority felt that the government had been out of line in its policies in the Council, a new procedure for the formulation of Danish EEC policies was agreed upon. According to this procedure the government must consult with the EU Committee before all important decisions in the EU Council, and it must present its point of view on the subjects to be discussed in the Council together with a proposal for a Danish policy on the subject concerned. The Committee then – after a discussion with the relevant minister – either accepts or rejects the proposal of the government, or it may itself formulate a mandate within which the Danish government is allowed to negotiate in the Council.[4]

In any case the Danish government must act within the limits of the mandate of the EU Committee; *inter alia*, this implies that if a result in the Council cannot be reached within the mandate of the EU Committee, the minister has to go back to the Committee to get

[4] The Committee does not take any formal votes, but on the basis of the debate in the Committee, the chairman concludes what the mandate of the government in each case is.

another mandate.[5] In order not to make this system too inflexible the mandates are, however, normally formulated in a relatively broad manner so that some room for negotiations is left for the government.

To some foreign observers this system has seemed to be too complicated to be workable in practice, but the general conception in Denmark is that it provides a reasonable balance between the influence of the Folketing and the possibilities of the government to engage actively in the EU decision-making procedures.[6] Also, there seem to be no indications that Danish interests are not taken into consideration to the same degree as the interests of any other member country.

The consultation procedure has been in effect since 1973 and has obvious benefits for both the government and the Folketing. If the government actually acts within the mandates laid down by the EU Committee, the government does not risk criticism after a decision in the Council for having misjudged the points of view of the Folketing, a criticism which might ultimately lead to a vote of no confidence. At the same time, the Folketing through the EU Committee becomes involved in the EU decision-making process at a time when it is still possible to influence the outcome of the process.

The effect of the procedure is that the government has achieved the *prior consent* of the Folketing to its EU policies, thus achieving a state of affairs very similar to the one required by section 19 of the Constitution concerning traditional foreign policy questions. Among the EU countries, this is an extraordinary form of cooperation between the government and parliament in EU matters, although several of the other member countries, too, have formed special European committees in their parliaments, but none of them has been given the same formal influence as the Danish committee.

However, it is important to notice that the initiative concerning the formulation of Danish EU policies still rests with the government. This will probably hold true no matter what kind of institutional arrangement is instituted with respect to the cooperation between the Folketing and the government, as the government has far greater administrative and investigative capacities than the

5 If the Danish government acts within the mandate, but the Council by a majority vote defeats the Danish points of view, there is, of course, no need to get another mandate from the EU Committee. This is not a question of the relationship between the Danish legislative and executive authorities, but a consequence of the voting rules of the EU treaties.

6 Jokingly it has been said that the EEC (before 1995) had 13, and not 12 members: the 12 member countries and the Danish EU Committee.

Folketing will ever have.[7] Furthermore, there is no doubt that the governing principle concerning all foreign policy matters (as expressed in section 19 of the Constitution) still is that the government is the principal actor in international affairs.

There has been general agreement in Denmark that the basic idea of the mandate-giving procedure is sound and in accordance with Danish parliamentary traditions. However, over the years the procedures have been amended in several respects in order to make the influence of the Committee more effective. One change occurred in the 1980s when it was decided that the mandates should be taken down in writing in the minutes of the Committee. Thus, there could be no discussion later on in the EU decision-making process of what the Committee had actually authorized the minister to agree to, as had been the case in a couple of instances.

Another weakness of the procedure agreed upon in 1973 was that the Committee exerted its influence at a relatively late point in the decision-making process. A procedure has therefore now been established whereby the Committee receives all proposals for new EU rules as soon as they have been translated into Danish, accompanied by factual notes prepared by the Foreign Ministry pointing out the implications of the proposals in relation to existing Danish law. If the proposals are changed during their passage through the EU machinery, new notes will be forwarded to the Committee. This procedure increases the possibilities of the Committee actually to influence the decision-making process in its early stages.

Furthermore, cooperation between the EU Committee and the other specialized committees in the Folketing has been improved. The committees now inform each other of what goes on in their respective committees concerning the EU proposals, but the EU Committee is still the only one that gives mandates to the Danish government. It thus plays a co-ordinating role in relation to the specialized committees.

Even if the increased role of the specialized committees is undoubtedly an advantage for the decision-making process in general, it has also given rise to a certain rivalry between the specialized committees and the EU Committee. The specialized committees normally enter the decision-making process earlier than the EU Committee, so even though the EU Committee is still the only one with formal power in relation to the government's EU policies, the specialized committees can in practice influence the ministers to such an extent that it would be difficult for them to

[7] The administrative apparatus of the Folketing has recently been increased considerably, but still it is small compared to the government administration.

change their point of view later on in the decision-making process without causing political trouble. Furthermore, the specialized committees will, of course, view matters from their specific point of view, whereas the EU Committee with its co-ordinating role will take broader political aspects into consideration.

As a consequence of the increased number of EU proposals and of the growing role of the EU Committee in the Danish decision-making process on these proposals, the staff of the Committee has also been increased in recent years. Today four university-educated assistants and a number of clerical workers assist the Committee in its work.[8]

## Practical Politics or Legal (Constitutional) Rule?

As indicated in the sections above, the Constitution contains no explicit provision securing the influence of the EU Committee (and of the Folketing in general) with respect to Danish EU policies. The influence of the Committee has not even been secured at statutory level as the provision of the Accesssion Act only requires – and constantly has been interpreted only to require – the government to inform, but not to consult the Committee or to accept its points of view. If the present procedure should, anyhow, be considered to be legally – or even constitutionally – binding, it must therefore be on the basis of customary law.

In order to accept a procedure as legally binding on the basis of customary law, Danish legal theory requires that the procedure is adhered to over a lengthy period of time, and that it is adhered to consistently during that time. This requirement seems to be met if developments from 1973 till today are considered.[9] However, even if these so-called *objective* requirements are met, this does not in itself constitute a legal rule, but could be a consequence of the political prudence of the government.

Thus, also a *subjective* requirement should be met, implying that the parties involved (*in casu* the government and the Folketing and its party groups) should feel legally obliged to follow the procedure. This is, of course, difficult to investigate, but on the basis of

8 In international comparison this may not seem very impressive. However, it should be compared to the ordinary parliamentary committees which have normally only one or two academic assistants.

9 Instances could be mentioned where the government was criticised for having overstepped its mandate, but this criticism was not supported by a majority in the Folketing, and generally this kind of criticism is rare.

authoritative statements from central politicians it was not possible to establish in 1989 that this requirement had been met.[10] Actually, influential politicians from several parties claimed that, in principle, the government had the sole responsibility for Danish EU policies – thus giving a strong indication that the subjective requirement had *not* been met.

However, the fact that the procedure has been consistently adhered to for another six years in itself suggests that the procedure is considered to be legally binding. Another factor pointing in the same direction is the fact that the mandate procedure has been amended several times (the last time being in 1994) by agreement between the government and the Committee – each time taking for granted that the basic features of the arrangement should be left unchanged. Finally, the Committe itself in a description of its work and functions claims that the mandate-giving procedure is part of Danish law.[11] With some caution it can therefore probably be concluded that it has become part of Danish law that the government must obtain the consent of the EU Committee before advancing Danish policies in the EU institutions.

If we accept this point of view, the question arises at what level in the legal order to place this legal rule – is the rule a constitutional or a statutory rule? The rule concerns an important part of the relationship between government and parliament, and this indicates that the rule should be considered a constitutional rule, as one of the basic functions of a constitution is to regulate this relationship – especially considering the crucial role that this relationship has played in Danish constitutional history. One of the consequences of characterizing the rule as constitutional would be that it can only be changed according to the Danish constitutional amendment procedure (section 88 of the Constitution), meaning that it would be very difficult to change, as a constitutional amendment requires the majority of two subsequent Folketing and the vote of 40% of the electorate in a referendum.[12]

On the other hand it is fairly obvious that even a rule at the constitutional level which is only based on customary law is more vulnerable to changing political circumstances than a written constitutional rule. Thus, if and when the Danish Constitution is revised, the position of the EU Committee (or another form of

[10] Jørgen Albœk Jensen, ***Parlamentarismens statsretlige betydning*** (København: Jurist- og Økonomforbundets Forlag, 1989) pp. 131–135.

[11] Europaudvalget, februar 1995, p. 3.

[12] Experience shows that public interest in constitutional questions is small, so the greatest obstacle for a constitutional amendment would probably be a low turnout in the required referendum.

parliamentary influence on the formulation of Danish EU policies) should be explicitly secured in the Constitution itself.[13]

## Other Institutions Influencing Danish EU Policies

As demonstrated, the government and the EU Committee play the crucial roles in the formulation of Danish EU policies. However, also other parts of the Danish political system influence this process to some degree.

Parliament as a whole has its most important function in connection with the implementation of EU directives. If Danish law does not already fulfill the requirements of EU directives, it must be changed. This requires the participation of the Folketing – either by passing acts that directly bring about the state of law required by EU law, or by giving statutory authorization to the government to issue administrative orders to that effect.[14]

The Folketing can also be involved in EU questions according to a rule which was enacted in connection with the European single market in 1986. Considering the great importance of some of the proposals relating to the single market, it was determined that before being decided in the EU Committee, the most important proposals might undergo a more principled discussion in the plenary Folketing. However, this possibility never achieved any practical importance.

In connection with the implementation of EU directives, the specialized committees of the Folketing should also be mentioned. Generally speaking, there is a specialized committee for each ministry, and the committees play a very important part in the ordinary legislative process as the bodies where the political negotiations on the contents of the acts take place. This is, of course, also the case in connection with acts implementing EU directives. As mentioned above, the specialized committees are also involved in the formulation of Danish EU policies in connection with new directives discussed in the EU institutions, but do not play the same crucial role here.

The Danish members of the European Parliament do not have any

[13] In connection with the most recent Constitution Day (5 June 1995) several speakers mentioned the role of the EU Committee as one of the points to be discussed in connection with a constitutional amendment.

[14] In the latter instance legislative power is delegated to the government. This is very common in Danish law – both generally and in connection with EU-related legislation.

formal connection to the national decision-making bodies except for the fact that they receive all documents officially that the EU Committee receives. But on a more informal level there is close contact between the MEPs and the national political scene. A few of the Danish members of the European Parliament are also members of the Folketing, and this naturally secures a close connection. However, in recent years most parties have banned this possibility of 'dual membership'. Even so, there is still close cooperation between the parties of the Folketing and their members of the European Parliament, eg by inviting the MEPs to participate in the meetings of national parliamentary groups, by exchanging information, and by personal informal contacts.

On the other hand, the influence of the MEPs is rather limited due to the fact that most Danish parties do not consider the work of the European Parliament to be too important. This has the consequence that those put up for election to the European Parliament are generally either rather unknown politicians or politicians wanting a kind of 'retirement job', meaning that their domestic political influence has peaked.

## Concluding Remarks

Developments since 1973 with regard to the formulation of the Danish EU policies show that it is possible to adapt existing political institutions to major changes in the conditions for policy making if there is the political will to safeguard the basic principles of the Constitution. The decision-making process of the EU created a problem in relation to the parliamentary principle of the Danish Constitution as the Constitution did not contain any provision to guarantee the formal influence of the Folketing on Danish EU policies.

By the institution of the mandate procedure, this problem has been solved in a satisfactory and flexible way – both from a political and practical point of view, and to a certain extent also from a legal point of view. At least in this respect there thus is no democratic deficit in the Danish relationship with the EU.

# The European Union: An Opportunity for the French Parliament to Recover Powers?

*Louis Dubouis*

1958 was a bad year for the French Parliament. On 1 January the Treaties of Rome came into force. On 4 October France adopted a new constitution. At the time, however, few noticed the relationship which was to grow between the birth of the Fifth Republic and the development of European integration with respect to the powers of the French Parliament.

What seemed important in 1958 was the weakening of Parliament and the corresponding increase in the power of the Executive caused by the constitution of 1958, especially through the limitation on the length of parliamentary sessions and the powers of the assemblies, the strengthening of the powers of the Executive to a point where the possibility of calling a vote of confidence had become a weapon for the Government rather than a means of control to be used by Parliament. As far as the role of the European Community was concerned, it did not seem important enough to establish a transfer of power from national to Community authorities. More importantly, this transfer did not seem necessarily to affect the internal equilibrium within French institutions, but only that between French and Community ones. The two spheres seemed to be complete strangers.

The constitutional amendment of 23 June 1992, made necessary by the Treaty of Maastricht, has just proven in a very clear way that European integration and the relationship between Parliament and the Executive are linked in significant ways. The French Parliament has seen some power to influence the making of European Union policy recognized, in accordance with Declaration no 13, in the annex to the Treaty of Maastricht, concerning the role of parliaments of Member States in the elaboration of European policy. However, this can only happen by granting Parliament new powers within the institutional framework of the Fifth Republic. Thus there is a link between the reconquest of power on a European and on a national level, and this indicates the difficulties which, in countries such as France, parliaments must overcome to become one day the cornerstones of European integration.

Elements of these problems concerning the relationship between Parliament and Community institutions are not unique to France. Therefore, in keeping with the theme of national models for parliamentary influence, this study will concentrate on national issues, that is to say the traditional instruments at the disposal of the French Parliament, the new instruments which it has given itself, an evaluation of their functioning and new propositions in the light of the inter-governmental conference of 1996.

## The Traditional Instruments and Their Weakness

Little by little, the great difference in the respective positions of Parliament and the Executive with respect to European integration has been felt. The former has experienced a transfer of power to the European Community which has not been compensated, as is the case for the latter, by active participation in the decision-making process of the Community. Clearly, until 1979, the two chambers benefited from the presence within the European Parliament of a real 'delegation' because their members were drawn from the National Assembly for two-thirds and from the Senate for the remaining third. But this representation, which some propose to recreate under the title of a European Senate, had power which was limited by the narrowness of that given to the European Parliament itself, which, except for the budget since 1970, until the enactment of the Single European Act, had a purely consultative function. This explains the fact that neither the National Assembly nor the Senate has, with few exceptions, ever paid much attention to what its members sitting in Strasbourg were doing.

If the two assemblies want to exert an influence over Community policy, they must make use of the instruments of information and control over the Executive which are available to them. This possible influence is limited by the superiority of the Executive over the legislative power which is a characteristic of the Fifth Republic.

This is all the more true in the field of foreign relations. The President of the Republic, over whom Parliament has no direct control, considers this domain, within which fall European matters, to be his exclusively, which is why he participates in European Councils. And the Government has a greater margin of autonomy here than where domestic matters are concerned.

The members of Parliament can use a whole series of procedures which allow them to get information concerning, among other matters, questions of European policy. The number of parliamentary questions, written or oral, varies from 300–400 from year to year.[1] Some of these questions force the Government to give information concerning Community policies being negotiated and to present its position. However, because these policies are the result of negotiation among 12 or 15 partners, it is easy for the Government to refuse to take a firm position, especially because the question cannot result in the passing of a resolution by the Assembly even if it is a question on which there is debate.[2] So in the absence of any committee on European matters, the information at the disposal of members of Parliament is often insufficient.[3]

The use of techniques to seek the approval of Parliament is not a very effective way for Parliament to control the policy followed by the Government in European matters. The 'majority factor' protects the Government from any unpleasant surprises. It can only be forced to resign by a majority of members of the National Assembly, and it was only during the 1967-1968 period and between 1988 and 1993 that it did not have a majority in the National Assembly which would protect it from such a threat. Only one motion of censure has been passed under the Fifth Republic, on 5 October 1962.

In practice, when the Government asks Parliament for approval, either through a vote of confidence on the programme or through a declaration of general policy under Art. 49.1 of the constitution, or by the adoption of a law under Art. 49.3 of the constitution, it is putting pressure on Parliament. This was the case on 25 November 1992 when the Prime Minister, Pierre Bérégovoy, asked for the approval of the National Assembly to strengthen his hand during the GATT negotiations.[4] When the initiative for a vote of approval comes from Parliament, it is governed by the restrictive conditions found in Art. 49.2 of the constitution. The vote has to be preceded

1 Dorothée Meyer, 'Le contrôle du Parlement français sur la politique communautaire sous la Vie République' (thèse, Université d'Aix-Marseille III, 1993) p. 46.

2 Thus, on the adoption of the directive 'Télévision sans frontière', questions by Mr Philippe de Villiers, JO Assemblée Nationale, Débats 12 avril 1989, pp. 126–127.

3 See Dorothée Meyer, op. cit. pp. 54 ff.

4 He also asked for the approval of the Senate under Art. 49-4 of the constitution.

by a motion of censure signed by at least one-tenth of the members of the National Assembly, who can only sign one motion per session, and adopted by a majority vote. This procedure has only been used twice with respect to European questions: once on 10 May 1989 in order to force the Government to inform Parliament about presidential policies, and a second time on 27 May 1992 in respect of the Common Agricultural Policy, when it was defeated by only three votes.

The application of its superiority in matters of European policy means that the Executive can prevail over any resistance on the part of Parliament, even when the latter has certain powers which apply since the adoption of the European rule in 1992.

This is true concerning the adoption of legislation to implement Community regulations. The best and most significant example is in the laws transposing Community directives into domestic legislation. The limitation on the competence of the legislature found in Articles 34 and 37 of the constitution result in the transposition being mostly by regulation and not by legislation. When legislation is required, the Government has at its disposal ways to impose respect for the primacy of Community law, in addition to the primacy which French courts accord to directives over domestic legislation.[5] On 30 November 1978, the National Assembly voted an *exception d'irrecevabilité* implementing the sixth VAT directive instituting a uniform basis on which VAT is calculated. The Government fought back against this rebellion which, according to Prime Minister Raymond Barre, undermined the international credibility of France. The bill was passed after being presented again on 6 December once the threat of a vote of confidence was raised.

The only possibility available to Members of Parliament is to ask the *Conseil constitutionnel* to declare unconstitutional a law implementing a directive. If such a measure succeeded, a very complex conflict could arise between constitutional and Community norms. In any case, the decision would not be taken by the two chambers.

Parliament has broader powers when it is asked to apply Community treaties because their ratification requires legislative approval (Art. 53 of the constitution) or a referendum (Art. 11). A refusal is conceivable, as shown by the vote of the National Assembly on 30 August 1954 on the Treaty of 27 May 1952 creating the European Defence Community. But this refusal took place under the

5 Conseil d'Etat 28 February 1992, S.A. Rothmans International France, Recueil des arrêts du Conseil d'Etat, p. 80, conclusions Laroque, 'L'actualité juridique Droit Administratif', p. 329, chronique C. Maugüé and R. Schwartz, *Revue française de droit administratif*, 1992, p. 425, note L. Dubouis.

Fourth Republic and when the Government had refused to call for a vote of confidence. A similar incident under the Fifth Republic is highly unlikely. Thus in 1977 the Government used all the measures available to it to obtain the ratification of the agreement concerning the election of the members of the European Parliament by universal suffrage reached at the Council of Ministers on 20 September 1976. Its theory, that Parliament cannot vote an amendment to a bill submitted to it because this would result in giving the Executive orders, prevailed. The Prime Minister thus obtained this ratification under the conditions of Art. 49.3 of the constitution.

## The New Instruments which Parliament Created for Itself

The lack of sufficient traditional means of control was felt more sharply when Parliament realized how important Community matters were becoming. It thus wanted to create something which was more efficient because it was better adapted to overseeing Community policies – the delegations for the European Communities, one for each house. These delegations have allowed the houses to maximise their right to information and to pass resolutions since the constitutional reform of 25 June 1992.

The parliamentary delegations for the European Communities, which since Act 94-976 of 10 June 1994 are called *delegations for the European Union*, were created by an Act of 6 July 1979 which underwent major changes in the Act of 10 May 1990.[6]

The delegations owe their existence to a double distrust: of the European Parliament and of the French Government. Members of parliament distrust the European Parliament, elected by universal suffrage, both because they fear that it will try to enlarge its powers and because they feel that it will become more and more foreign. The quite recent unfortunate incident concerning the implementation of the sixth VAT directive made them regret that they had not been informed in time of the question of the harmonization of VAT and thus had to deliberate in haste. The delegations had as their essential function to inform their assemblies about Community questions.

6 Gilles Cottereau, 'Les Délégations parlementaires pour les Communautés européennes', *Revue de droit public*, 1982, p. 35; Hervé Groud, 'Les Délégations parlementaires pour les Communautés européennes', R.D.P. 1991, p. 1309; Stephane Pierre Caps, 'L'adaptation du Parlement français au système communautaire', *Revue française de droit constitutionnel*, 1991, p. 254.

The failures experienced in this function caused by a lack of means put at the disposal of the delegations and by inadequate information from the Executive led to a strengthening of the institution in 1990. Now each Delegation consists of 36 members (instead of 18 in 1979) chosen in the same proportion as the members from each party in Parliament. The delegates can also be members of the European Parliament, contrary to the rule at first.

The delegations are supposed to

> follow the workings of the institutions of the European Community in order to inform their colleagues concerning European developments.[7]

This information is furnished by the Government which must communicate all draft directives, regulations or other actions, as well as all relevant documents from the Communities, as soon they are transmitted to the Council of Ministers. Moreover, the Government must keep the delegations informed concerning negotiations in progress. Finally, the delegations can ask to hear ministers and representatives from European Community institutions. This corresponds to a well-established practice, but the Government was never very enthusiastic about sending its ministers before the delegations.

The delegations remain, however, very different from parliamentary committees. Three times, in 1979, 1990 and then in 1992 when the constitution was being reformed, the question was raised whether to have not just simple delegations but real permanent committees, that is to say, bodies which would participate in the drafting of legis-lation. This would imply the amendment of Art. 43 of the constitution which limits to six the number of committees for each assembly.

The hostility of the standing committees, especially the Foreign Affairs Committee, in addition to the hesitation of the Government being unwilling to submit itself to yet another committee, put an end to this initiative. Not only do the delegations have no constitutional existence, but they appear to be subordinated to the committees. In the beginning, the only power the delegations have is to transmit to the appropriate parliamentary committee the information received, with their analysis and advice if they feel it necessary, even about Community actions, and to reply to requests for information from parliamentary committees concerning any decision or proposed decision or proposed domestic legislation in the European field.

The constitutional amendment of 25 June 1992 represents a

[7] Article 4 of the Act of 10 May 1990.

particularly important step towards the reconquest of power by the French parliament.[8] Parliament, with the initiative coming from the Senate, took advantage of the fact that any proposed constitutional amendment had to be passed in identical terms by both houses when an amendment was made necessary by the decision of the *Conseil constitutionnel* (no 92-308 of 9 April 1992, deciding that a certain number of articles of the Treaty of Maastricht were incompatible with the constitution) to ask for something in exchange for their vote. It introduced in title XV on 'The European Communities and the European Union', in accordance with Arts. 88-1, 88-2 and 88-3, which make the modifications made necessary by the Treaty, Art. 88-4 which reads as follows:

> The Government puts forward to the National Assembly and to the Senate, as soon as they reach the European Council of Ministers, proposals for Community legislation.
>
> During or outside parliamentary sessions, resolutions may be passed as provided in this article, according to the procedure established by each house.

Article 88-4 is the result of a parliamentary initiative which forced the Executive to accept an enlargement of the revision of the constitution and to abandon its principle of 'the Treaty, only the Treaty, and nothing but the Treaty'. It had to give in to Parliament's 'hunger to reform' which led members of Parliament to ask a price for their support.

The provisions of Art. 88-4 show the desire of Parliament to intervene at the earliest possible moment in the production of Community legislation by giving it the right to receive proposals for legislation as soon as they reach the European Council of Ministers. More importantly, these dispositions recognize a new power, that of both houses to send resolutions to the Government, whereas previously, according to the decisions of the *Conseil constitutionnel*, in order to protect the power of the Government, they could only do so for matters concerning their internal workings (CC. 2DC 17, 18 and 24 June 1959, Rec. 58). It is true, however, that when the *Conseil constitutionnel* has had the opportunity to check, as it must under Art. 61 of the constitution, the constitutionality of the standing orders adopted by each house in pursuance of Art. 88-4(2),

[8] Robert Ladrecht, 'Europeanization of Domestic Politics and Institutions: The Case of France', *Journal of Common Market Studies*, 1994, vol. 32, no.1, pp. 76 ff; Peter Oliver, 'The French Constitution and the Treaty of Maastricht', *International and Comparative Law Quarterly*, 1994, vol. 43, 1, pp. 16 ff.; Marie-France Verdier, 'La révision constitutionnelle du 25 juin 1992 nécessaire à la ratification du traité de Maastricht et l'extension des pouvoirs des assemblées parlementaires françaises', *Revue de droit public*, 1994, pp. 1137 ff.

it has done this strictly in order not to encroach upon the prerogatives of the Government.

In its decisions DC 92-314 of 17 December 1992[9] concerning the standing orders of the National Assembly and 315 DC of 11 January 1993 concerning those of the Senate, the *Conseil constitutionnel* cut short all discussion concerning the legal effect of the resolutions when it declared that 'each house has the faculty to give an opinion (*avis*) in adopting a resolution', whereas the Senate had voluntarily replaced the term '*opinion*' by '*resolution*'. During debate, the senators were quick to deny that the resolutions had any binding legal effect, but without reducing them to simple opinions.[10] The *Conseil constitutionnel* added that the passing of a resolution

> could not either diminish the prerogatives which belong to the Government under the constitution nor lead to questioning its responsibility which remains exclusively governed by articles 49 and 50 of the constitution.

Among other things, the *Conseil constitutionnel* has recognized the right of the Government to exercise a certain amount of control of the agenda of both houses when it agreed that the Government can set a time limit for action on a proposed resolution (one month according to the standing orders of both houses) and can decide, as in legislative matters, that a proposed resolution be given priority status on the calendar. Finally, the *Conseil constitutionnel* rejected the Senate's practice of meeting outside the normal sessions, which means that during this period resolutions may be passed only in committees.

## Which Influence Can Parliament Exert?

Of course, in order to have the maximum influence over the evolution of European policy, Parliament has to use all the instruments at its disposal. It has not hesitated to do so. But, until now, some instruments have seemed to be used less than others because they have proved to be less effective.

This is the case for ties with the European Parliament. Very few members of the French parliament are now members of the European Parliament and those who are there are split up among

9 *Revue française de droit constitutionnel*, 1993, no. 13, pp. 131 ff., chronique P. Gaïa.

10 See M. Gaillard, 'Le retour des résolutions parlementaires', *Revue française de droit constitutionnel*, 1993, no. 16; B. Rullier, 'L'article 88-4 de la Constitution: un premier bilan', *Revue de droit public*, 1994, p. 1698.

many political groups, which lessens their impact. Moreover, the Conference (*Assises*) of 27-30 November 1990 in Rome proved that there was competition between the European Parliament and national parliaments in the attempt to bring more democratic accountability to the European Union. The discussion which began between the Delegation of the National Assembly and the Commission on the subject of domestic markets for gas and electricity was difficult and brief.

The relations among national parliaments have become closer since the creation of the Conference of Specialised Bodies of the Community Assemblies (COSAC) held in Paris on 16-17 November 1989 in which the European Parliament was also represented. But until now COSAC has been more a body for debate than for taking decisions.[11]

It is within the national framework, ie in the relationship between Parliament and the Executive, that Parliament exerts the most influence. Since 1993, it has tried to use in the best possible way the new instruments at its disposal. If it is too early to draw any final conclusions, we can speak of several tendencies.

The parliamentary delegations of the European Union have become an essential instrument of parliamentary control because of their specialization and also because they receive all the information and propositions concerning European actions. The National Assembly, since the decision of the Presidents' Committee of 20 April 1993, implemented by the reform of the standing orders of the National Assembly of 26 January 1994, and the Senate since 12 October 1994, have both taken this path. Each delegation now systematically examines all propositions for Community decision and studies in depth those which involve provisions of a legislative nature.

Act 94-976 of 10 June 1994 ensures in addition that the delegations will receive propositions concerning the second and third pillars of the European Union: Common Foreign and Security Policy (CFSP) and Cooperation in justice and home affairs. And the delegations themselves have the right to propose resolutions.

The delegations have been very active since the beginning of the present legislature (March 1993), especially the Delegation of the National Assembly, thanks to the strong impulse given by Philippe Séguin president of the Assembly. During the past two years, it has held 99 meetings and adopted 86 reports. The great majority of the resolutions adopted by the National Assembly come from the

[11] Ch. Lequesne, 'Paris Bruxelles – Comment se fait la politique européenne de la France' (Paris: Presses de la Fondation nationale des sciences politiques, 1993) p. 256.

delegation's propositions. On the other hand, the information concerning the Union remains in the hands of a few dozen members of parliament; the others do no feel involved, except when the issue is of special interest to them.

The implementation of the powers contained in Art. 88-4 has resulted in several differences of opinion between Parliament and the Government. Most of these differences, however, are resolved and Parliament has undoubtedly scored some points and won some ground in its attempt to influence the Government's European policy.

A procedure for the transmission of propositions concerning Community actions containing provisions of a legislative nature has been established. The *Conseil d'Etat* decides which texts must be transmitted to the two houses: those which will require an act of Parliament to be implemented in French law and also those which, directly or indirectly, would have required the intervention of the legislature if they were adopted on the national level without a decision by the Community. Involving the distinction between texts of a legislative order (Art. 34 of the constitution) and those requiring only regulations (Art. 37 of the constitution), the disagreements between the houses of parliament and the Government are minor.

On the other hand, the houses have protested vigorously against what M. Pandraud, President of the Delegation of the National Assembly has called a too literal ('*notariale*') interpretation of Art. 88-4 which deprives Parliament not of the information but of the right to pass resolutions concerning propositions which have great political importance.

As a matter of fact, the Government eliminates decisions of the European Commission under the pretext that they are not submitted to the Council of Ministers. The same literal interpretation allows it to exclude the decisions within the framework of the second and third pillars because they are not Community actions. This is strictly true, but deprives the houses of all power concerning decisions which are politically important, for example, concerning border controls, a situation which provoked a letter of protest signed by the presidents of both houses on 19 April 1994.

Lastly, inter-institutional agreements such as those of 1993 concerning the procedures for the application of the principle of subsidiarity and budgetary discipline and the improvement of procedure for budgetary matters are not transmitted under Art. 88-4 either. The Government undoubtedly wants to leave itself some room to manoeuvre in the delicate negotiations involved in this type of decision.

As for time limits for transmission, the houses have justly complained that they are often informed too late and have just a few days to give their opinions, or even no time at all once the decision of the Council of Ministers has been taken.[12] The complaints on this subject seem to be subsiding. The Government and its services are making more of an effort to act in a timely manner. Most importantly, after being unfavourably inclined for a long time, the Government has now agreed to invoke before Community bodies the need for parliamentary examination. This is a kind of scrutiny reserve.

In the circular of 19 July 1994 concerning the role of the Parliament in the elaboration of Community actions, the Prime Minister declared that when the inclusion of a decision on the agenda of the Council of Ministers is requested less than 14 days before it is to meet, the permanent representative will oppose it if the decision is in the process of being examined by Parliament and Parliament has shown its intention to make its opinion known on the subject. The French Government did this for the first time on 26 and 27 July 1994 when the COREPER was discussing the granting to South Africa of a generalised tariff preference in commercial matters. When the inclusion is requested at least 14 days before the meeting, the permanent representative will either ask for a postponement or say that the final position of France will be adopted after hearing from Parliament.

The evaluation of the results of this system is most delicate. The houses have adopted resolutions. From January 1993 to 31 March 1995 there were 35 in the National Assembly and 20 in the Senate covering various subjects from the application of VAT to the conveyance of persons to the Uruguay Round or structural funds or the Community budget. This rhythm seems to have been maintained since then. In general these resolutions invite the Government to adopt a specific position in Community negotiations which is never very different from the text proposed by the Delegation whether the resolution is adopted in committee or in the full house. Informal cooperation between the two houses almost always ensures that the two resolutions converge.

But what is the impact of these resolutions on the position which the Government adopts? The circular of 19 July 1994 states that the resolutions will be examined by an interministerial committee on European affairs which will meet once a month. A circular of 21 March 1994 announced this examination in order to take into consideration during European negotiations resolutions passed by the houses. Members of Parliament are kept informed of the fate of their resolutions. The Minister of European Affairs, M. Lamasoure,

[12] See the report of the Délégation de l'Assemblée Nationale no. 1436 of 28 June 1994, presented by M. Robert Pandraud, and that of the Délégation du Sénat no. 224 of 15 février 1995, presented by M. Jacques Genton.

even said that he once followed the advice of Parliament rather than that of the Prime Minister.[13]

Nevertheless, a resolution is not a mandate. If the Government agrees, the resolution may be a trump for it in European negotiations. If it disagrees, the Government is not bound by the resolution. The judgment of the president of the Delegation of the National Assembly, M. Pandraud, is laconic: the Government could 'do better' but isn't responsible for EU decisions which more and more often are taken by a majority vote. He concludes that any real progress towards parliamentary control of actions of the European Union will be necessarily global and integrated into the decision-making process of the Union.[14]

## Towards New Propositions

In France, as in other countries of the Union, the perspective of the inter-governmental conference of 1996 during which reform of the institutions will be considered has caused intense analysis concerning the role of national parliaments in these institutions. Moreover, the Delegation of the National Assembly has indicated that it hopes that the national parliaments as well as the European Parliament will be consulted by the study group in charge of the preparation for the conference. Time constraints, in particular the perspective of the Council of Ministers meeting in Cannes in June 1995 and presidential elections, mean that at present, we have only the broad lines of a position. Nevertheless, several propositions are not without interest.

It will surprise no one that the two houses agree on the absolute necessity to reinforce the role of national parliaments in the decision-making process of the Union. They continue to refute the idea that it is only the European Parliament that should be called upon to bring more democratic accountability to the European Union. They therefore feel that the Maastricht Treaty, and in particular the two annexes concerning the parliaments, represent only a very timid beginning. It has been pointed out that the Declaration on the Conference of the Parliaments has never been implemented concretely[15] and that the Declaration on the Role of

[13] Declaration before the National Assembly, 29 June 1994. See rapport Pandraud, p. 384.

[14] Rapport Pandraud, p. 88.

[15] Nicole Catala and Nicole Ameline, 'Quelles réformes pour l'Europe de demain?, Assemblée Nationale, Délégation pour l'Union Européenne', *Rapport d'information* no. 1939, p. 92.

National Parliaments in the European Union was not binding either on national governments or on community institutions.[16]

Within the framework of the 1996 revision, the propositions of course concern the reform of the institutions of the European Union and not of the national system. Nevertheless, the Delegation of the Senate believes that the present system could be improved by integrating into the Treaties the Declaration on the Role of National Parliaments in the European Union. This text provides that

> the governments of the member-States will ensure, *inter alia*, that national Parliaments receive Commission proposals for legislation in good time for information or possible examination.

We have already seen that consultation is often impossible because the Commission submits proposed decisions to the Council of Ministers too late. Incorporating the Declaration into the Treaties would give the idea of time needed for information and examination by the national parliaments a binding character in order to reinforce its observance by the Commission.[17]

Important differences exist between the National Assembly's and the Senate's propositions concerning the way to associate national parliaments with the decision-making process of the Union.

The President of the National Assembly, Philippe Séguin, proposes a bicameral European Parliament in which the national parliaments would constitute the lower house and the European Parliament the upper house. Each national parliament would have a number of votes equivalent to that of its country in the Council of Ministers. Once the text was definitely drafted by the Council, it would be sent to each parliament which would have one month to respond, otherwise the text would be deemed to be approved.[18]

Instead of this complex proposal, the Delegation of the National Assembly prefers the creation of an interparliamentary committee. This committee would be a transformation and a reinforcement of COSAC which would be composed of a small and equal number of representatives from each member state designated by the different houses of parliament. Each member state would have a block vote. The question of the equality or weight to be given is still open. The Committee would be consulted concerning major decisions affecting the Union: revision of treaties, international agreements, enlargements, the budget, justice and home affairs, monetary and

[16] Yves Guéna, 'Rapport d'information sur la réforme de 1996 des institutions de l'Union européenne', Rapport *Genton*, p. 24.

[17] Rapport *Genton*, p. 75.

[18] Philippe Séguin, 'Pour un mémorandum français sur l'Europe, le Figaro', 7 décembre 1994.

defence questions as well as *a priori* control of the principle of subsidiarity through the possibility of making an objection on the grounds of subsidiarity. It would vote yes or no and would have no power to amend. Its vote would be purely consultative.

This proposition also shows a desire to avoid the creation of a second European house. The committee would only meet one or two days a month, limiting itself to votes on principle preceded by brief debate. Is this a realistic solution where the questions are important and national parliaments divided as to the right answer?

The Delegation of the Senate chose a different system, based on the distinction between the Community pillar and the two other pillars of the European Union.

In matters concerning the three Communities, the Delegation proposes that the Council be composed in such a way that national parliaments might be consulted. This would concern, for example, the community budget, agreements of association or adhesion: a representative might be a member of the national Delegation, alongside the Minister or even in his place.

As for decisions taken in the framework of inter-governmental pillars, the CFSP and justice and home affairs, they would be submitted to the control of a European Senate representing the national parliaments whose representation would reflect the weight of votes in the Council of Ministers, each member of Parliament being free to vote as he wished. The Senate would restrict itself to giving its opinion concerning the projects examined by the Council and to sending recommendations.

This proposal seems to be a good idea from two points of view, the first national and the second Community. From a national point of view, it acknowledges that in France at least the Government does not submit projects concerning the two inter-governmental pillars to Parliament and attempts to fill this gap. From a Community point of view, the Senate would intervene in areas in which the European Parliament does not have much power. The authors of this project point out that there would be no risk of recommendations going back and forth endlessly between the two houses and that there would even be a clarification of the decision-making process. The European Parliament would still be concerned with first pillar matters, the Senate would concern itself with the two other pillars.

This system, however, ignores the powers which the Treaty on the European Union gives to the European Parliament in the field of inter-governmental cooperation. Articles J7 and K6 give Parliament the right to be informed, consulted, to ask questions, to make recommendations and add that the Presidency should ensure that the views of the European Parliament are 'duly taken into consideration'. Thus the competence of the two houses would overlap and they would therefore be in competition. The project of a European Senate could only avoid the serious criticism which has been directed against it from the beginning if the European Parliament lost some of its competence.

• • •

European policy seems to have anticipated the 'revaluation' of Parliament announced by President Chirac and it will benefit from the President's policy. What can we expect? It is too soon to say. By virtue of the amendments of the French constitution adopted on 31 July 1995, we know that Parliament will have longer sessions, a reform which may reinforce its capacity to control the executive. But its relations with this branch will still depend very much on political factors such as the size or the cohesion of the majority in the National Assembly and the will of the Government to cooperate with Parliament.

It is undoubtedly for this reason that the two houses of the French Parliament are keeping 'two irons in the fire' and will attempt to reinforce their role within both the institutions of the European Union and those of the Fifth Republic.

# The German Parliament and European Integration

*Meinhard Hilf* and *Frank Burmeister*

## The Democratic Deficit

One of the key questions facing the European Union is the effective and democratic legitimation and control of European legislation. The forthcomming revision of the Treaty on European Union (TEU) in 1996[1] is the point of reference for resolving this question. One reason for feeling uncertain about the process of European integration is the alleged *lack of democratic legitimacy*.[2] Although

1 Cf. Art. N para. 2 TEU; see O. Schmuck, Die EU-Regierungskonferenz 1996: Zum Stand der Reformdebatte, *Integration* 1995, pp. 68 ff. and J. Lipsius (pseud.), 'The 1996 Intergovernmental Conference', *European Law Review* 1995, pp. 235 ff.

2 See C. D. Classen, 'Europäische Integration und demokratische Legitimation', *Archiv für öffentliches Recht*, vol. 119, 1994, pp. 238 ff.; K. Featherstone, 'Jean Monnet and the "Democratic Deficit" in the European Union', *Journal of Common Market Studies* 1994, pp. 149 ff.; M. Hilf, 'Die rechtliche Bedeutung des Verfassungsprinzips der parlamentarischen Demokratie für den europäischen INTEGRATIONSPROZEß', *Europarecht* 1984, pp. 9 ff.; P M. Huber, 'Die Rolle des Demokratieprinzips im europäischen INTEGRATIONSPROZEß', *Staatswissenschaften und Staatspraxis* 1992, pp. 349 ff.; I. Pernice, 'Maastricht, Staat und Demokratie, *Die Verwaltung* 1993', pp. 449 ff.; P. Raworth, 'A Timid Step Forwards: Maastricht and the Democratisation of the European Community', *European Law Review* 1994, pp. 16 ff.; A. Randelzhofer, 'Zum behaupteten Demokratieprinzip der Europäischen Gemeinschaft', in P. Hommelhoff/P. Kirchhof (eds.), *Der Staatenverbund der Europäischen Union* (Heidelberg:

the European Parliament was given a more important role in the decision-making process by the TEU, the increase in its powers seems to be inadequate given the extent of legislative responsibilities which have been entrusted to the European Community (EC) by the TEU.

The democratic legitimacy of the European Union is undermined by *structural shortcomings*: it lacks a European-wide body of public opinion and a distinctive political and social infrastructure (common media, language etc.). Although political parties have formed umbrella organisations on the European level, there is no European party system in which policy options can be thrashed out between government and opposition.[3]

However, against this background, democratic legitimacy in the Union cannot come about in the same way as within a national state order.[4] The only way of establishing a sufficient legitimate basis for the Union is via a *system of dual representation*, in which the European and the national legitimacy are suitably combined. Different sources of political legitimacy will have to come together: on the one hand, the doubtlessly existing legitimacy of the European Parliament, on the other hand the legitimacy of the Member States, represented by their national parliaments.

For that reason, it will be discussed to what extent the German Parliament, the *Bundestag*, is set to cooperate in European affairs at the same time as the Federal Government is responsible for exercising the membership rights within the EU (Art. 32 para. 1 of the Basic Law [*Grundgesetz – GG*]). But in light of the fact that the Federal Republic of Germany is not a unitary state, attention must also be paid to the role of the *Länder* in European affairs. In Germany's federal system the *Länder* have the quality of states and sole or at least specific responsibilities in a number of policy fields, such as cultural affairs, education, the media, public security and environmental policy as well as in the field of administration even with respect to most legislative acts adopted on the federal level.

Therefore, two forms of cooperation in European affairs will have to be distinguished: first the cooperation of the *Bundestag* and

*cont.*
C.F. Müller, 1994) pp. 39 ff.; G. Ress, 'Über die Notwendigkeit der parlamentarischen Legitimierung der Rechtsetzung der Europäischen Gemeinschaften', in W. Fiedler et al, *Gedächtnisschrift für W.K. Geck* (Köln: Carl Heymanns Verlag, 1989) pp. 625 ff.; M. Zuleeg, 'Demokratie in der Europäischen Gemeinschaft', *Juristen-Zeitung* 1993, pp. 1069 ff. and recently W. Kluth, *Die Demokratische Legitimation der Europäischen Union* (Berlin: Duncker & Humblot, 1995).

3 See W. Weidenfeld (ed.), *Europe '96: Reforming the European Union* (Gütersloh: Bertelsmann Stiftung, 1994) pp. 30 ff.

4 See BVerfGE 89, 155 at 182; for details on this decision, see below.

secondly the cooperation of the *Länder*. But unlike the *Bundestag*, the parliaments of the *Länder* (*Landtage*) have no direct influence on European affairs. Only the governments of the *Länder* are represented on the federal level in the *Bundesrat* which comprises 68 members from the various governments (Arts. 50 and 51 GG). For that reason, only the *Land* governments have the ability to control their members' votes in the *Bundesrat*, but not the parliaments of the *Länder*.[5] Thus, a considerable loss of powers with respect to the parliaments of the *Länder* can be determined.[6]

In connection with the recent process of ratification of the TEU the *Bundestag*'s and the *Bundesrat*'s role in European affairs has been explicitly regulated by constitutional law. The newly inserted Art. 23 GG (see below) and, correspondingly, the Federal legislative Acts on Cooperation in European Union Matters give detailed provisions on this subject. These texts may be considered as a major achievement to enhance the involvement of the German Parliament comprising the *Bundestag* and the *Bundesrat* in European affairs.

The following contribution will first try to explain the development of parliamentary cooperation since the creation of the European Communities, then analyse the current legal situation, and finally give a review of the consequences resulting from the Maastricht Decision of the Federal Constitutional Court (*Bundesverfassungsgericht – BVerfG*).[7] The contribution will draw some conclusions and perspectives for both the *Bundestag* and the *Bundesrat* concerning their cooperation in European Union matters.

## The Evolving Influence of the German Parliament

The influence of the German Parliament evolved gradually in obvious relation to the growing impact of EC affairs on domestic policies.

5 See BVerfGE 8, 104 at 120 ff.; see also Chr. Dästner, 'Zur Aufgabenverteilung zwischen Bundesrat, Landesregierungen und Landesparlamenten in Angelegenheiten der Europäischen Union', *Nordrhein-Westfälische Verwaltungsblätter* 1994, pp. 1 ff. at p. 3.

6 See S. Magiera, 'Die Grundgesetzänderung von 1992 und die Europäische Union', *Juristische Ausbildung* 1994, pp. 1 ff. at p. 9; M. Müller, 'Die Mitwirkung der Landesparlamente in Bundesrats- und Europaangelegenheiten', *Die Öffentliche Verwaltung* 1993, p. 103; M. Schweitzer, 'Beteiligung der Bundesländer an der europäischen Gesetzgebung', *Zeitschrift für Gesetzgebung* 1992, pp. 128 ff. at p. 129; T. Stein, 'Europäische Union: Chancen oder Gefahren für den Föderalismus in Deutschland, Österreich und der Schweiz?', in *Veröffentlichungen der Vereinigung der Deutschen Staatsrechtslehrer*, vol. 52, 1994, pp. 26 ff. at p. 37.

7 See BVerfGE 89, 155 ff.; for an English version, see *Common Market Law Review* 1994, pp. 1 ff.

## 1. The Bundestag's Cooperation in European Affairs

Until the ratification of the TEU, the *Bundestag*'s direct influence on the Federal Government's position in European affairs was rather limited. The legal basis for the participation of the *Bundestag* was Art. 2 of the Act of Ratification of the Treaties of Rome.[8] According to this Act, the Federal Government was to give the *Bundestag* comprehensive *information* concerning all European projects. The information referred to so-called '*EG-Vorlagen*', which first of all comprised proposals of the EC Commission. However, only a minor part of these documents became the subject of debates in the *Bundestag*.[9] For that reason, the *Bundestag* changed the procedure in 1977 that only the more important proposals of the Commission had to be sent to the *Bundestag*.

The handling of these proposals was as follows: the '*EG-Vorlagen*' were sent to the *Bundestag*'s administration by the Ministry of Economic Affairs. This took place approximately two or four weeks after receipt of the EC Commission's proposals by the Council of Ministers. A covering letter indicated when the Council of Ministers was expected to decide on the proposal. Regularly, the relevant period was rather short, mostly some six weeks.

Shortly after receipt, the *Bundestag*'s administration distributed the '*EG-Vorlagen*' to the relevant Committees of the *Bundestag* which were thought to be interested. Depending on the importance of the document, the competent Committee would recommend to the *Bundestag* either just to take note of the proposal or to adopt a *resolution*. In most cases, the *Bundestag* followed the Committee's recommendations. However, the Federal Government was not obliged to take the *Bundestag*'s resolutions into account when negotiating within the Council.

As a result of the *Bundestag*'s intention to improve its influence on European affairs, in 1983 the *Bundestag* established a *Commission on European Affairs* (*Europa-Kommission*), which comprised members of the *Bundestag* and of the European Parliament. The Commission was instructed to work out recommendations for European policy-making. In the course of its activity, this Commission was dealing with important initiatives concerning the reform of the Communities, eg the European Parliament's Draft of the Treaty

[8] Act of 27.7.1957 (BGBl. II, p. 753).

[9] See S. Hölscheidt, 'Parlamentarische Mitwirkung bei der Europäischen Rechtssetzung', *Kritische Vierteljahresschrift für Gesetzgebung und Rechtswissenschaft* 1995, pp. 405 ff. at p. 419.

on European Union (1984) and the Single European Act (1986).[10] However, the influence of the Commission within the *Bundestag* was fairly limited owing to its lack of a power to adopt resolutions. Therefore, the Commission was dissolved in 1987.

In 1991 the *Bundestag* created a permanent EC Committee (*EG-Ausschuß*).[11] The decisive reason for establishing the Committee was the forthcoming Conference on reforming the Communities. In creating such a Committee the *Bundestag* intended to strengthen its influence on the Federal Government's negotiating position. The EC Committee consisted of 33 members of the *Bundestag*. Furthermore, 11 German members of the European Parliament had the right to participate, but were not authorized to vote.

The Committee dealt with amendments of the EC Treaties, institutional matters and cooperation between the European Parliament and the national parliaments. Furthermore, the Committee had the right to adopt resolutions regarding the above-mentioned '*EG-Vorlagen*', in so far as no specific Committee of the Bundestag was competent.[11a]

## 2. *The Cooperation of the Länder in European Affairs*

According to Art. 2 of the Act of Ratification of the Treaties of Rome (1957) the *Bundesrat* was also entitled to receive information on European affairs. In the course of the years rather far-reaching changes took place regarding this procedure of cooperation between the Federal Government and the *Länder* concerning European affairs.[12]

The main step in this process was the *regulation on cooperation* between the Federation and the *Länder* in European affairs adopted on the occasion of the ratification of the Single European Act in 1986.[13] The Federal Government's obligation to pass on information

10 See R. Kabel, 'Die Mitwirkung des Deutschen Bundestages in Angelegenheiten der Europäischen Union', in A. Randelzhofer et al. (eds.), *Gedächtnisschrift für E. Grabitz* (München: C. H. Beck, 1995) pp. 241 ff. at p. 249.

11 Between 1987 and 1991 a Committee dealing with European projects was part of the Committee on Foreign Affairs (*Ausschuß für auswärtige Angelegenheiten*); see Kabel, op. cit. p. 250.

11a See Kabel, op. cit. p. 251.

12 See R. Hrbek, 'The German Länder and EC Integration', *Revue d'intégration européenne/Journal of European Integration* 1992, pp. 173 ff.

13 Art. 2 of the Act of 19.12.1986 (BGBl. 1986 II, p. 1104). For details see G. Ress, 'Das deutsche Zustimmungsgesetz zur Einheitlichen Europäischen Akte – Ein Schritt zur "Föderalisierung" der Europapolitik', *Europäische Grundrechte-Zeitschrift* 1987, pp. 361 ff.

was extended and the government was obliged to give the *Bundesrat* ample opportunity to comment within an appropriate period of time. The Federal Government was furthermore committed to take the *Bundesrat's* comments into account when conducting negotiations within the EC Council.[14]

## Art. 23 of the Basic Law and the Acts on Cooperation in European Union Matters

A major change in the above-mentioned procedures took place on the occasion of the recent procedure of ratification of the TEU in 1992. For the first time the constitution was amended in order to underline the importance of the participation of the German parliament in European affairs. The Basic Law was amended to ensure that it was compatible with the provisions of the TEU (eg Arts. 28 and 88 GG), and vice versa, that the TEU would pass any test of constitutionality. Therefore, *inter alia*, the new 'Article on Europe' 23 was inserted into the Basic Law which is relevant to the procedures on cooperation:[15]

Article 23 (The European Union)

(1) With a view to establishing a united Europe the Federal Republic of Germany shall participate in the development of the European Union, which is committed to democratic, rule-of-law, social and federal principles as well as the principle of subsidiarity, and ensure protection of basic rights comparable in substance to that afforded by the Basic Law. To this end the Federation may transfer sovereign powers by law with the consent of the Bundesrat. The establishment of the European Union as well as amendments to its statutory foundations and comparable regulations which amend or supplement the content of this Basic Law or make such amendments or supplements possible shall be subject to the provisions of paragraphs (2) and (3) of Article 79.

(2) The Bundestag and, through the Bundesrat, the Länder shall be involved in matters concerning the European Union. The Federal Government shall inform the Bundestag and the Bundesrat comprehensively and as quickly as possible.

(3) The Federal Government shall give the Bundestag the opportunity to state its opinion before participating in the legislative process of the European Union. The Federal Government shall

[14] For details see Hrbek, *supra* note 12, pp. 178 ff.

[15] Act amending the Basic Law of 21.12.1992 (BGBl. I, p. 2086).

take account of the opinions of the Bundestag in the negotiations. Details shall be the subject of a law.

(4) The Bundesrat shall be involved in the decision-making process of the Federation in so far as it would have to be involved in a corresponding internal measure or in so far as the Länder would be internally responsible.

(5) Where in an area in which the Federation has exclusive legislative jurisdiction the interests of the Länder are affected or where in other respects the Federation has the right to legislate, the Federal Government shall take into account the opinion of the Bundesrat. Where essentially the legislative powers of the Länder, the establishment of their authorities or their administrative procedures are affected, the opinion of the Bundesrat shall in this respect prevail in the decision-making process of the Federation; in this connection the responsibility of the Federation for the country as a whole shall be maintained. In matters which may lead to expenditure increases or revenue cuts for the Federation, the approval of the Federal Government shall be necessary.

(6) Where essentially the exclusive legislative jurisdiction of the Länder is affected the exercise of the rights of the Federal Republic of Germany as a member state of the European Union shall be transferred by the Federation to a representative of the Länder designated by the Bundesrat. Those rights shall be exercised with the participation of and in agreement with the Federal Government; in this connection the responsibility of the Federation for the country as a whole shall be maintained.

(7) Details regarding paragraphs (4) to (6) shall be the subject of a law which shall require the consent of the Bundesrat.

Article 23 para. 1 GG has the effect of formulating and confirming a mandate for the Federal Republic of Germany to be committed to further supporting the process of integration and to participate actively in the establishment of the European Union. It gives guidelines with regard to the *basic values and principles* to which the European Union ought to conform. Among these principles are the principles of democracy, federalism and the principle of subsidiarity. In addition, the Union ought to guarantee the rule of law and, above all, ensure adequate protection of fundamental rights.[16]

[16] For further details concerning Art. 23 para. 1 GG, see U. Everling, 'Überlegungen zur Struktur der Europäischen Union und zum neuen Europa-Artikel des Grundgesetzes', *Deutsches Verwaltungsblatt* 1993, pp. 936 ff.; U. di Fabio, 'Der neue Art. 23 des Grundgesetzes', *Der Staat* 1993, pp. 191 ff., W. Fischer, 'Die Europäische Union im Grundgesetz: der neue Art. 23', *Zeitschrift für Parlamentsfragen* 1993, pp. 32 ff.; T. Oppermann/C.D. Classen, 'Europäische Union: Erfüllung des Grundgesetzes', *Aus Politik und Zeitgeschichte* 28/1993,

The further paragraphs relate to rather detailed provisions for the decision-making procedure in European affairs at the national level. The general provision (Art. 23 para. 2 GG) stipulates that the *Bundestag* and, through the *Bundesrat*, the *Länder* shall be involved in matters concerning the European Union. The Federal Government is obligated to inform them comprehensively and as quickly as possible.

Thus, for the first time, the Basic Law acknowledges the right of the *Bundestag* and the *Bundesrat* to participate in the law making and the administration with respect to all relevant aspects of European Union affairs.

## 1. Provisions relating to the Bundestag

The more detailed provisions in Art. 23 para. 3 GG state the influence of the *Bundestag*. Correspondingly, the *Bundestag* (and paradoxically the *Bundesrat*) enacted the 'Act on Cooperation between the Federal Government and the Bundestag in European Union Matters'.[17] Section 3 of this Act repeats the constitutional obligation on the Federal Government *to inform the Bundestag as quickly as possible*. Section 4 refers to proposals on the European level which can be important for the *Bundestag*, especially proposals for EC directives and regulations.

Section 5 specifies the Government's obligation to give the *Bundestag* the opportunity to state its opinion. The opinion of the *Bundestag* 'shall be the basis' for the negotiations of the Federal Government, though the opinion is not binding on the Federal Government.[18] Thus, there is no legal possibility to formally instruct the respective ministers with respect to Council meetings. But, of

*cont.*

pp. 11 ff.; R. Scholz, 'Europäische Union und Verfassungsreform', *Neue Juristische Wochenschrift* 1993, pp. 1690 ff.; K. P. Sommermann, 'Staatsziel "Europäische Union". Zur normativen Reichweite des Art. 23 Abs. 1 S. 1 GG n.F.', *Die Öffentliche Verwaltung* 1994, pp. 596 ff.; P. Wilhelm, 'Europa im Grundgesetz: Der neue Art. 23', *Bayrische Verwaltungsblätter* 1992, pp. 705 ff.

17 Act of 12.3.1993 (BGBl. I, p. 311). For details, see M. Brenner, 'Das Gesetz über die Zusammenarbeit von Bundesregierung und Deutschem Bundestag in Angelegenheiten der Europäischen Union', *Thüringer Verwaltungsblätter* 1993, pp. 196 ff.; F. Möller/M. Limpert, 'Informations- und Mitwirkungsrechte des Bundestages in Angelegenheiten der Europäischen Union', *Zeitschrift für Parlamentsfragen* 1993, pp. 21 ff.

18 O. Rojahn, in I.v. Münch/P. Kunig (eds.), *Grundgesetz-Kommentar*, vol. 2 (München: C. H. Beck, 3rd ed., 1995), Art. 23 marginal note 62; but this question is not undisputed, see, eg, Magiera, *supra* note 6, pp. 10 ff. and Möller/Limpert, *supra* note 17, pp. 28 ff.

course, the *ex post* parliamentary accountability of the entire Federal Government through the person of the Federal Chancellor (not of individual ministers) with respect to the conduct of European affairs remains untouched (Arts. 65 and 67 GG).

In connection with the Federal Government's obligation to inform the *Bundestag*, an additional Agreement between the *Bundestag* and the Federal Government is under negotiation.[19]

Furthermore, Art. 45 GG has been inserted into the GG in order to give a constitutional basis for the above-mentioned EC Committee of the *Bundestag*. Art. 45 GG determines that the *Bundestag* shall appoint a Committee on European Union (*Ausschuß für Angelegen-heiten der Europäischen Union*).[20] The *Bundestag* may empower the Commitee to excercise the *Bundestag's* rights in relation to the Federal Government. Accordingly, the Committee on European Union was established in 1994.[21] There may be doubts as to whether this delegation of decision-making powers to a committee can withstand constitutional scrutiny as only a limited number of members of the *Bundestag* are represented in the said Committee. But it has to be taken into consideration that the transfer of powers to the Committee can be repealed at any time. Thus the provision is still constitutional.

## 2. Provisions relating to the Bundesrat

The constitutional basis for the involvement of the *Bundesrat* in European affairs is Art. 23 paras. 4 to 6 GG. These provisions are much more detailed and thus more complicated than the provisions relating to the *Bundestag*. According to Art. 23 para. 4 GG the *Bundesrat* shall be involved in the decision-making process of the Federation in so far as it would have to be involved in a corresponding internal matter or in so far as the *Länder* would be internally responsible.[22]

Article 23 paras. 5 and 6 GG give even more influence to strengthening the cooperation of the *Bundesrat* in the fields in

[19] See Hölscheidt, *supra* note 9, p. 421.

[20] See also section 2 of the above-mentioned Act.

[21] See Hölscheidt, *supra* note 9, p. 421.

[22] For details see U. Neßler, 'Die "neue Ländermitwirkung" nach Maastricht', *Europarecht* 1994, pp. 216 ff.; A. Randelzhofer, in Th. Maunz et al. (eds.), *Kommentar zum Grundgesetz*, vol. 2 (München: C.H. Beck 1995), Art. 24 marginal notes 200 ff.; Rojahn, *supra* note 18, marginal notes 64 ff.; I. Winkelmann, 'Innerstaatliche Kompetenzverteilung bei Vertragsabschlüssen in Angelegenheiten der Europäischen Union', *Deutsches Verwaltungsblatt* 1993, pp. 1128 ff.

which the respective powers of the *Länder* may be concerned. In such cases the opinion of the *Bundesrat* has to be taken into account by the Federal Government. If powers of the *Länder* were to be affected their opinions have to be considered with particular attention. On the other hand, the *Bundesrat* has to take into account the overall responsibility of the Federal Government for the state as a whole.

With respect to the revised Art. 146 of the EC Treaty[23] Art. 23 para. 6 GG allows the representation of the Federal Republic of Germany in the Council of Ministers by a *Land* representative to be appointed by the *Bundesrat*.

Article 23 para. 6 GG is most criticized with respect to the cooperation of the *Bundesrat* in European affairs. The critical point is the *lack of parliamentary control* of the respective representatives of the *Länder* acting within the EC Council.[24] Who is to control them? Neither the *Bundestag* nor the respective *Land* parliament have a constitutional basis for exercising any sort of parliamentary accountability. This remains therefore an open question.

In accordance with Art. 23 para. 7 GG the *Bundestag* and the *Bundesrat* enacted the 'Act on Cooperation between the Federation and the Länder in European Union Matters' (*Gesetz über die Zusammenarbeit von Bund und Ländern in Angelegenheiten der Europäischen Union*).[25] It amounts to a fairly complicated and detailed weighing up of different interests. On the one hand the Federal Government does not want to negotiate under any sort of instruction when acting within the EC Council. On the other hand the *Länder* will look for a more decisive role in European affairs if their respective internal powers may be affected by secondary EC legislation.

However, an initial overall assessment of these provisions was fairly negative. Taking the wording of the provisions into account,

[23] Art. 146 of the EC Treaty was amended by the TEU. The revision of this provision was a key demand of the *Länder*, see K.H. Goetz, 'National Governance and European Integration: Intergovernmental Relations in Germany', *Journal of Common Market Studies* 1995, pp. 91 ff. at 106 ff.

[24] See R. Breuer, 'Die Sackgasse des neuen Europaartikels (Art. 23 GG)', *Neue Zeitschrift für Verwaltungsrecht* 1994, pp. 417 ff. at p. 428; C.D. Classen, 'Maastricht und die Verfassung: kritische Bemerkungen zum neuen "Europa-Artikel" 23 GG', *Zeitschrift für Rechtspolitik* 1993, pp. 57 at 60; M. Hilf, 'Europäische Union: Chancen oder Gefahren für den Föderalismus in Deutschland, Österreich und der Schweiz?' in, *Veröffentlichungen der Vereinigung der Deutschen Staatsrechtslehrer*, vol. 52, 1994, pp. 7 ff. at 15 ff.; A. Sattler, *ibid.*, pp. 141 at 142; I. Pernice, 'Europäische Union: Gefahr oder Chance für den Föderalismus in Deutschland, Österreich und der Schweiz?', *Deutsches Verwaltungsblatt* 1993, pp. 909 ff. at p. 917.

[25] Act of 12.3.1993 (BGBl. I, p. 313).

the influence of the Government within the EC Council may have been weakened. In some cases the provisions stipulate a binding *commitment* of the Federal Government to the *Bundesrat*'s opinion. Supposing that these provisions might not be interpreted restrictively, the principle of community loyalty (Art. 5 of the EC Treaty) would be in danger if the Federal Government were no longer able to cooperate in the search for a compromise at the EC Council. In addition, the competence of the Federal Government in foreign affairs (Art. 32 GG) might be called into question.[26]

But even on the basis of a restrictive interpretation there is certainly enough room for public debate and for the ability of the *Bundesrat* to give strong recommendations to the Federal Government.[27] The first practical experiences on the basis of these provisions seem to have produced rather satisfactory results.[27a]

In a first Decision of 22 March 1995 the Federal Constitutional Court ruled on the *Länder*'s rights of participation in European Union matters and on the obligation of the Federal Government to respect and follow the opinion of the *Bundesrat* when participating in the negotiations in the EC Council.[28] The Court stressed that it was a matter for the Federation to safeguard German interests within the European Union. If the Union took action in a policy field for which the *Länder* were internally competent, the Federation had to represent the interests of the *Länder* as a trustee (*Sachwalter*). According to the Court the Federal Government and the *Länder* had to cooperate in a spirit of loyalty. In the given case the Court found that the Federal Government had violated the relevant rights of the *Bundesrat*.

For matters concerning the European Union the Basic Law provides for a specific Chamber for European affairs (*Europakammer*) whose decisions are to be considered decisions of the *Bundesrat* (Art. 52 para. 3 a GG). This Chamber is composed of

[26] See Hilf, *supra* note 24, p. 18: Section 5 para. 3 of the Act which binds the Federal Government in case of EC legislation on the basis of Art. 235 EC Treaty seems to be unconstitutional; see also J. Schwarze, 'Das Staatsrecht in Europa', *Juristen-Zeitung* 1993, pp. 585 ff. at p. 590.

[27] In this connection an additional Agreement between the Federal Government and the Länder was concluded on 29.10.1993 (Bundesanzeiger no. 226 of 2.12.1993); for details, see M. Borchmann, 'Neue Bund-Länder-Vereinbarung über die Zusammenarbeit in Angelegenheiten der Europäischen Union', *Europäische Zeitschrift für Wirtschaftsrecht* 1994, pp. 172 ff.

[27a] Cf. the detailed account and well balanced survey by G.-B. Oschatz/H. Risse, 'Die Bundesregierung an der Kette der Länder?', *Die Öffentliche Verwaltung* 1995, pp. 437 ff.

[28] The decision has been published in *Europäische Zeitschrift für Wirtschaftsrecht* 1995, pp. 277 ff. with annotation by U. Häde, *ibid.*, p. 284 ff. It relates to the EC Directive 89/552/EEC, O.J. 1989 L 298/1.

members of the various governments of the *Länder*. It is mootable whether this Chamber will be able to effectively lobby the Federal Government's position in the EC Council, especially if such positions have to be taken under a specific time constraint – as is often the case.[28a]

## The Maastricht Decision of the Federal Constitutional Court: The Enhanced Role of the German Parliament

On 12 October 1993, the Federal Constitutional Court passed its judgment on the compatibility of the Maastricht Treaty with the Basic Law.[29] As is well known the Court declared the constitutional complaints unfounded. However, there are several quite remarkable passages dealing with the *democratic legitimacy* of the European Union.

The Court ruled, *inter alia*, that the democratic principle did not prevent the Federal Republic of Germany from becoming a member of the European Union, but it had to be *in the first place* the citizens of the Member States through their national parliaments who were to legitimize this process of integration.[30] Therefore, democratic legitimation could be assured through the feed-back with respect to the actions of the European institutions provided by the parliaments of the Member States; within the institutional structure of the European Union there was only an 'additional factor' for the provision of democratic legitimation by means of the European Parliament.[31]

[28a] See, however, Oschatz/Risse, *supra* note 27a, pp. 448 ff. for practical arrangements in order to have the Chamber's position even at short notice.

[29] BVerfGE 89, 155 ff.; see, eg, annotations by M. Herdegen, 'Maastricht and the German Constitutional Court: Constitutional Restraints for an "Ever Closer Union"', *Common Market Law Review* 1994, pp. 235 ff.; P. Kirchhof, 'Das Maastricht-Urteil des Bundesverfassungsgerichts', in: Hommelhoff/Kirchhof, *supra* note 2, pp. 11 ff.; R. de Lange, 'Het Bundesverfassungsgericht over het Verdrag van Maastricht: een nieuw Solange?', *Sociaal-Economische Wetgeving* 1994, pp. 418 ff.; J. Schwarze, 'La Ratification du Traité de Maastricht en Allemagne, l'Arrêt de la Cour constitutionnelle de Karlsruhe', *Review du Marché commun et de l'Union européenne* 1994, pp. 293 ff. at 298 ff.; H. Steinberger, 'Anmerkungen zum Maastricht-Urteil des Bundesverfassungsgerichts', op. cit. pp. 25 ff.; Chr. Tomuschat, 'Die Europäische Union unter der Aufsicht des Bundesverfassungsgerichts', *Europäische Grundrechte-Zeitschrift* 1993, pp. 489 ff.

[30] BVerfGE 89, 155 at 185 ff.

[31] *Ibid.*

The Court stressed, furthermore, that if the peoples of individual Member States provided for democratic legitimation through their national parliaments, limits to the extension of the Communities' functions and powers were then set by virtue of the democratic principle. From that it followed that *functions and powers of substantial importance* had to remain with the *Bundestag*.[32]

The Court explained that the necessary influence of the *Bundestag* was guaranteed, in the first place, under Art. 23 para. 1 GG concerning Germany's membership in the European Union. Any future development of the Union through a *fundamental treaty amendment* or an extension of its powers, required the two-thirds majority in the *Bundestag* and the *Bundesrat*. In addition, the *Bundestag* participated in the exercise of German membership rights within the European institutions. It cooperated in the formation of the will of the Federation in these matters, in accordance with Art. 23 paras. 2 and 3 GG and the Act on Cooperation between the Federal Government and the *Bundestag* in European Union Matters. These interrelated competences were to be exercised by the Federal Government and the *Bundestag* in a 'spirit of institutional loyalty' (*Organtreue*).[33]

The Court stated finally, that the *Bundestag* also influenced the European policy of the Federal Government through the latter's *accountability* to the *Bundestag* (Arts. 63 and 67 GG).[34] Due to this initiation and control function of the *Bundestag* the general public and the political parties could take different positions on the Government's European policy, and thus might determine and influence the citizens when voting in elections.

It is conspicuous that the Court did not mention the role of the *Bundesrat* in this context.[35] The reason for this may be that the Court only had to deal with individual complaints arguing that through the TEU the competences of the *Bundestag* are reduced in a way which is to be considered as unconstitutional.

## Conclusions and Perspectives

This overview has shown that *parliamentary control* in European affairs on the national level is intrinsically complex. It may be

[32] *Ibid.*

[33] *Ibid.*, p. 191.

[34] *Ibid.* with reference to BVerfGE 68, 1 at 109 ff.

[35] J. Kühn, 'Die Koordinierung der deutschen Europapolitik' (Bonn: Zentrum für Europäisches Wirtschaftsrecht der Rheinischen Friedrich-Wilhelms-Universität, 1994) p. 13.

doubtful whether the new Art. 23 GG and the Acts on Cooperation in European Union Matters can alter the predominant and decisive role of the Federal Government. The extent of parliamentary influence by the *Bundestag* is limited. As has been noted, unlike Denmark's *Folketing*, the *Bundestag* has no power to bind the Federal Government with respect to its opinions on European policy-making.[36]

Moreover, the *Bundestag*'s debates and opinions on European Union matters are often reduced to a *German point of view*. European interests are often neglected. The *Bundestag* due to its composition has no call to voice the interests of the peoples of all Member States. A recent debate of the *Bundestag* on European agricultural policy sets a compelling example: the entire *Bundestag*, the opposition as well as the majority supporting the Government, urged the competent Minister of Agriculture to prevent the adoption of some European Commission proposals concerning annual prices which might negatively affect German producers.[37] This may demonstrate that the *Bundestag*'s cooperation in European affairs is certainly not an adequate and overall control of EC legislation on the whole as it only takes a one-sided position from the angle of national interests. This statement, however, does not minimize the involvement of the national parliaments in the constitution-making process of the EU (cf. Art. N TEU) or the implementation of EC directives on the national level.[38]

Even the case law from the European Court of Justice has made a contribution to the influence of national parliaments in European affairs. The Court ruled that the implementation of EC directives simply by way of administrative instructions or ordinances was not sufficient; always acts of parliament binding the national courts were required.[39]

Nevertheless, democratic control of European affairs by national parliaments has its inherent limits. The suggested 'ratification' of EC regulations by national parliaments seems to be more than problematic: if unanimity in the Council were provided for, the process of integration might be hampered; if a regulation could be passed by majority vote in the Council, it would seem rather absurd to expect any Member State to respect the given regulation if its

[36] Cf. the contribution in this volume relating to Denmark and W. Kaufmann-Bühler, 'Deutsche Europapolitik nach dem Karlsruher Urteil: Möglichkeiten und Hemmnisse', *Integration* 1994, pp. 1 ff. at p. 11 note 9.

[37] See debate of 18.5.1995.

[38] See *European Commission*, Rapport sur le fonctionnement du Traité sur l'Union européenne, doc. SEC (95) 731 final, p. 17.

[39] Case C-59/89, *Commission./.Germany*, ECR 1991, pp. 2567 ff.

own national parliament had refused to 'ratify' such a regulation. The *Bundestag*, for example, would probably never have 'ratified' the recent regulation on bananas.[40] Thus, any voting on EC secondary legislation by national parliaments would not lead to 'more' democracy but to a rather inefficient, if not chaotic, situation and thus finally to a demise in democratic legitimacy.

Likewise, the suggested requirement of the European Parliament's consent to any treaty amendment under Art. N TEU might be questionable for the time being.[41] The German Federal Constitutional Court clearly required that the Member States had to remain Masters of the Treaties (*Herren der Verträge*).[42] Thus, it seems that a sort of veto or required consent by the European Parliament would be excluded. This, however, does not exclude a major involvement of the European Parliament in the proceedings of any Intergovernmental Conference.

We have seen that European affairs in Germany are not only a matter of the *Bundestag*. The *Länder* are more and more affected by European legislation and, indeed, the *Bundesrat* is determined to make its own contribution to the evolution of European integration.

However, the given provisions of the Constitution pertaining to the *Bundesrat* are fairly complicated. The *Länder* will try to extend even further their influence and to safeguard their powers by adopting new demands in connection with the upcoming Intergovernmental Conference in 1996. In its resolution of 31 March 1995, the *Bundesrat* demanded to be involved in the preparation of the Conference as soon as possible.[43] Furthermore, in the opinion of the *Länder* the Federal Government should work out the German basis for negotiations in collaboration with the *Länder*. The Federal Government already declared its consent to the demand of the *Länder* to have two seats in the German delegation for the Intergovernmental Conference. However, the request of the *Länder* to be represented in the Reflection Group had been met with disapproval.

Finally, when discussing the influence of the *Länder*, it must be taken into consideration that attempts by the *Länder* to strengthen

[40] Regulation 93/404/EEC, O.J. 1993 L 47/1; for details of this EC regulation see H.-D. Kuschel, 'Die Bananenmarktordnung der Europäischen Union', *Recht der Internationalen Wirtschaft* 1995, pp. 218 ff.

[41] See *European Commission*, Rapport sur le fonctionnement du Traité sur L'Union européenne, SG (95) D/33026, p. 5; see also the *Bundesrat*, Resolution of 31.3.1995, *Europäische Zeitschrift für Wirtschaftsrecht* 1995, pp. 325 at 326: 'The results of the Intergovernmental Conference should be implemented in cooperation with the European Parliament'.

[42] BVerfGE 89, 155 at 190.

[43] *Supra* note 41.

their role in European affairs focus exclusively on the governments, but not on the parliaments of the *Länder*. Again the predominance of the executive seems to be untouched.

• • •

The debate on the Intergovernmental Conference in 1996 will centre, at least in Germany, on the question whether the above-mentioned rights and prerogatives of the German Parliament have been respected – or to what extent the German Parliament might have been given a continuing adequate role in European integration.

It remains to be seen whether the present constitutional framework for cooperation in European affairs under Art. 23 GG will function satisfactorily. It is assumed that in practice the more intense involvement of both the *Bundestag* and *Bundesrat* will finally strengthen the democratic legitimacy of the European Union despite all the practical difficulties which will have to be resolved.

# The UK Parliament and EU Institutions – Partners or Rivals?*

*Colin R. Munro*

## Introduction

On one view, the European Community involves 'an ever closer union among the peoples of Europe',[1] in which the participating parties have pooled their sovereign powers in a joint enterprise to preserve peace and assist economic and social progress. The engines which would drive these aims and activities would be supranational, the Community's institutions. The institutions remaining in Member States would have diminishing roles, as Community competence (often exclusive) was extended. But those institutions in the Member States would also be called in aid by the Community, for example so as to carry into effect Community directives[2] or to enforce pecuniary obligations on persons.[3] Indeed, there is the general duty to take 'all appropriate measures ... to ensure fulfilment of the obligations arising out of this Treaty or resulting from action taken by the institutions of the Community'.[4] On this

* The author is grateful to his colleague, Mr Peter Cullen of the Europa Institute in the Faculty of Law, University of Edinburgh, for helpful comments on a draft.

1 Treaty Establishing the European Community (hereafter 'EC Treaty'), Preamble; Treaty on European Union, Article A.

2 Article 289, EC Treaty.

3 Article 192, EC Treaty.

4 Article 5, EC Treaty.

view, the institutions of the Member States are intended to act as *partners* in the Community enterprise. But their role is subordinate: they are junior partners, expected to carry out unquestioningly the policies of the senior partners who sit at the top of the table and take the decisions.

Another view is also possible. The European Union (as in its widened form it has become) is an international organisation, in which nation states have participated, to further their own interests or for their own reasons, some to prevent another war between European countries, some for security reasons, some for economic reasons. The agreement involves a customs union and a common market, and some associated areas of economic activity, and in these spheres entrusted to the Community a harmonisation of national laws has been accepted. However, on this view the institutions of the nation states remain important players. In areas which have come within Community competence, the institutions of the nation states may nonetheless seek to modify supranational decision-making in deference to national interests. In areas which are not, or not clearly, within Community competence, the institutions of the nation states will seek to maintain and assert their own pre-eminence and perhaps their own exclusivity. On this view, the institutions of the Community and the institutions of the Member States are apt to view each other as *rivals*.

These are, of course, only two rather simplified models of the relationships which exist or which are possible. Nevertheless, they help to explain some of the tensions which have existed, at least since the United Kingdom and others joined the Community in 1973. Some of these tensions go back further. Indeed they may be said to be inherent in the structure, because the institutions of the Community in themselves represent a balance between supranationalism and the different concept of intergovernmentalism.[5] There have been earlier periods when the balancing was awkward, such as in the 1960s when President de Gaulle's hostility to supranationalism led to the Empty Chair crisis and some years of stalling.

But these tensions have been especially evident since 1992, when the Treaty on European Union was signed at Maastricht. Some of the features of that Treaty bear witness to these tensions. The principle of subsidiarity[6] is one of these, and the placing of two pillars of the European Union (foreign and security policy, and justice and home affairs)[7] on an intergovernmental basis is another. So too may be

5 See J. Weiler, 'The Community System: the Dual Character of Supranationalism', (1981) 1 *Yearbook of European Law* 267.

6 Article 3b, EC Treaty.

7 Titles V, VI, Treaty on European Union.

regarded the United Kingdom's 'opting out' of the Protocol on Social Policy, and negotiation of a protocol permitting it to opt out of the third stage of economic and monetary union, involving a single currency.[8]

However, the tensions are not only evident in the Treaty itself, but are also visible in the ambivalent reception given to it in different countries of the Community. This ambivalence was apparent not only in the United Kingdom (where the passage of the necessary legislation in Parliament was troublesome, with the Prime Minister having to use the suicide threat of a vote of confidence to bring his party rebels into line) and in Denmark (where a second referendum had to be held, following upon declarations and clarifications agreed at the Edinburgh European Council meeting), but also in France, where the referendum vote was narrow, and in Germany, where the Federal Constitutional Court adjudicated upon the legal challenge brought there.[9]

## Britain and Europe[10]

Perhaps the lesson to be drawn from the Maastricht aftermath is that the enthusiasts for integration (sometimes, but perhaps confusingly, described in Britain as 'federalists') have been going too far or too fast for most of the people of Europe. However that may be, in any discussion of the tensions between different conceptions of the relations between the Community and Member States, the United Kingdom is likely to feature prominently. It might be suggested that British institutions are particularly prone to regarding Community institutions, not as partners in a common enterprise, but as rivals to be carefully watched. Cartoonists may have found it convenient to depict Mrs Margaret Thatcher, handbag at the ready, in this mode, but younger observers (perhaps to their surprise) will be finding that Mr John Major betrays similar attitudes, while older observers will recall that Britain's ambivalence pre-dates the Conservative administrations which have governed Britain since 1979.[11]

8 Protocol on Social Policy, Protocol on Certain Provisions relating to the United Kingdom of Great Britain and Northern Ireland.

9 *Brunner v The European Union Treaty* [1994] 69 CMLR 57.

10 Neither of these terms is accurate. The state is correctly the United Kingdom of Great Britain and Northern Ireland, but the shorter term is sometimes convenient. That state is, of course, in the continent of Europe, but (perhaps significantly) British people often use the word 'Europe' to refer to the continental land mass or the rest of Europe.

11 See generally Stephen George: *An Awkward partner* (Oxford University Press, 2nd ed., 1994).

The Bill which became the European Communities Act 1972, by which entry to the Communities received the approval of the United Kingdom Parliament, was passed by a majority of only eight in the House of Commons, although the previous general election had given the Conservatives a majority of 43 over Labour. Neither of the two main political parties was united in its attitude to membership then, and indeed it may be suggested that intra-party disunity, if sometimes relatively hidden, has persisted ever since.[12]

The Labour Party adopted the more aggressive stance in its manifesto for the February 1974 general election and following their victory the Prime Minister, Mr Harold Wilson, was obliged to fulfil his promise to open a 're-negotiation' of the terms of British membership. At the Dublin meeting of Heads of Government in 1975, the re-negotiation was concluded with some minor adjustments and, in fulfilment of another promise, the result was then put to the British electorate in the form of a referendum on continued membership in June 1975. The normal rule of collective responsibility was suspended by the Prime Minister so that members of his government, as well as other politicians, were free to adopt and promote their own views outside Parliament. With the backing of most organs of the press, and with support from British industrial and financial circles which allowed £1.5 million to be spent on the 'Yes' campaign against £133,000 on the 'No' campaign, there was a 67%–33% vote in favour of continued membership.[13]

The referendum device has rarely been used in British government, and the 1975 referendum is the only occasion where the electorate's view on a European Community issue has been specifically and officially tested. Opinion polls had previously suggested that a majority of British people was against membership and the referendum vote can be viewed as a passing moment of public favour, as the opinion polls were soon afterwards showing a majority against again. However, in recent years, especially as a generation accustomed to membership has grown up, the opinion polls show more favourable attitudes.[14]

At some subsequent general elections there was at least the possibility of the electors choosing between parties on the basis of their policies on the issue as the Labour Party (led by Mr Michael Foot) in 1983 proposed to withdraw from the Communities. But,

[12] See Nigel Ashford, 'The Political Parties', in, Stephen George (ed.), *Britain and the European Community* (Oxford: Clarendon Press, 1992), ch. 6.

[13] On a turnout of 64.5%. See D. Butler and U. Kitzinger, *The 1975 Referendum* (London: Macmillan, 1976).

[14] See Neill Nugent, 'British Public Opinion and the European Community', in Stephen George (ed.), *Britain and the European Community*, op. cit. ch. 8.

following Labour's massive defeat in that election and some changes of attitude, the process began (under Mr Kinnock's leadership) of extricating the party from that commitment.

When the 1992 general election was held, it was harder to discern any fundamental difference of view between the two main parties, although by then, in differences of tone, Labour appeared more pro-European, as it does at the moment. The Conservative Party may appear more obviously divided in its attitudes currently,[15] but the visibility of its divisions is heightened by its being the party in government and sharpened by its small working majority in the House of Commons. In fact, a case can be made that numerically, at least, the Parliamentary Labour Party is more seriously divided than the Conservatives.[16]

Why was Britain ambivalent about membership in 1972? Why has there been continuing ambivalence?

Perhaps fundamentally the answers lie in geography and in history. Britain is geographically at the periphery of the continent, and moreover is an island. A certain insularity might be expected, therefore, and it would not be surprising if these features affected attitudes on matters such as fisheries, immigration and foreign affairs. The historical experience is also profoundly different. Britain has not been conquered or successfully invaded since 1066, and has not suffered revolutions since the seventeenth century. During the Second World War, the six founding members of the Community suffered either from Fascism or from enemy occupation or from both. Britain suffered neither, and victory in war was apt to reinforce patriotism, which is at least related to nationalism. Wartime allies included the United States of America, which is English-speaking, and most of the countries which are today the other members of the Commonwealth, many having English as a first or second language. In these characteristics and contrasts, there are deep-seated psychological factors which help to explain a persistent difference in attitudes.[17]

It may also be observed that, as *Vernon Bogdanor* puts it, Britain 'was committing herself to membership of an organisation whose

[15] See D. Baker, A. Gamble and S. Ludlum, 'Whips or Scorpions? The Maastricht Vote and Conservative MPs' (1993) 46 *Parliamentary Affairs* 151, and 'The Parliamentary Seige of Maastricht 1993: Conservative Divisions and British Ratification' (1994) 47 *Parliamentary Affairs* 37.

[16] In the parliamentary process following the Maastricht meeting, 66 Labour MPs defied the party whip and voted against the treaty at the third reading stage.

[17] A recent and telling example was seen when there was friction between Canada and Spain over Spanish fishing practices. British media coverage was more sympathetic to Canada.

constitution was likely to be both unfamiliar and uncongenial'.[18] Many of the other Member States, by reason of their constitutional arrangements, are accustomed to a division of powers between different levels of government, and regard politics as a co-operative activity in which multi-party arrangements represent the norm. By contrast, in the United Kingdom coalitions are regarded as an aberration; in the Westminster Parliament, there is executive dominance and politics is frequently adversarial; and powers are not divided or shared but merely devolved at the will of Parliament. The functioning of the Court of Justice, too, has been rather alien to British traditions and expectations of the judiciary. Thus in addition to the more deep-seated differences of view, British politicians are likely to find the Community's institutions and arrangements difficult to comprehend. For these reasons, it may seem natural to conceive of the Community institutions as being in competition with, rather than complementary to, Westminster, or rivals rather than partners.

In this catalogue of misunderstandings, a principle of the British constitution has also played a part, when it ceased to be a 'merely legal conception'[19] and became a weapon in political discourse.

## Parliamentary Sovereignty[20]

There are of course different meanings of the term 'sovereignty' but a well-known principle of the British constitution, perhaps its leading principle, is the supremacy or (as it is often termed) sovereignty of Parliament. In the classical exposition of Professor A. V. Dicey in the nineteenth century, what this means is that

> Parliament has the right to make or unmake any law whatever, and no person or body is recognised by the law of England as having a right to override or set aside the legislation of Parliament.[21]

In Britain we noted that the Community treaties do not expressly deal with conflicts between Community law and national law. Therefore, when the European Court of Justice began to espouse

[18] V. Bogdanor, 'Britain and the European Community', in J. Jowell and D. Oliver (eds.), *The Changing Constitution* (Oxford: Clarendon Press, 3rd ed., 1994), ch. 1 (at p. 3).
[19] A. V. Dicey, *Introduction to the Study of the Law of the Constitution* (London: Macmillan, 10th ed., 1959), p. 72.
[20] See generally C. R. Munro, *Studies in Constitutional Law* (London: Butterworth, 1987), chs. 4–6.
[21] A. V. Dicey, *Law of the Constitution*, op. cit. p. 39.

the doctrine that Community law always prevails, it was making a political judgment rather like the United States Supreme Court did in *Marbury v Madison*.[22]

However that may be, it is fair to say that the doctrine of the primacy of Community law, as elaborated by the Court of Justice in *Costa v ENEL*,[23] was well understood by the British government at least, when membership negotiations were commenced.[24] When a Bill was put before the British Parliament, where perhaps the nature of Community law was less well understood, the Bill's supporters may have been guilty of some dissembling. In what has been called 'a masterpiece of drafting, designed to minimise political controversy',[25] the government preferred subtlety to grandiloquence. In the European Communities Act 1972, Section 2(1), Parliament gave the force of law in Britain to directly effective Community law, and in Section 2(2) provided for the implementation of other Community laws. Then, by Section 2(4), it was provided that 'any enactment passed or to be passed ... shall be construed and have effect subject to the foregoing provisions of this section'. Further, by Section 3(1), questions as to the validity, meaning or effect of any Community instrument were (if not referred to the European Court) to be decided in accordance with the principles laid down by that court.

It may be thought that these provisions conveyed sufficiently clearly that it was the will of Parliament to make domestic laws subject to the laws of the Community in the areas of its competence. However, the language of the Act could not in itself resolve the matter, since the very question at issue was whether any Act was capable of detracting from the capacity of a future Parliament to do whatever it liked.

In the years immediately following our accession, the courts wavered in their response to these provisions, and some of Lord Denning's *obiter dicta* were characteristically teasing. An important decision in 1979 was *Macarthys Ltd v Smith*,[26] where in an equal pay case a discrepancy appeared between Article 119 of the EEC Treaty and the construction given domestically to our own Equal Pay Act 1970. In the Court of Appeal, Cumming-Bruce and Lawton LJJ simply took the view that Community law would prevail over domestic law, if there were adjudged to be an inconsistency. Lord

22 1 Cranch 137 (1803).
23 [1964] CMLR 425.
24 See J. Forman, 'The European Communities Act 1972: the Government's Position' (1973) 10 *Common Market Law Review* 39.
25 Stephen Weatherill and Paul Beaumont, *EC Law* (London: Penguin, 2nd ed., 1995) p. 317.
26 [1979] 3 All ER 325.

Denning MR preferred to regard Section 2(4) of the European Communities Act 1972 as laying down a rule of construction, but of a special kind. In construing our statutes, he said, 'we are entitled to look to the Treaty as an aid to ... construction; but not only as an aid but as an overriding force'.[27]

The 'rule of construction' approach was adopted by the House of Lords in *Garland v British Rail Engineering Ltd*[28] and *Pickstone v Freemans plc*,[29] Lord Diplock suggesting in the former case that in the event of inconsistency national courts must still construe domestic law to conform, 'however wide a departure from the *prima facie* meaning may be needed to achieve consistency'.[30]

Occasionally, however, the conflict between Community law and domestic law may be so clear and so wide that the two cannot be reconciled. In *Macarthys Ltd v Smith*, Lord Denning conceded that in that eventuality the courts would be under a 'bounden duty to give priority to Community law [as a] result of S. 2(1) and (4) of the European Communities Act 1972'.[31]

It is in the light of this history that in a case in 1991 Lord Bridge was able to say that:

> Under the 1972 Act it has always been clear that it was the duty of a United Kingdom court, when delivering final judgement, to override any rule of national law found to be in conflict with any directly enforceable Community law.[32]

The case was *Factortame*,[33] where the House of Lords, after the European Court of Justice had affirmed[34] that national courts were required to consider whether interim protection should be given to putative Community rights and, where necessary, to do so by setting aside any rule of national law which might be an impediment, restrained a Minister from enforcing the provisions of the Merchant Shipping Act 1988. The Act, which had been intended to protect the British fishing industry, was eventually found to be in breach of

27 *Ibid.* at p. 329.
28 [1983] 2 AC 751.
29 [1989] AC 66. Another striking example was *Litster v Forth Dry Dock* [1990] 1 AC 546.
30 [1989] 2 All ER 402, 415.
31 [1979] 3 All ER 325, 329.
32 [1991] 1 All ER 70, 108.
33 *Factortame v Secretary of State for Transport (No. 2)* [1991] 1 All ER 70, [1990] 3 CMLR 375.
34 *R v Secretary of State for Transport, ex parte Factortame* (Case C-213/89) [1990] ECR 1-2433.

Articles 7, 52 and 221 of the EEC Treaty,[35] and the British courts were effectively forced to disapply it.

More recently, in the *EOC* case,[36] the House of Lords held that provisions in the Employment Protection (Consolidation) Act 1978, concerning the rights of part-time workers, as they were indirectly discriminatory against women, were incompatible with Article 119 of the EC Treaty and Council Directive 75/117 (the equal pay directive).

So the willingness of British courts to set aside domestic legislation, even subsequent legislation, in favour of Community law cannot be denied, and there are those who regard these developments as the death knell of Parliamentary sovereignty.[37]

However, many British constitutional lawyers have a less cataclysmic view of events, and the conclusions to be drawn rather depend on what we mean by 'parliamentary sovereignty'. In *Macarthys,* Lord Denning also added the significant rider that:

> If the time should come when our Parliament deliberately passes an Act with the intention of repudiating the Treaty or any provision in it or intentionally of acting inconsistently with it and says so in express terms, then I should have thought that it would be the duty of our courts to follow the statute of Parliament.[38]

Lawton LJ also observed that:

> Parliament's recognition of European Community law and of the jurisdiction of the European Court of Justice by one enactment can be withdrawn by another.[39]

In *Garland,* Lord Diplock in the House of Lords appeared to support the possibility of express repeal of Community law.[40] Thus, there is nothing in the case law[41] to prevent Parliament from overriding Community law by expressly stating that it intends to do so. Nor is

[35] As they then were (references to the EEC Treaty, before amendment by the Treaty on European Union).

[36] *Equal Opportunities Commission v Secretary of State for Employment* [1994] 1 All ER 910.

[37] Decisions affirming or conceding the supremacy of Community law are still apt to be greeted with alarm, outrage and (more surprisingly) surprise by some politicians. For a reaction from a neo-Diceyan constitutional lawyer, see H. W. R. Wade, 'What Has Happened to the Sovereignty of Parliament?' (1991) 107 *Law Quarterly Review* 1.

[38] [1979] 3 All ER 325, 329.

[39] [1979] 3 All ER 325, 334.

[40] [1983] 2 AC 751, 771.

[41] *Factortame* (note 32, above) and *EOC* (note 35, above) included. Neither case involved a deliberate override.

there anything in the European Communities Act 1972 to protect it from being repealed or amended. It may therefore be argued that the essential core of parliamentary sovereignty has been preserved.

It is true that the ordinary rules of implied repeal (which normally result in later legislation superseding earlier to the extent of any inconsistency, even when not expressly so provided) will not operate so as to repeal Community laws. By such an undramatic accommodation, lip service has been given to the primacy of Community law. Even this may be regarded as a matter of statutory interpretation, rather than as being a constituent of 'sovereignty'.[42]

Moreover, it should always be remembered that it is only by virtue of the European Communities Act 1972 that Community law enjoys the status it has in the law of the United Kingdom. The judges have often emphasised that what they are doing is done on the authority of Parliament itself, and the courts have shown no inclination to accept Community law's view of itself, as a new legal order having force by reason of its own specific nature.[43]

## Westminster and the European Constitution

With the background we have seen, it might be expected that the British Parliament's interests in (or concerns about) Community affairs would be at their highest when the larger questions of structure or what might be called the Constitution of the European Union are at stake. For example, any extension of Community competence is liable to provoke jealousy or sensitivity at Westminster, which would stand to lose what the Community institutions gained. Any extension of majority voting in the Council, involving the risk of a British minister being outvoted, has a consequential effect on accountability of ministers at Westminster.

Accordingly, it may be suggested that the United Kingdom Parliament is most obviously concerned with Community developments when constitutional changes of substance are in prospect, through amendment of the treaties. In practice, matters of that kind are dealt with rather differently from the more routine secondary legislation of the Community (which will be considered in the following section).

But does Parliament necessarily or obviously have any role in

[42] As argued by T. R. S. Allan, 'Parliamentary Sovereignty: Lord Denning's Dexterous Revolution' (1983) 3 *Oxford Journal of Legal Studies* 22.

[43] See, for example, ***Macarthys Ltd v Smith*** [1980] 3 WLR 929, 948 (Lord Denning): *Factortame v Secretary of State for Transport (No. 1)* [1989] 2 All ER 692, 700.

connection with the treaty-making power? In the British constitution it is Ministers, acting in the name of the Crown and under the royal prerogative, who have the sole powers to negotiate, enter into and ratify a treaty,[44] while Parliament clearly cannot amend executive treaties.

There is a convention (called the Ponsonby Rule) to the effect that the text of a treaty entered into by the Crown is laid before Parliament at least 21 days prior to its being ratified. By this concession of governments, Parliament is at least kept informed, but its role is essentially passive. There is no general rule requiring the legislature's consent to treaties, such as is found in some form in the constitutions of many other states.[45]

But there is an important qualification to this apparent dichotomy of functions, which stems from the strongly dualist character of the United Kingdom's legal systems. Treaties are not self-executing. The making of treaties does not alter the law, unless and until they are incorporated into the law by the intervention of, or under the authority of, Parliament.[46] Therefore, whenever it is necessary to alter the law and create rights and obligations enforceable in domestic courts, there must be legislation.

Technically, it need not always be primary legislation. Under the terms of the European Communities Act 1972,[47] new treaties and amendments to treaties can be implemented in law (to the extent that it is necessary) by the government by Order in Council, a form of delegated legislation. If that procedure is used, a draft of the Order in Council has to be approved by resolutions of both Houses of Parliament, but as the procedure does not allow amendments to be moved, the matter is simplified (and the time spent shortened).

In practice, however, if the changes are of importance, governments would not use their delegated powers to legislate, but would introduce a Bill. There is a general constitutional convention to that effect, and the sensitivity of Parliament to issues of relations with the Community would ensure its observance.

However, perhaps reluctant to trust entirely to governments' discretion, the Westminster Parliament has also begun to create

[44] *Blackburn v Attorney-General* [1971] 1 WLR 1037. The exercise of prerogative powers has been held subject to judicial review in principle, but the treaty-making power has been held unjusticiable: *Ex parte Molyneaux* [1986] 1 WLR 331.

[45] See F. G. Jacobs and S. Roberts (eds.), *The Effect of Treaties in Domestic Law* (London: Sweet & Maxwell, 1987).

[46] *J. H. Rayner (Mincing Lane) Ltd v Department of Trade and Industry* [1990] 2 AC 418. See R. Higgins, 'United Kingdom', in F. G. Jacobs and S. Roberts (eds.): *The Effect of Treaties in Domestic Law*, op. cit. ch. 7.

[47] Section 1(3).

some exceptions to the general rule that its consent to treaties is not required. When the European Parliamentary Elections Act 1978 was passed, the Labour government sought to assuage backbench fears with what became Section 6(1), providing that:

> No treaty which provides for an increase in the powers of the European Parliament shall be ratified by the United Kingdom unless it has been approved by an Act of Parliament.

This was recognised as a constitutional novelty, a device by which the government's prerogative powers in connection with treaties had been manacled by a parliamentary fetter. It becomes an additional constitutional requirement in the terms of Art. N(1) of the Treaty on European Union (replacing Art. 236, EEC Treaty), providing that amendments to the founding Treaties must be ratified by the Member States in accordance with their respective constitutional requirements.

A similar technique has more recently been employed on the specific question of the third stage of economic and monetary union. Mr Major's government introduced it in order to reassure members that 'Parliament still retained sovereignty in this matter',[48] as he explained it. Section 2 of the European Communities (Amendment) Act 1993 provides that the government may not give notification of intending to move to the third stage unless a draft of the notification has first been approved by Act of Parliament. So, as in some other states, there has been a reinforcement of parliamentary ratification procedures in the post-Maastricht trauma.

When Parliament is concerned with a Bill which is regarded as being of major constitutional importance, its procedures may also be varied on that account. For example, the committee stage in the House of Commons, where clauses are given detailed consideration, may on a motion be referred to a 'committee of the whole House'[49] – that is the chamber in plenary session – instead of to a standing committee as is usual. The European Communities Act 1972 and the European Communities (Amendment) Act 1993 were treated in that way, and it could possibly be argued that there is a constitutional convention to that effect.[50]

The role of the national Parliament in respect of changing the European Constitution at first sight appears minimal and merely *ex post facto*. When legislation is not required – as it was not for the

[48] HC Deb, Vol. 208, col. 264.
[49] Under Standing Order 61.
[50] Mr Rippon told the House of Commons in July 1972: 'I thought it right to have the whole Bill discussed on the Floor ... '. HC Deb, Vol. 840, col. 1954.

inter-governmental pillars of the Treaty on European Union[51] – then Parliament can effectively be by-passed by the executive. But when legislation is needed, then by reason of the dualist legal systems, conventional expectations, and statutorily imposed pre-ratification requirements, there is scope for extensive parliamentary debate and (from a government's view) opportunity for trouble. Parliament's weapon is the bludgeon of veto, not the surgeon's knife for effecting alterations, which might in some ways be even more dangerous. But in this way the British Parliament exercises an important influence on the British government's actions, and the influence is not merely *ex post facto*, because anticipation of the limits of Parliament's tolerance will affect the negotiating position. In some respects the long struggle to secure parliamentary approval for ratification of the Maastricht Treaty bears witness to this, even if in other respects (for example, the debates being held in the shadow of legal proceedings in the English courts) the circumstances were more novel.[52]

## Influencing Community Affairs

National parliaments have to deal with more mundane Community affairs as well as high constitutional matters. Of course, they have no formal part in the Community's legislative process. But they may seek to influence the national government or other actors, and they have a role in implementation of Community law. In this section and the following one we shall consider how the United Kingdom Parliament fulfils these two functions.[53]

The government, through the Foreign Secretary in particular, has the responsibility of providing Parliament with information on Community activities. The government makes monthly forecasts of the agenda for Council meetings, and every six months publishes a white paper on developments within the Communities. Ministerial

[51] The 1993 Act makes no provision for these pillars, on the basis that no rights or obligations were created. Similarly, the provisions in the Single European Act on foreign policy co-operation and the role of the European Council were not covered in the European Communities (Amendment) Act 1986.

[52] See Richard Rawlings, 'Legal Politics: The United Kingdom and Ratification of the Treaty on European Union' [1994] *Public Law* 254 and 367.

[53] See generally Philip Norton, *Does Parliament Matter?* (Hemel Hempstead: Harvester Wheatsheaf, 1994), ch. 7; Vernon Bogdanor, 'Britain and the European Community' (note 18 above); Stephen George, 'The Legislative Dimension', in Stephen George (ed.), *Britain and the European Community* (note 12 above), ch. 4; Eileen Denza, 'Parliamentary Scrutiny of Community Legislation' [1993] *Statute Law Review* 56.

statements are usually made in Parliament after meetings of the Council. The Prime Minister reports to the House of Commons on meetings of the European Council, and two days each session are devoted to debates in advance of such meetings. So Community matters may figure in the ordinary procedures of Parliament. There are still debates on some of the more important documents from the Community in the House of Lords and sometimes on the floor of the House of Commons. Select committees may examine European issues or questions with a Community dimension, and some of them, such as the Commons Select Committees on Agriculture and Environment, do so quite often.

However, more specific procedures have also been adopted. The House of Commons appoints a Select Committee on European Legislation to consider draft proposals by the Commission, and other documents published by it which go to the Council.[54] The Commission proposals are sent, with an accompanying explanatory memorandum, from government departments. The Committee has 16 members, and is served by three full-time specialist staff, a clerk and other supporting staff. It has a substantial workload, and considers some 600–900 documents a year in order to decide whether they are of importance and, if so, warrant debate. It recommends about 15% for further consideration.

Documents recommended for further consideration can be referred for debate to the House, but since 1991 there have been set up each session two European standing committees for this purpose, each with 13 members. One committee deals with agriculture, forestry, the environment and transport, the second with everything else. The procedures allow for the relevant government minister to be questioned for up to one hour, prior to the usual debate. They remain, however, deliberative committees, not investigative.

The House of Lords Select Committee (called the European Communities Committee) has wider terms of reference, which extend to consideration of the merits of legislation.[55] Also, whereas the Commons Committee merely sifts documents so as to select for debate elsewhere, the Lords Committee compiles reports. The European Communities Committee is chaired by a salaried office-

[54] See J. A. G. Griffith and M. Ryle, *Parliament: Functions, Practice and Procedures* (London: Sweet & Maxwell, 1989) pp. 436–439; T. St. J. N. Bates, 'European Community Legislation before the House of Commons' [1991] *Statute Law Review* 109.

[55] *Ibid.*, pp. 490–492. See also C. Grantham and C. Moore Hodgson, 'The House of Lords: Structural Changes: The Use of Committees', in Philip Norton (ed.), *Parliament in the 1980s* (Oxford: Blackwell, 1985), pp. 125–127.

holder of the House, and is aided by two legal advisers, a specialist assistant, five clerks and five secretaries, as well as *ad hoc* expert advisers. The Committee comprises 24 peers, and meets fortnightly. But most of the work is conducted through five subcommittees (with some 50 or so others in their membership). Four of these operate in particular policy fields, while the fifth, chaired by a member of the judicial committee of the House, considers legal and institutional issues.

In the Lords, the committee chairman does the initial sifting. On average, about one-third of the Community documents received are selected for further consideration, which may vary from brief scrutiny to quite substantial inquiries, with evidence taken from the government, specialists, interests groups, the EC Commission and sometimes MEPs. In addition to pre-legislative scrutiny, which often ranges widely over the subject, the committee also instigates *ad hoc* inquiries from time to time, at the rate of about one per year.

The House of Lords Select Committee is more influential and more admired than its Commons counterpart. Its reports, which are sent to EC institutions, are generally acknowledged as thorough and authoritative. They inform the participants in legislation and seem to have influenced policy on occasions, although *Philip Norton* observes that 'in practice, the reputation of the committee probably exceeds its impact'.[56]

The ulterior purpose of pre-legislative scrutiny is to seek to influence decision-making in the Council of Ministers. Most obviously, the United Kingdom Parliament will seek to influence the British minister. The particular mechanism developed for the protection of Parliament is the so-called scrutiny reserve. Following a resolution of the House of Commons in 1980, agreed to by the government, ministers are expected to withhold assent to any proposal in the Council which one of the Select Committees has recommended should be debated, but has not yet been debated, unless the committee has indicated that agreement need not be withheld or the minister concerned considers that 'special reasons' obtain. As may be seen, this conventional obligation incorporates some flexibility in its operation. The government has claimed as special reasons factors such as the desirability of introducing measures beneficial to Britain into force as quickly as possible and the need to avoid a legal vacuum.

In practice, moreover, there are some proposals which are accepted by the Council even when the scrutiny reserve should

[56] Philip Norton, *Does Parliament Matter?*, op. cit., p. 126.

have been applied.[57] British ministers may be reluctant to delay legislation if there is general eagerness, and eagerness in the chair, to speed its passage.

The responsibility of ministers to Parliament is one of the most important conventions of the British constitution.[58] But, just as within domestic affairs the responsibility of ministers becomes attenuated in practice as the individual's own degree of involvement and responsibility becomes less, so in international and Community affairs. Where unanimity is required for decisions, ministerial responsibility to Parliament may operate in more or less the traditional way. But when the Council operates by majority voting, it follows that a minister may be outvoted, and then can scarcely be held responsible for a decision which was opposed by him or her. The institutional changes made by the Single European Act and the Treaty on European Union, by reducing the veto powers of national governments, simultaneously weaken the powers of national parliaments to influence Council decision-making by the most obvious route.

Incidentally, so far as the other two pillars of the Union are concerned, it has already been requested by a House of Commons committee that the House should be consulted before any important decisions are taken by a minister on behalf of the country.[59] However, in areas such as foreign and security policy and justice, when viewed from a domestic perspective, there is often scope for governmental action without parliamentary consent, by virtue of prerogative or other powers.

If in Community affairs it has become more precarious to rely on seeking to mandate or influence national ministers, then the lesson for national parliaments is surely that they will have to try harder to influence the Commission or the European Parliament at earlier stages. The UK Parliament has been at the back of the field in that race. Its connections with the EC institutions have been rather minimal, especially in the case of the House of Commons, and most of the blame for this state of affairs lies with the British Parliament. There are, of course, some inter-parliamentary links such as COSAC (*Conférence des organes specialisés dans les*

57 This has been calculated as between 2% and 9% in a year: Select Committee on Procedure, House of Commons (1989): Fourth Report from the Select Committee on Procedure: The Scrutiny of European Legislation, HC 622 (1988–89).

58 It is more correctly a cluster of conventions. See generally Colin Turpin, 'Ministerial Responsibility: Myth or Reality?', in J. Jowell and D. Oliver (eds.), *The Changing Constitution*, op. cit. ch. 5.

59 Foreign Affairs Committee, House of Commons (1993), Second Report of the Foreign Affairs Committee: Europe After Maastricht, HC 642–1 (1992–93).

*affaires communautaires*) and the Conference of Presidents and Speakers of Parliaments, which may be built on. However, the prospects for regular conferences of parliaments (following the model of the 'Assises' held in Rome in 1990), even with a Declaration appended to the Treaty on European Union to give encouragement to the practice, remain doubtful, with there being little enthusiasm in the UK Parliament, amongst others. In general, it may be concluded that there is some understanding in Britain of the need to exert influence on the Commission and Parliament more effectively, but as yet insufficient evidence as to how this might, let alone whether it will, be achieved.[60]

## Implementing Community Legislation

As EC regulations are directly applicable, national parliaments have no need to take action to implement them. With EC directives, however, national authorities are servants with regard to implementation, as they are bound to accomplish the desired result but 'the choice of form and methods' is at their discretion.[61] Occasionally, legislation is not required.[62] If legislation is required, in the United Kingdom it may be done by Act of Parliament (since anything may be done by Act of Parliament) or, with certain exceptions,[63] it may be effected by subordinate legislation, as allowed by Section 2 of the European Communities Act 1972. The choice of method turns partly upon imprecise conventions or understandings – for example, if an important change of principle is involved, then it should be done by Act of Parliament – but partly upon practical factors (such as room in the parliamentary timetable) and expediency.

More often subordinate legislation is used. The government has

60 See Fourth Report from the Select Committee on Procedure, 1988–89. The Scrutiny of European Legislation, HC 622 (1988–89); Foreign Affairs Committee, House of Commons (1993), Second Report of the Foreign Affairs Committee: Europe After Maastricht, HC 642–1 (1992–93). See also, on the interparliamentary arrangements, Martin Westlake, 'The European Parliament, the National Parliaments and the 1996 Intergovernmental Conference' (1995) *Political Quarterly* 59.

61 Article 189, EC Treaty.

62 Changes in administrative practices and procedures may be sufficient. For example, directives on public sector contracts were met in Britain by alterations in the procedures for advertising and awarding contracts.

63 European Communities Act 1972, S. 2 and Schedule 2: the exceptions relate to taxation, retrospective legislation, sub-delegated legislation, and the creation of new criminal offences.

delegated powers to make statutory instruments subject to the approval or, more usually (and at their choice), the absence of disapproval of the two Houses of Parliament. In practice, when this method is used, there is diminished parliamentary participation and scrutiny. There is scrutiny of the instruments (along with other statutory instruments) by a committee, the Joint Committee on Statutory Instruments, but it is restricted to considering and reporting on legal and procedural matters, and may not examine the merits.

The quality of the subordinate legislation, judged technically, seems to have been rather mixed, for various reasons (including different traditions in legislative drafting).[64] But, judged by rate of implementation, the United Kingdom's record has been good. Mrs Thatcher, addressing the European Parliament in 1986, used this point to stress that Britain was 'fully *communautaire*', and studies have largely vindicated the claim in this respect,[65] although differences in implementation rates are not as great as is sometimes implied and are perhaps explicable by differences in national politics or national procedures.

So far as procedures for post-legislative monitoring or scrutiny are concerned, the British government co-operates with the Commission in its activities in this regard. Otherwise, there are no formal or systematic procedures in place, although the general remit of officials in government departments partially fills the gap.

## The Inter-Governmental Conference and After

In the United Kingdom, as in other Member States, there is currently discussion and debate concerning what will occur and what should occur at the inter-governmental conference in 1996, although interest probably does not extend much beyond some political and academic circles. As the last British general election was in April 1992, it is likely that the Conservative government, by exploiting its term to or nearly to the five year maximum, will still be in office, at least for its early stages.

In considering what is the British position, we are strongly reminded that it is primarily a matter for the government, rather

[64] See *Making the Law* (1993: Report of the Hansard Society Commission on the Legislative Process), ch. 8.

[65] See Heinrick Siedentopf and Jacques Ziller (eds.), *Making European Policies Work: The Implementation of Community Legislation in the Member States* (London: Sage, 1988). See also Commission of EC, Eleventh Annual Report on Monitoring the Application of Community Law, OJC 154, 6 June 1994.

than for Parliament. The British government's proposals and negotiating stance have been developed within the Cabinet committee system, apparently by a subcommittee chaired by the Foreign Secretary which has reported to an overseas and defence policy committee chaired by the Prime Minister, which in turn reports to the Cabinet.

The precise lines of the government's thinking will probably not be made public,[66] partly because – rightly or wrongly – it seems to be considered to be tactically advantageous not to disclose one's hand too plainly, but perhaps more generally because a culture of secrecy is prevalent in British government.

The general lines of the government's approach, however, are fairly clear.[67] The British government intends to maintain its Maastricht opt-outs and resist any attempts to change the inter-governmental bases of foreign and security policy and justice and home affairs co-operation. It will resist any increase of powers for the Commission, and may even possibly try, if there is any support, to claw back some areas of competence in favour of the Member States. Some of the more extreme proposals of the Euro-sceptics[68] for wider repatriation (for example, of agriculture and fisheries) have, however, been rejected as unrealistic. The government may try to limit the powers of the Court of Justice, for example, as regards retrospective rulings. It will generally be opposed to extensions of majority voting in the Council of Ministers, although compromises may be necessary or possible if there are changes in the voting rules to favour the larger states.

The British government is also generally opposed to increasing the powers of the European Parliament. Some persons consider that increasing the European Parliament's role is the key to removal of 'the democratic deficit'. But British governments and Parliaments have tended to adopt a different perspective. Since any

66 At the time of writing, it is unclear whether some statement of the government's position might be published in the form of a White Paper. Some MPs are pressing for that to happen, and in a parliamentary reply, the Prime Minister indicated that he was giving it consideration: 260 HC Deb, col. 149. At a minimum, the Foreign Secretary will reveal something of the position in statements or in answering questions.

67 Briefings and 'leaks' provide us with a partial picture, and the information here is mainly drawn from national newspaper reports in summer 1995.

68 Several groups of MPs and others published their own views and proposals in attempts to influence the national debate. For an example of the 'Euro-sceptical' approach, see Martin Howe, *Europe and the Constitution after Maastricht* (Oxford: Nelson & Pollard, 1993). One prominent 'Euro-sceptic' MP, Mr. William Cash, has also introduced a private member's Bill, the European Communities (Reaffirmation of Sovereignty of the United Kingdom Parliament) Bill (HC Bill 55, 1994–95).

strengthening of the more supranational institutions of the Community is liable to be at the expense of either the Council of Ministers or national institutions, the British authorities are apt to be ambivalent at best and hostile at worst.

These attitudes might to an extent be different if reform of the European Parliament involved some stronger link with national parliaments or national parliamentarians, as some proposals have envisaged.[69] The British Prime Minister, Mr Major, in outlining his approach in the House of Commons in May 1995 did say that one of the government's proposals for the 1996 conference was 'a strengthened role for national parliaments',[70] but there is also an awareness in government circles that some of the other national parliaments are significantly more integrationist in tone than Westminster.

It is not yet clear what precisely will be proposed, still less what will result. Some commentators fear that the proposal to enhance the national parliaments' role is likely to remain as merely a 'pious hope',[71] which will be swept aside by more pressing concerns. In the light of earlier conferences and summits, such pessimism is difficult to dismiss, although predicting is a risky business. However, there are some reasons to *hope* that national parliaments will be given greater prominence, if one believes that the modern liberal state remains the fundamental basis for establishing and maintaining democracy and the rule of law in a way that is meaningful to individuals and consistent with their sense of identity. This perspective acknowledges that national parliaments may function as necessary brakes at times, even if their role is different at other times.

There are some recent signs, as in the Commission's modest White Paper on Social Policy, that the concept of subsidiarity may be taken seriously and that Community institutions will rein back the centralising tendencies which they have so often displayed. If that were to occur, perhaps in conjunction with a strengthened role for national parliaments, therein lies the best hope that the UK Parliament, if it cannot conceive of Community institutions as partners, may at least conceive of them as friendly rivals rather than as opponents.

69 See Karlheinz Neunreither, 'The Democratic Deficit of the European Union: Towards Closer Cooperation between the European Parliament and the National Parliaments' (1994) 29 *Government and Opposition* 299; Martin Westlake, 'The European Parliament, The National Parliaments and the 1996 Intergovernmental Conference' (1995) *Political Quarterly* 59.

70 260 HC Deb, col. 148.

71 Peter Riddell, *The Times*, 15 May 1995.

# Preserve or Abolish the Democratic Deficit?

*Sverker Gustavsson*

I present three points on the following pages. All relate to the much-discussed weakening of national parliamentarism in the Member States of the European Union, which is not matched by a parallel growth in democratic accountability at the European level. Irrespective of whether the so-called democratic deficit is an *intended* or an *unintended* consequence of European integration, a considerable element of suprastatism has in fact been instituted – without a corresponding shift in the technique for achieving democratic accountability. The problem is not so much whether such a deficit does in fact *exist*, but rather how it should be *evaluated*, and what constitutional policy is to be *recommended vis-à-vis* the resulting imbalance between power and responsibility.

I begin – as illustrated in Figure 1 below – by (1) sketching an overall picture of the European normative debate over the democratic deficit. The object is to place the problem within a larger perspective by distinguishing between strategies aimed at *preserving* and those aimed at *abolishing* the deficit. The latter idea is not, empirically speaking, nearly as dominant as it might seem normatively correct to assume.

I then proceed (2) to distinguish, within the category of abolitionist strategies, between approaches focused on strengthening the *European* Parliament and those seeking to reinforce the *national* parliaments.

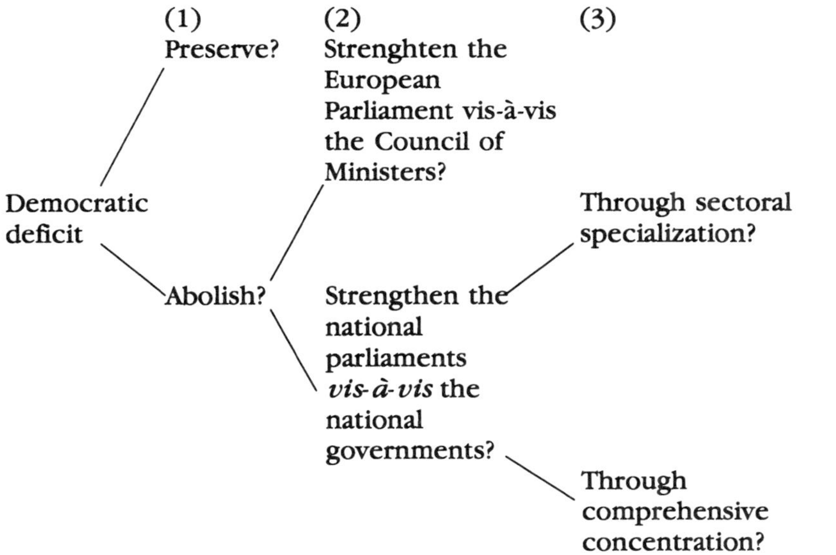


**Figure 1. Three normative questions about the democratic deficit.**

Last on the list comes (3) a report on what the Swedish Riksdag has done to regain what it lost through EU membership. What is most interesting here is that, rather than dividing the various components of EU policy among the *specialised* standing committees of the Riksdag, Swedish parliamentarians have chosen to assign EU policy as a whole to a *general* committee for European Union affairs. I question whether leading Swedish politicians actually wanted to strengthen the Riksdag in relation to the government. Both the specialising and the general strategy have been *presented* as means for diminishing rather than increasing the relative strength of the government within the Swedish system of power-sharing. Neither need in fact be true, either in the sense that a strengthening of the Riksdag is *intended* or in the sense that the chosen solution *actually works* in that direction.

The thrust of my threefold argument is that it cannot be excluded – as a matter of normative definition – that influential politicians are more anxious to preserve than to abolish the weakness of parliaments. A precaution against taking idealism for granted seems to be needed in two instances: when discussing the lack of parliamentarism at the European level, and when assessing proposals said to strengthen parliament at the expense of government at the national level.

## 1. Symmetry is Not Necessarily Better than Asymmetry

For at least the last 15 years, the so-called democratic deficit has been a central theme in West European debate. The expression has entered general usage, serving as an umbrella term for critical viewpoints of all kinds. Even so, the heart of the matter – the question most interesting from the standpoint of principle – is relatively easily discerned. The critical thing is the *constitutional asymmetry* characterising the European Union. The degree of legal development within the Union in a suprastatist direction is not matched by any corresponding democratic accountability on the part of its governing organs.[1]

The lack of constitutional balance emerges with particular clarity if we compare with federal states like the United States, Canada, Switzerland, Germany and Austria. For these systems contain a large suprastatist element as well. In these countries, the federal authorities make decisions on a majority basis against which the constituent states have no right of veto. Federal law has direct effect within the states, and enjoys precedence over state law as well. A distinct form of accountability corresponds to the degree of legal development in the direction of suprastatism. The peoples of the US, Canada, Switzerland, Germany and Austria enjoy the last word in deciding the political course taken on the federal level. They do this by voting in presidential and congressional elections in the United States, and in elections to the *Bundestag* or its equivalents in the other countries. The electorate can hold the federal leadership

[1] Pierre Pescatore, 'Les exigences de la démocratie et la légitimité de la communauté européenne', *Cahiers de Droit Européen* 10 - 1974, pp. 499–514; David Marquand, *Parliament for Europe* (London: Jonathan Cape, 1979); Georg Ress, 'Über die Notwendigkeit der parlamentarischen Legitimierung der Rechtsetzung der Europäischen Gemeinschaften', in: Wilfried Friedler and Georg Ress (Hrsg.), *Verfassungsrecht und Völkerrecht. Gedächtnisschrift für Wilhelm Karl Geck* (Köln: Carl Heymanns Verlag, 1989) pp. 625–684; Joseph H. H. Weiler, 'The Transformation of Europe', *Yale Law Journal*, 100 - 1991, pp. 2403–2483; Joseph H. H. Weiler, Ulrich R. Haltern and Franz C. Mayer, 'European Democracy and its Critique' in Jack Hayward (ed.), *The Crisis of Representation in Europe* (London: Frank Cass, 1995), pp. 4–39; Mario Teló, Démocratie internationale et démocratie supranationale en Europe' in Mario Teló (ed.), *Démocratie et construction européenne* (Bruxelles: Éditions de l'Université de Bruxelles, 1995), pp. 1–70; Philippe C. Schmitter, 'If the Nation-State Were to Wither Away in Europe, What Might Replace It? in Sverker Gustavsson and Leif Lewin (eds.), *The Future of the Nation-State* (London: Routledge, 1996), pp. 211–244; Peter Graf Kielmansegg, 'Integration und Demokratie' in Marcus Jachtenfuchs and Beate Kohler-Koch (Hrsg.), *Europäische Integration* (Opladen: Leske + Budrich, 1996), pp. 47–71.

democratically account-able – for the latter must stand down, should the voters so desire.

Voting out the leadership of the European Union, on the other hand, is impossible. For in this particular body, it is not the European Parliament but rather the Council of Ministers, the Commission and the Court that exercise power. This power is applied through the legitimate exercise of authority by the government of each member country. There is, in other words, no collective accountability. On the contrary, the strength of this construction is thought precisely to lie in the absence of a European electorate as the final arbiter *vis-à-vis* the central organs. The European Parliament and European elections must be regarded as a facade. The real power lies with the other three European-level organs, the authority of which does not derive from European elections, but rather from the governments and heads of state of the various member countries. The heart of the matter, in other words, is not the lack of a democratic power base as such. The point is rather that such a base is lacking despite the fact that European law, in federal fashion, has direct effect and precedence within the Member States.

Before examining what can and should be done about this imbalance, I would like to answer two objections often put to the idea that constitutional asymmetry should be regarded as *at all* problematic. According to the first objection, the democratic principle is fulfilled in that the participating countries are themselves democratic. The Member States have ratified the treaties in accordance with their constitutions, and the majority of these countries meet strict democratic criteria to boot. The problem therefore does not exist, according to this objection. The deficiency of this argument is that it focuses solely on the constitutional *origins* of the legal order whose democratic character has been called into question. It does not follow, because a certain institution was founded by a collection of democracies, that said institution is itself democratic.

The second objection to viewing constitutional asymmetry as problematic is based on the view that the democratic principle is satisfied through the positive *impact* which the imbalance on the supranational level might be thought to have on democracy in the Member States. This applies despite – or maybe thanks to – the lack of an adequate procedure for ensuring democratic accountability on the European level. Whether we speak of peace or of prosperity, the Union contributes to the stability of democracy in the Member States. Indeed, it is assumed to be this favourable impact which in practice sustains the confidence of the public in the Union as a historical project.

Even if we accept that the Union's *modus operandi* has such a positive impact on democracy in the Member States, the objection is nevertheless irrelevant to the question under examination here. The question I have posed is whether the structure of the Union is *democratic,* not whether it can be considered, in a sociological sense, to be *legitimate*. The difference becomes clear if we recall an extreme example. The Hitler regime, towards the end of the 1930s, was eminently legitimate in the eyes of the German people. Yet this circumstance did not render it, from a democratic standpoint, the slightest bit more acceptable. The support of public opinion and the practice of universal and equal suffrage did not suffice to qualify that regime as democratic. For freedom of speech and association could not be found there. The constitution itself, furthermore, decreed that the government could not be dismissed.

Instead of concentrating on the *modus operandi*, the formalist chooses to speak of origins, and the result-oriented politician focuses on effects. Neither of these are uninteresting, of course. But they are and remain peripheral questions, and they should not be allowed to take the place of an analysis of the real issues. The *modus operandi* is of great and lasting interest independently of origins and effects. The questions of provenance and of impact are possibly easier to answer in a reassuring manner. But this hardly helps if the discussion in fact has to do with the more troublesome issue of the *modus operandi*.

What, then, do I mean by my assertion that the *modus operandi* within the European Union is suprastatist in respect to trade and commercial policy? And why do I argue that this suprastatist feature is matched by no democratic counterweight as in the United States or Germany? Neither of the underlying principles in question – 'suprastatism', 'democracy' – has a definition accepted by all. Every delimitation involves taking a normative position. Let us not, however, exaggerate the difficulties of communication following from this. For the present purpose it suffices to try to capture the essential. I will content myself with recollecting what stands at the centre of each of these concepts. More peripheral aspects I choose to let alone.

I base my definition of the concept of suprastatism on three criteria.[2] The first is that decisions binding on all Member States are taken on the basis of simple or in various ways qualified majorities. The constituent states thus have no right of veto, as in a confederation (in which decision-making in principle is always consensual). A second distinguishing feature is that suprastatal legal developments enjoy precedence over competing developments

[2] Hans-Peter Ipsen, 'Die Bundesrepublik Deutschland in den Europäischen Gemeinschaften', in Josef Isensee and Paul Kirchhof (Hrsg.), *Handbuch des Staatsrechts der Bundesrepublik Deutschland. Band VII* (Heidelberg: C. F. Müller, 1992) pp. 767–815 at p. 774.

initiated by parliaments and courts in the Member States. *Bundesrecht bricht Landesrecht*, as Article 31 of the German constitution puts it. Thirdly, the concept of suprastatism means that the legal provisions in question are applied in the Member States directly, and that they bind individual legal subjects there. Suprastatal precedent becomes valid law in the Member States, without the necessity for any corresponding action on the part of the national authorities themselves.

Among the possible criteria for democracy, I choose here to focus on three. A first general requirement is that freedom of speech and association prevail. This precondition is not relevant to the present discussion, but of course it is basic to democratic government. A second requirement is for universal and equal suffrage. It bears noting, however, that a federal form of government always involves a greater or lesser departure from the principle that all votes are to count alike. This follows from the fact that the size of the constituent states is never exactly the same. Federal states always contain an element of one-state-one-vote as a counterweight to the principle of one-person-one-vote. The third criterion, finally, is that those who have conferred power on the leaders are able to hold the latter accountable. The citizens of a state, an association or a municipality cannot be considered bound by the decisions taken if the leadership of the body in question cannot be forced, upon having lost their confidence, to part with its position. Freedom of speech and association is not enough, not even if combined with universal and equal suffrage. The electors must also be able to convert their lack of confidence in a given set of policies – as they express this in general elections – into an effective choice of another set of policies.

The European Union does not, in respect to its suprastatal features, satisfy the requirements of democracy. This conclusion is evident if we take our starting point in the definitional criteria above. The norm-giving power of the Union is exercised in a high degree by the governments of the Member States acting in common. The leadership is thereby in practice immune from democratic accountability at the European level. The interesting thing for our present discussion, however, is not this fact in and of itself. The question sooner concerns which practical conclusions this constitutional asymmetry should give rise to. Should we work to *abolish* this disparity? Or should we seek rather to *preserve* the lack of symmetry as regards the prospects for holding the suprastatal authorities democratically accountable? The purpose in the latter case could be to safeguard the interest of the participating democracies in self-determination, and to maximise the possibilities for accountability within each individual country.

There is also a 'yes-side' and a 'no-side', in other words, when it comes to democracy at the European level. But 'yes' and 'no' mean something different here from what they meant in last year's referenda in Austria, Finland, Sweden and Norway. The current question – now that membership is an accomplished fact for the first three countries mentioned – is whether we wish to say 'yes' or 'no' to furnishing the suprastate with its own democratic power base. It is far from being a matter of course, be it noted, that one who says 'yes' to membership also says 'yes' to democratisation. Or vice versa. For example, many Danish debaters who said 'no' in the referendum of 1992 on the Maastricht Treaty returned after the referendum of 1993 as champions of the 'yes-side' in respect to the democratisation of the Union.[3]

Whether one is positive or negative to the democratic deficit depends, in other words, on which perspective one takes. I would like therefore to delineate four schools of thought (illustrated in Figure 2 below), each with a different recommendation regarding the democratic deficit: *federalism, constitutional liberalism, functionalism* and *confederalism*. These ideal types are defined by the answers given to two basic questions: should the suprastate have a democratic power base of its own and should more and more issue-areas eventually be integrated into the sphere of suprastatal governance?

| | | Stronger suprastate? | |
|---|---|---|---|
| | | Yes | No |
| Suprastate with its own power-base? | Yes | Federalism | Constitutional liberalism |
| | No | Functionalism | Confederalism |

**Figure 2. Four recommendations regarding the democratic deficit**

At the same time, these four recommendations represent two different approaches to the question of a stronger suprastate. According to the common view of federalists and functionalists, the right of veto should increasingly be superseded in favour of majority decisions. The movement is towards drawing an increasing number of questions into the constitutional sphere in which the guiding ideas are direct effect and the precedence of Union law over national law. The counterpart to this position is the standpoint

[3] Asger Baunsbak-Jensen et al., *Tag Europa alvorligt* (København: Tiderne skifter, 1993).

championed by both constitutional liberals and confederalists, who stand guard over the right of veto and work to counteract all tendencies towards majority voting and the development of suprastatal law.

Constitutional liberals want to furnish the suprastate with a democratic power base in order to limit the use of majority rule more effectively.[4] Federalists, on the other hand, see the point of democratisation as lying precisely in the political possibilities it offers for enlarging the powers and responsibilities of the suprastate. What they have in mind are matters above and beyond the free movement of capital, goods, services and labour. A stronger suprastate can be used to conduct an active policy against the socially and culturally undesirable side-effects of intensified economic competition. Confederalists, for their part, concentrate on the questions of national sovereignty and democracy in the Member States. Functionalists, finally, are action-oriented pragmatists and expansionists. Just as for the federalists, a deepening of integration for them means not just a reduced scope for the right of veto, but also that co-operation is strengthened and broadened to include more and more policy areas.

These are ideal-typical recommendations, of course. They are seldom, if ever, encountered in a pure form in one and the same person. At the same time, I hope, these positions are not so bereft of contact with political realities that they cannot help us to orient ourselves within the politics of European integration. An area for their application lies close at hand: the preparations for the intergovernmental conference (IGC) which, according to Article N, Point 2 of the Maastricht Treaty shall be convened in 1996. On this occasion, the criteria for new Member States – together with the future scope, orientation and organisation of European co-operation in well-nigh every aspect – will be up for discussion.

What demands will then be placed on new and old Member States is a critical question, which is reflected in the view of different actors as to the decision-making structure. There will be some hard nuts for the IGC to crack, not least the order of succession between large and small states in connection with the rotating presidency, and the number of votes assigned to each country in the Council of Ministers. For it is not just a question of reaching reasonable compromises between governments. Any and all changes in the Maastricht Treaty must be ratified in *all* of the Member States,

[4] Peter Bernholz et al., *A Proposal for a European Constitution* (London: European Policy Forum, 1993); Roland Vaubel, 'Demokratisierung ohne Zentralisierung', in Manfred Brunner (Hrsg.), *Kartenhaus Europa?* (Bonn: Verlag Bonn Aktuell, 1994) pp. 215–223.

according to the constitutional rules applying in each. This grants a strong negotiating position to defenders of minority views.

As the number of Member States grows, the governments of the larger countries are becoming more and more anxious to introduce a structure of decision-making that reflects the population size and economic strength of each country. Yet these same governments wish to avoid making the Union democratic, in the sense of furnishing the suprastatal organs with their own democratic power base. The conflicts we are therefore likely to witness are, I believe, amenable to interpretation in terms of the four ideal-types whose general content I have indicated.

It is far from being self-evident, in other words, that the democratic deficit should be regarded as an evil. Which of the above standpoints one adopts is decisive for how one judges this question. It is the federalists and constitutional liberals who want to abolish the deficit. For functionalists, by contrast, the deficit is the very point. In the degree the thing is problematic at all, it is in the area of public opinion. The deficit is not, that is, a problem in its own right. As far as confederalists are concerned, on the other hand, the issue touches on matters of principle. But their recommendations vary according to whether the object of their attention is the structure at the European level or the relationship between government and parliament in the political system of each state.

## 2. Which Parliament Should an Abolitionist Seek to Strengthen – The European or the National?

In the degree the functionalist (for reasons of pragmatism) or the constitutional liberal, the federalist or the confederalist (for reasons of principle) view the democratic deficit as a problem, the question becomes along what lines he or she wishes to abolish it. Should this be done by strengthening the European Parliament? Or is the right method instead to strengthen each national parliament in relation to its government in the Council of Ministers?

Practical politicians have a tendency to want to sit on two stools at the same time. They are tempted, in an effort to please as many as possible, to try to satisfy different groups whose opinions are incompatible. In some way this lies in the nature of the thing, and the matter under examination is no exception. Politicians claim to want both to promote democracy within the Union and to defend the influence of their own country. Such a double strategy is hard to present in a credible manner. Such a position can only be defended if one recommends a federalist or a constitutional liberal course of action. But in political practice these standpoints are very rare.

The constitutional liberal outlook is too extreme to attract even the right-wing parties of Europe. It rests, furthermore, on a somewhat Utopian and unrealistic assumption – that the peoples of Europe would be willing, within the foreseeable future, to place their fate in the hands of a constituent assembly specially convened for the purpose of giving Europe a new constitution. Such things only happen in connection with revolutions or a complete loss of political self-respect. The creation of the West German constitution in 1949 had the latter as a precondition. But this is not the normal way of things. The shape of the European Union following the IGC of 1996 will be decided on the basis of the rules applying within each country for the conclusion of international agreements. It is not politically possible, at any rate for the time being, for the people of Europe as a whole to acquire a new constitution. The possibilities are limited in practice by the provisions applying within each Member State for the ratification of treaties.

The federalist approach, for its part, suffers from the same weakness. It is easy to sympathise with the idea of a federal state as final goal and as constitutional construction. But this helps matters little, if those embracing the doctrine cannot indicate any method for its realisation. Only an extremely impractical idealist can disregard the need for a practicable method for giving the suprastate its own democratic legitimacy. For the problem is that the Union is founded on treaties which can only be changed through the adoption of identical resolutions by each and every Member State. How can all of the competing requirements in each of these constitutions – for referenda, qualified majorities, etc – be cleared out of the way? As the Danes showed in 1992, a single country can stop any effort in that direction. Federalism needs, in other words, to stop the 'clock of history' in order to achieve the constitutional 'new start' or 'qualitative leap' held out by orthodox adherents of this view as the key to future progress.

Parliamentarism at the European level is the common denominator of constitutional liberalism and of federalism. But that road seems in practice to be closed. Ordinary common sense forbids us to embrace ideas without any basis in reality. One can warmly appreciate the long-term objectives of constitutional liberalism and of federalism from a variety of points of view. But that hardly helps. For the way there presumes an extreme deepening of the crisis – to the point that the situation is perceived, by hundreds of millions of Europeans, as revolutionary.

If the 'way out' offered by constitutional liberalism and federalism is closed, then the remaining choice stands between confederalism and functionalism. As so often in real-life politics, it feels like a choice between the devil and the deep blue sea. Neither position is attractive on its face. Yet it is so that the problem must be posed, it seems to me. Confederalism calls for a Union of sovereign national states. It views European co-operation as a component in each state's foreign policy. Everything having to do with democracy is to be taken care of on the national level. In the field of foreign affairs, consensual agreements may be concluded, which then become valid law through decisions made in accordance with each country's constitution.

A drawback seen from a consistent federalist point of view is an advantage for a consistent confederalist. If the Member States of the Union refuse to submit to the majority principle on the European level, no suprastatal arrangements can arise. Common laws and practices will in that case be adopted at the rate desired by the least cooperation-inclined country. The guiding principle of functionalism, on the other hand, is not the notion of the federal state, but rather the desirability of the greatest possible 'integration'. What this means in political terms is the highest possible degree of suprastatism without parliamentarism. The right of veto should be restricted, says the functionalist. But this must not lead to the federalisation of cooperation, for down that road lies democratisation. Integration would then risk grinding to a halt, on account of the excessive dependence on public opinion resulting from the power which democratisation would grant to the population of the Union to vote the European 'government' out of office.

Integrating is like riding a bicycle, functionalists are in the habit of saying. It goes well as long as one keeps moving forward at a certain speed. If the pace of integration slackens, however, the political mechanism making for continued forward movement no longer functions. It is therefore critical to move forward continuously, and to avoid giving any 'unnecessary' encouragement to a broader discussion. The functionalist does not ask first of all how well the principle of democracy is fulfilled, but rather what cooperation leads to in practice. The results that count are peace, prosperity and a good environment. This attitude is familiar from what in a domestic context is usually referred to as corporatism. Also that phenomenon, at its best, yields results which in practice help indirectly to strengthen democracy in a country. But arrangements such as these are often dubious, on account of the departure they entail from such democratic staples as the one-person-one-vote principle and the idea that it must be possible to vote the holders of governmental power out of office.

The political problem is how to combine suprastatism on the one hand with democratic accountability on the other. Having clarified the issue in the light of the above four approaches, I would like to present the reader with the argument that federalism and constitutional liberalism are historically and politically out of the question. To give the suprastate a democratic power base of its own, as federalists and constitutional liberals prescribe, would seem to require *un nouveau pouvoir constituant*. For such a new constituent assembly to become a realistic political option, however, existing national governments would have to suffer a severe political crisis resulting in a lack of democratic legitimacy. Only when the peoples of all the Member States decide actually to disregard their national authorities and to demand a new constitutional framework are we likely to see developments along the lines preferred by federalists and constitutional liberals.

Such a general breakdown of Member State authority does not seem especially likely. Nor could such a political crisis be justified, normatively speaking, as a tolerable means for realising a desirable outcome. In practice, therefore, the problem of the democratic deficit has to be solved according to the idea of *les pouvoirs déjà constitués*, i.e., nothing can be done which is not legitimised through the already legitimate constitutional orders of the Member States.

The assumption that the Member States are masters of the treaties leaves us, then, with functionalism and confederalism as the only politically feasible options. Confederalism would mean a retreat from the degree of suprastatal governance already instituted. To the extent a partial suprastate is the kind of governance we really want, we must keep trying to solve the problem of democratic accountability *within* rather than *outside* the theoretical limits of functionalism, i.e., suprastatism without parliamentarism at the European level. Solving the problem of democratic accountability within functionalist theory remains the challenge, for federalism and constitutional liberalism are not available, and confederalism is not desirable.

From a functionalist point of view, the problem is the well-known fact that the European Union *resembles* a constitutional democracy without actually *being* or *becoming* one. This basic discrepancy – between what the Union appears at first glance to be and what it really is – has been with us ever since the 1950s. The increasing public awareness of the discrepancy, however, is rendering the constitutional arrangements of the Union increasingly problematic. After the cold war, the ratification of the Union Treaty, and the membership referenda in Austria, Finland and Sweden, public awareness of these matters has become a huge problem on the political agenda. Constitutional facts about the structure and meaning of the Treaty are less and less easily hidden from the public. Moreover, the gap between rhetoric and reality is made still wider by the fact that none of the really powerful actors is particularly eager (and indeed many are actively unwilling) to push the European Union in a democratic direction.

To a great extent, this politically embarrassing discrepancy is a matter of language. Participants in this discussion are forced to adopt the language of democracy, for the long-established rhetoric has it that 'the peoples of Europe' 'elect' a 'parliament', before which the 'European government' should be 'accountable'. In terms of such a rhetoric, it would seem reasonable to expect that this 'European government' be replaceable as a consequence of shifting majorities in European elections. And since all the Member States are democratic, an obvious parallel example lies close at hand. In the same way as within a Member State, then, the majority of 'the European people' is supposed to be able to 'throw the rascals out'.

In practice, the language of democracy and parliamentarism exacerbates the problem of constitutional asymmetry. The rhetoric offers a *standard* against which the real distribution of power and responsibility is measured, and when judged against this standard, the prevailing structures seem to make no provision for democratic accountability. If the rhetoric had instead been that of an ordinary international organisation, and if no suprastatal jurisdiction and sphere of decision-making existed, the problem would never have arisen. Nor would this problem have appeared if the European Union had been *truly* federal, or if it had at least been *on its way* towards some sort of parliamentarism or presidentialism at the European level. As we know, however, *neither* is in fact the case.

What makes the established Treaty so attractive to the governments of all the Member States is the fact that decision-making and jurisdiction at the European level are *not* hampered by democratic accountability to the European Parliament. The need for responsiveness to parliament is being sharply reduced at the national level, *without* being increased at the European level. That is where matters stand today. It is also, I believe, why national bureaucracies find the system so convenient for day-to-day purposes.

For federalists and constitutional liberals, this asymmetry between power and responsibility is a clear and undeniable deficiency. The deficit is something we should try to abolish.

For functionalists and confederalists, on the other hand, such an answer is not so obvious. Functionalists see these possible problems of democracy as a question of the EU's media image, sooner than as a question of constitutional theory. Their basic idea – to the extent they have one – is that the deficit is precisely what we should seek in the highest possible degree to maintain, on both the European and national levels. For the whole point is to make possible governments which are *stronger* – in the sense of being more resistant to the influence of parliaments and popular opinion at *both* the European and the national level. Confederalists, on the other hand, take a mixed approach. They see the deficit on the European level as something to be preserved. On the national level, however, they recommend that the government's participation in the Council of Ministers be subjected to the most effective possible control of parliament.

## 3. Strengthening Parliament in the Swedish Context – Through the Regular Standing Committees or Through a General EU Committee?

In the Swedish political context – as in most other national contexts, I believe – very few people actually address the problem of the democratic deficit in the light of constitutional theory at the European level. As might be expected, the practical problem in Sweden has been thought to concern how the Swedish Riksdag can regain what it lost in relation to its own government through EU membership.

Swedish Riksdag members and cabinet ministers are neither federalists nor constitutional liberals. Most belong to the functionalist or confederalist schools of thought. Very few active politicians regard democratisation on the European level as either realistic or desirable. For the functionalist or confederalist, the important question is not the structure of decision-making at the European level, but rather how the government in one's own country is to be controlled.

Irrespective of the background and political motivations involved, the immediate problem has to do with the internal organisation of the Riksdag. Should consultations between the government and the Riksdag on European questions take place in a special EU committee in which the handling of all EU questions is concentrated? Or should they be organised on a sectoral basis instead, within the framework of the system already established – with its standing committees for agriculture, trade, energy and other such broad areas?

In other words, the discussion so far has only to a very limited extent touched on the problem of European accountability in regard to *l'acquis communautaire*, i.e., what has been achieved in the area of European integration already. The focus has rather been on a corollary of this concept, *la perte de la souveraineté parlamentaire nationale*, i.e., the power that the national parliament has lost. The Riksdag has concentrated on controlling, in the highest possible degree, the conduct of the government in the Council of Ministers. The question – which is new for parliamentarism – is how the government administers the norm-giving power lost by the Riksdag through EU membership, rather than how the all-European norm-giving power can be made accountable to the European Parliament.

The Swedish system for cooperation between the government and the Riksdag[5] falls with the category usually described as strictly parliamentarian.[6] The Riksdag is sovereign, and the head of state wields no actual power (unlike in presidential or semi-presidential systems). There is, furthermore, virtually no separation of powers between the Riksdag and the government. The daily work of politics is based on legislative-executive power-sharing.

Before Sweden became a member of the EU, just two models for power-sharing between the government and the Riksdag were found in that country. The first – the *domestic-policy* model of power-sharing – applies to the exercise of the national norm-giving and taxing powers, i.e., to legislation, taxes and the budget. The Riksdag is organised for these questions as a mirror image of the government. The division of the government into *ministries* along chiefly sectoral lines (agriculture, education, taxes, culture, etc) is matched by the division of the Riksdag into *standing committees* for the same areas.

The symmetry between ministries and standing committees is not total. But the present discussion gains in clarity and overarching perspective if things are presented in this fashion. The ministries work out government bills with proposals for how the Riksdag should decide over the use of the norm-giving and taxing powers. The bills are then examined in detail by the standing committees of the Riksdag, which issue thick reports containing the final proposals on which the Riksdag decides. These reports furnish the real basis for the Riksdag's formal decisions.

Complementary proposals – in the form of private members' motions – are also examined by the standing committees. Motions consisting of counter-proposals or amendments relating to government bills may be submitted within 15 days of the date on which the bill was submitted to the Riksdag. The committees work for a number of weeks until their reports are complete. These reports then continue to the Riksdag for decision in a plenary sitting.

The second, *foreign-policy* model for power-sharing applies to the more important questions arising in connection with treaties. In the autocratic state, foreign policy was regarded as a matter primarily for the king. The breakthrough of democratic and parliamentary principles led to the establishment in 1921 of the

5 Nils Stjernquist, 'From Bicameralism to Unicameralism: The Democratic Riksdag, 1921–1986', in Michael F. Metcalf (ed.), *The Riksdag: A History of the Swedish Parliament* (New York: St. Martin's Press, 1987) pp. 223–303 at pp. 243 ff.; Erik Holmberg and Nils Stjernquist, 'Introduction', in *The Constitution of Sweden 1989* (Stockholm: The Swedish Riksdag, 1990) pp. 9–36 at pp. 17 ff.

6 Giovanni Sartori, *Comparative Constitutional Engineering* (London: Macmillan, 1994) pp. 101 ff.

Foreign Affairs Advisory Council, which was to provide a permanent forum for deliberations (but not the preparation of business) in the foreign policy field.

> The Government shall keep the Foreign Affairs Advisory Council continuously informed of those matters relating to foreign relations which may be of importance to the Realm, and shall confer with the Council in these matters as often as is necessary. In all foreign policy matters of major importance, the Government shall if possible confer with the Council before making its decision.[7]

The Foreign Affairs Advisory Council differs from the usual standing committees in more than the fact that it does not prepare business for the Riksdag. It is also important to note that it consists of just ten members, which means in practice that the parties are not proportionately represented. In addition, no minutes are kept which are immediately made public. On the contrary, a member must 'exercise caution in communicating to others what he has learnt in such a capacity'. In delicate situations, moreover, members have an 'unconditional obligation to maintain silence'.[8]

In sum, this means that consultations in the Foreign Affairs Advisory Council do not issue in any publicly available documents concerning what has been agreed to, or showing how discussions have proceeded between representatives for the government and the opposition. The Council's political function lies in its role as a bridge for the establishment of mutual confidence and minimum consensus between the leaders of the political parties. The top representatives of the opposition acquire knowledge thereby of how the government is reasoning. The other members of the Riksdag, however, and the general public as well, obtain but indirect knowledge of the arguments behind the Swedish viewpoints defended in various international settings.

Against the background of these two models for power-sharing, a third has now become established in the Swedish political system, as a direct result of membership in the EU. This emerging system – which is applied to consultations between the government and the Riksdag in EU questions – represents something of a cross between the domestic- and foreign-policy models. The Advisory Committee on European Union Affairs resembles the existing Foreign Affairs Advisory Council inasmuch as its prerogatives, formally speaking, do not include preparing business for the Riksdag; rather, its functions are purely deliberative. But it differs from the latter in that, like the

[7] The instrument of Government, Ch. 10, art. 6.
[8] The instrument of Government, Ch. 10, art. 7.

usual standing committees, it has 17 members, thereby affording proportionate representation to the parties.

> The Government shall inform the Advisory Committee on European Union Affairs about issues that are intended to be dealt with by the Council of the European Union. The Government shall also consult with the Advisory Committee about how negotiations in the Council shall be conducted in matters judged by the Government to be of importance, and in other matters as decided by the Committee.[9]

Moreover, 'at sessions of the Committee, stenographic records shall be kept of the Committee's deliberations with the government'.[10] And not only that. These stenographic records become publicly available as soon as they have been adjusted, i.e., after three or four weeks. The only exceptions to this rule are the fall-back positions discussed by members of the government with the committee on the eve of sessions with the Council of Ministers. These remain classified as long as they are judged to carry political significance.

That the government and Riksdag would choose this model – this middle way – was less than obvious. All throughout the process, until the decision was reached in December 1994, there were voices calling for solutions much closer to either the domestic- or the foreign-policy model.

Why leading Swedish politicians chose this middle way is something for future historians and political scientists to examine more closely. I content myself here with concentrating on one particular question discussed in connection with the decision to adopt the solution finally chosen, and which I judge to be of lasting interest. I have in mind the choice between the third model and the domestic-policy model. Decision-making in the Council of Ministers has in all essentials to do with sectoral questions which in a national perspective would seem to be domestic-policy matters. Would not the Riksdag have secured an even stronger position in relation to the government, then, if it had pressed the demand that consultations with the government be done through the regular standing committees in their respective areas?

The explanation for why this did not happen lies – at least viewed superficially – in how the problem had been discussed in the years immediately preceding.

In the spring of 1991, the Social Democratic government had initiated preparations for membership by charging a parliamentary commission of inquiry under the leadership of political science

[9] The Riksdag Act, Ch. 8, art. 15.

[10] The Riksdag Act, Ch. 8, art. 19.

professor Olof Ruin with the task of clarifying in what degree, and in what manner, the constitution would need to be changed in order to make membership possible. The work of the commission proceeded for two years, and issued in an official report. The only provision the commission thought absolutely necessary to change was the paragraph prescribing that the competence to make decisions binding in Sweden could only 'to a limited extent' be made over to an international organisation.[11] EU membership must be considered to involve such a transfer to more than a 'limited extent', in the view of the commission, in which case said expression had to be removed from the constitution before any legislation joining Sweden to the Union could be placed before the Riksdag.

Above and beyond this, the commission under Olof Ruin's leadership analysed a long series of other constitutional problems which, although important in their own right, did not necessitate any changes in the Instrument of Government. Among these other issues could be found the problem – to which this section of the present paper is devoted – of the consequences for the Riksdag's *modus operandi*. The judgment was ventured in the course of the commission's work[12] that Sweden ought to choose the Danish model – with a general EU committee. Somewhat later, an internal parliamentary inquiry into the Riksdag's working methods arrived at the same judgment,[13] as did a special commission of inquiry on the framing of the requisite law on accession to the Union.[14]

The conclusions reached by these various inquiries were concordant, not to say co-ordinated. All three inquiries saw three options – to assign consultation with the government on EU questions to the earlier-established Foreign Affairs Advisory Council, or to the established structure of committees for domestic-policy questions, or to a new general EU committee. And all three inquiries came to the conclusion that the third option – a general EU committee – was to be preferred. The reason offered for not assigning European policy to the Foreign Affairs Advisory Council

[11] The Instrument of Government, Ch. 10, art. 5 i.e. in its *pre*-1994 wording. In its *post*-1994 wording another constitutional technique has been chosen. The European Union is now being mentioned as a special case among international organisations. The principle 'to a limited extent' remains in force only for international organisations in general. As to the European Union an exception is being made. From 1995 and onwards, *all* parts of Sweden's national sovereignty can be transferred to the European Union, provided the Union is respecting human rights to the same extent as the Swedish constitution.

[12] SOU 1993: 14. *EG och våra grundlagar* [EC and our Constitution] pp. 242 ff.

[13] Förslag till riksdagen 1993/94: TK 3 [Proposal to the Riksdag from the Speaker's Conference] pp. 29 ff.

[14] SOU 1994: 10. Anslutning till EU [Sweden's Accession to the EU] pp. 84 ff.

was the risk for an excessive work load, and for a consequent distortion in the Council's work (especially in view of the demands posed by ordinary foreign policy). The reasons adduced against using the established structure of domestic-policy committees were also practical in nature – such as the excessive work load that would ensue, and the lack of an overarching outlook on European policy on the part of the individual committees.

About a year later – late in the Autumn of 1994, after the referendum of 13 November – it was time for the Riksdag to decide on its own working methods. The critical document for studying what was decided then, and which considerations were officially cited for the chosen construction, is the report submitted by the Standing Committee on Constitutional Affairs.[15]

It was here that the provision – which will likely prove extremely important in the future – on public stenographic minutes of the proceedings in the Advisory Committee on European Union Affairs was added. The formal decision in response to the report submitted by the Constitutional Affairs Committee was made by the Riksdag on 15 December,[16] and the requisite changes were introduced into the Riksdag Act.[17] EU membership, finally, came into force on 1 January 1995.

The leading politicians in the government and the Riksdag seem to have opted at an early stage for the model with a general EU committee. One might reasonably guess that their decision on this question was an expression of the general desire expressed by the leadership of the various parties to strengthen their position at the expense of the politicians active in the regular standing committees. I believe a fruitful research hypothesis could be that the party leaders eagerly seized the opportunity offered by EU membership. Evidence suggesting such a background can be found in the summary of motives which concluded the report of the Constitutional Affairs Committee on 7 December 1994. The critical section merits quotation in full:

> In the view of the Standing Committee on Constitutional Affairs, it is necessary to heed the knowledge and viewpoints of the regular standing committees in the procedures of consultation. It is a question here of mutuality between the regular standing committees

[15] Konstitutionsutskottets betänkande 1994/95: KU22, dated 7 December 1994. Samverkan mellan riksdag och regering med anledning av Sveriges anslutning till Europeiska unionen. [Report of the Standing Committee for Constitutional Affairs of the Swedish Riksdag: Co-operation between the Riksdag and the government in connection with the accession to the European Union].

[16] Riksdag Minutes 1994/95: 43, pp. 9 ff.

[17] The Riksdag Act ch. 3, art. 6; ch. 4, art. 10; ch. 8, arts. 14–19.

and the EU committee. The regular committees should of course be able to present formal statements to the EU committee, both at the request of the EU committee and at their own initiative, but other methods may often be more suitable. As regards statements from the regular committees to the EU committee, the difficulty can arise, in the opinion of the Constitutional Affairs Committee, that there is no item or direct proposal to which the statement can be connected.

The important thing, in the view of the Constitutional Affairs Committee, is that the standing committees' members and officials keep abreast of events in the European Union touching on their respective areas, and also that the members and officials of the EU committee regard it as important to call attention to issues and agendas expected within the EU. However, these forms for consultation should not, according to the Constitutional Affairs Committee, mean that – in the absence of active regulation by the Riksdag Act – consultation takes place only on the EU committee's terms.

The important role of the standing committees in our parliamentary system means that, under normal circumstances, it would be fitting for these committees to handle EU matters up to the point at which the latter come up for consideration in the Council of Ministers. The EU committee should also be aware of the positions of the Riksdag and the standpoints of the standing committees when the government, in accordance to 8 ch. 15, confers with it.

The Constitutional Affairs Committee does not now wish, however, to recommend that the forms for consultation and exchange of information between the EU committee and the standing committees be regulated in closer detail. Rather, the Constitutional Affairs Committee takes the view that the lessons of experience should be awaited. If, however, it has proven the case after one year – ie, at the close of 1995 – that the interplay between the standing committees and the EU committee does not reflect the notion of mutuality entertained by the Constitutional Affairs Committee, then the latter aims in the Riksdag to move that the Riksdag Act be amended to specify the duty of the EU committee to consult with the standing committee charged with a question to be taken up by the Council of the European Union.[18]

The conflict between the party leaders and the standing committee politicians is here resolved on the basis of a compromise founded on the idea of a *period of grace*. The EU committee has been established in the manner desired by the party leaders. But the presumption is that informal contacts between the standing committees and the EU committee will develop. If this proves not to have happened, when 1995 has come to a close, the Constitutional Affairs Committee will return to the issue and propose a

[18] 1994/95: KU 22, op. cit. pp. 22 f.

formal specification in the Riksdag Act of the duty of the EU committee to maintain close contacts with the standing committees on the questions that concern them.

Now, in the summer of 1995, half of this period of grace has elapsed, and a picture of how the EU committee works in practice has begun to take shape. If we begin by examining the composition of the committee, we find that the 17 regular and 17 substitute members are also members of the standing committees in a systematic and overlapping way.

The same close connection to the standing commitees is also found when studying the number of meetings and the intensity of preparations for them. During the spring of 1995, the EU committee met almost every Friday. The committee's rhythm and agenda is governed by the work schedule of the Council of Ministers. On the whole, one can say that the EU committee meets on every Friday preceding a week in which a meeting of the Council of Ministers is to take place. On Wednesday and Thursday each week, moreover, COREPER (*Comité des représentants permanents*) discusses those questions which are ripe for treatment as A- or B-points at the following week's meeting of the Council of Ministers. (A-points are issues on which decisions can be taken; B-points are items for discussion.) COREPER formulates proposals for the agenda of the various minister meetings. When the EU committee meetings open at 10.00am on Friday mornings, the members can usually base their work on the latest information about which questions will come up for discussion at the ministers' meeting, and they can take account as well of what representatives of the different member countries have said on the various issues in COREPER.

Since contacts are established with COREPER immediately following its meeting on Thursday, corrections can be made in the written materials which had been received by the members of the committee from the six person-strong secretariat on Monday, four days earlier. (The secretariat consists of a director, three address-holders and two assistants.) Agenda proposals with brief comments are distributed on Mondays. According to what has been agreed to in the committee, these short comments should be sufficiently detailed that members can decide whether they wish to request further information and possible consultation (if, for example, they make a judgment different from the government's on a particular question's importance). All of the standing committees, furthermore, receive the agenda for Friday's meeting of the EU committee at the start of the week.

An internal report on the working methods of the EU committee stresses that, when especially important questions are on the agenda for meetings of the Council of Ministers, the government makes special memoranda available. These can resemble the basic information issued earlier on the same question, but complemented now with information on what has taken place in the decision-making process. The memoranda might report, for example, on changes proposed or carried out, on the viewpoints of different Member States or organisations, etc.

> These memoranda are distributed as a rule to committee members on Monday of the same week during which the committee will be convened. They are a compromise between, on the one hand, the desire to obtain information as early as possible, and on the other, the need for correct and current facts'.[19]

A review of the minutes of the EU committee meetings during the spring of 1995 reveals that these meetings follow a definite pattern week after week. They normally treat impending gatherings of the various ministerial councils. This is matched, on Swedish soil, when the relevant ministries – represented by their responsible minister or his/her under-secretary, together with one or two officials – submit a report on the agenda for the ministerial meeting, and explain how they plan to act there.

Representatives for the parties then ask questions and issue comments, after which – in varying degrees – vehement and stimulating exchanges ensue. The chairperson, Social Democrat Berit Löfstedt, concludes each such session by summarising in general terms what has been said. Newspaper reports came out towards the end of the spring, according to which, she said that she tries to wrap up the various points by 'stating that the government has a majority for its position'.[20]

On the other hand, it can scarcely be determined – without an extremely thorough examination of a number of questions – in what degree the viewpoints expressed in the EU committee are co-ordinated with the deliberations undertaken in the various standing committees. The implicit guideline, according to Berit Löfstedt, is that the EU committee exercises the influence of the Riksdag in regard to short-term decisions week for week. In regard to long-term decisions and politics in a larger sense, on the other hand, it is up to the various committees and committee groups to co-operate with the government, in order that Sweden's policy in the Council of Ministers is co-ordinated in the best possible way with the national-level utilisation of the norm-giving and taxing powers.

[19] Bengt Ohlsson Riksdagens EU-nämnd – en presentation (The Secretariat of the Advisory Committee on European Union Affairs of the Swedish Riksdag: Internal mimeo, 13 March 1995), p. 7.

[20] Dagens Nyheter, 20 May 1995.

Otherwise put, one could say that the dealings of the EU committee with these questions are relatively speaking more formal, while those of the standing committees are more factual.[21]

Berit Löfstedt's distinction between short-term and formal on the one hand, and long-term and factual on the other, is of great interest from the standpoint of political science. It should, in my view, be taken as the point of departure for a more in-depth investigation into the practices which are emerging in Sweden as a result of the strategic choices made by party leaders and the Constitutional Affairs Committee during 1993 and 1994. Whether or not the Constitutional Affairs Committee will seek, at the end of 1995, to have the interplay between the standing committees and the EU committee formally regulated in the Riksdag Act must be considered as yet an open question.

Regardless of the position taken by the Swedish Constitutional Affairs Committee when the period of grace has run out, the problem in Sweden does not differ from, e.g., that in Denmark[22] or in Germany.[23] It is far from obvious which strategy for dealing with the democratic deficit in the national context – through a general EU committee or through the regular standing committees – is the most effective one. The larger and more fundamental question is whether the model employed within a national form of government can help to abolish the democratic deficit within the Union as a whole. As I see it, it is far from clear that *either* of these forms of control at the national level can reduce the democratic deficit, as long as power is exercised in common by the governments of the European Union, and not within each country separately.

The discussion of the internal organisation of the national parliaments in relation to their respective governments should not, in other words, be allowed to obscure a more profound and structural precondition. For what these parliaments have lost in terms of their participation in the exercise of the norm-giving and taxing powers – *la perte de la souveraineté parlamentaire nationale* – is not necessarily an unintended consequence of EU membership. A reasonable alternative hypothesis is that this effect is in fact intended – that it is a corollary of *l'acquis communautaire*, i.e., already achieved EC laws and common policies. Seen in a European perspective, the combination of these two inverted key

[21] Interview with Berit Löfstedt, Chairman of the Advisory Committee on European Union Affairs of the Swedish Riksdag, 5 May 1995.

[22] Peter Nedergaard, *Organiseringen av Den europæiske Union* (København: Handelshøjskolens Forlag, 1994) pp. 302 ff.

[23] Sven Hölscheid and Thomas Schotten, 'Der Unionsausschuß des deutschen Bundestages – Gestaltungsprobleme', *Integration*, 17 – 1994, pp. 230–233.

concepts of gain and loss – *l'acquis* and *la perte* – appears as the very quintessence of the governing functionalist logic. The internal organisational problems of the Riksdag, the Folketing and the Bundestag are certainly important on the practical level and on the margins. But in principle, and in respect to the main event, the battle seems irrevocably lost.

The battle was lost in that moment when the various European parliaments gave their consent to the accession of their country to the Union. It was thereby decided that a significant part of the norm-giving powers would be exercised in common by the governments in the Council of Ministers. In some decisive way, *la perte* cannot be regained by anything less than that the European Parliament recaptures this power on behalf of the principle of democratically constituted authority. And this – as I noted earlier – can scarcely be done unless the crisis deepens into an overall breakdown of Member State authority.

## Conclusion

My threefold argument can be summarised, finally, in the following brief fashion:

1. It is not at all self-evident – as seems to have become politically correct to assume – that influential politicians really want to abolish the democratic deficit. In their own view, they have good reasons for preserving it.
2. As far as compensating for the loss of parliamentary influence is concerned, a misunderstanding is close at hand. Strengthening national parliaments in relation to their respective governments – irrespective of method – has little to do with the question of preserving or abolishing the democratic deficit in the Union as a whole.
3. It is far from self-evident – as seems normatively reasonable to assume – that government and opposition leaders really want to compensate their parliaments for the influence lost due to EU membership. Government and opposition leaders may also want to use membership as a means for marginalising other leading figures within their parties who sit on the specialised standing committees.

# The Norwegian Parliament and European Integration – Reflections From Medium-Speed Europe*

*Fredrik Sejersted*

## Introduction

The European integration processes are not, and have never been, confined to the Member States of the European Union. On the one hand, the processes are due to broader changes affecting all of Europe. Even the development of a common European legal system is something that goes beyond Community law, encompassing *inter alia* the European Convention on Human Rights and a number of other treaties. On the other hand, developments inside the EU are affecting all other European states, and Community law is increasingly being adopted by non-Member States. There already exists a multi-speed Europe.

In this Europe, the remaining EFTA-members of the EEA Agreement – Norway, Iceland and Liechtenstein – represent a medium-speed alternative. They are not full members of the EU, but they are a legally integrated part of the single market. Under the

* Thanks to Hans Petter Graver, Ola Mestad, Johan P. Olsen, Eivind Smith and Ulf Sverdrup for valuable comments on a draft. The fact that I have not been able to follow up on all their comments is my own loss. As will become obvious to the reader, this essay is not the outcome of a finished process of reflection, but rather a piece of work in progress.

Agreement, Norway has adopted a large part of the *acquis communautaire*, including almost all legislation on the four freedoms, competition and state aid. Norwegian authorities have undertaken to implement and administer the Community rules as loyally as do the Member States, and to respect the relevant case-law of the European Court of Justice (ECJ). In this way Norway is able to reap the benefits of the internal market, without being part of the political system.

There is, of course, a catch. Through the EEA Norway has gained not only the advantages, but also many of the disadvantages of European integration. De-parliamentarizations is one of them. Like national parliaments inside the Union, the position of the Norwegian Parliament (the *Storting*) has been weakened on two levels. First, the EEA means a massive transfer of real, if not always formal, power from the Storting to the Community institutions, through the EEA organs. Second, it has led to a shift in the balance of power on the national level, weakening parliament and strengthening the government and the administration, as well as the courts. Like their colleagues in the Member States, Norwegian Parliamentarians face the challenge of regaining power lost.

It is primarily the *legislative* function of the Storting that is weakened by the Europeanisation process, and this is what I will focus on. The Community is a regulatory system, and it is through the impact of Community law that the decision-making powers of the Storting are most affected. Unlike parliaments in the Member States, the Storting has not transferred any formal legislative powers, but as I will show, the ceding of real legislative power is vast, and for most practical purposes the Storting is much in the same position as other national parliaments.

Other functions of the Storting are less affected by European integration. The financial and budgetary powers of parliament are not reduced as much as in the Member States.[1] The importance of the Storting as an arena of public debate and long-term policy formulation has probably increased because of the heated interest taken in European affairs by all political actors, but this is not the main theme here.

There seems today to be a general feeling throughout the Union

1 The financial powers are less affected because the EEA does not cover the EMU or the taxation policy. The budgetary powers are less restricted because the entrance fee to the EEA is small, as neither the CAP nor the structural policy of the Union are included. Use of the budget as an instrument of governance is however affected by other community rules included in the Agreement, *inter alia* the rules on state aid, government monopolies and public procurement. Compared to many other countries the Storting enjoys great control over the state budget, and uses this as a major power-base.

that in some way or another national parliaments have to be more included in the integration processes. There is less agreement on why and how this should be done.[2] To the proponents of further integration, some involvement of national parliaments is necessary in order to improve the shaky legitimacy of the supranational decision-making processes, but their actual influence should be kept at a minimum in order not to reduce efficiency. To the opponents of further integration, national parliaments constitute more of an alternative, and should be strengthened in real terms in order to counterbalance the supranational institutions.

Both perspectives could also be applied to the EEA alternative, though this is not yet seen as clearly as in the EU. The Agreement also suffers from a democratic deficit and subsequent problems of legitimacy that are bound to impair its efficency. For those in Norway, including the present government, who want to further strengthen and develop the EEA alternative, the Storting is crucial as a source of legitimacy. For those who want to weaken the ties to the Union, the Storting is arguably the most important fighting arena for doing so.

Strengthening the role of national parliaments is not easy, neither in the EU nor in the EEA. EU-led integration is a process that partly takes place in independent, supranational institutions, and partly in the form of negotiations and co-operation between nation states, represented by their ministers and civil servants. Integration presupposes agreement and compromise, and different decisions often have to be linked in larger packages. This is only if at all possible in confidential meetings between a relatively small number of representatives with wide mandates, not by involving 15 or more national assemblies. A national parliament is constructed as the supreme legislative institution of a state, not to represent the state externally, nor to lead in detailed and continuous negotiations with other states. Furthermore, parliaments are geared to national and local policy interests, not to take account of supranational considerations. National parliaments are cornerstones of European integration to the extent that their participation has been constitutionally and politically necessary to ratify the basic treaties, but as soon as co-operation has been established, they rather risk becoming stumbling-blocks.

In this article the problem of parliamentary influence is seen from the EEA perspective. To many this may seem of little comparative interest, since the Agreement today only remains important to Norway, Iceland and Liechtenstein. Hopefully, such is not altogether the case. First, the EEA alternative might serve to highlight aspects

[2] For a better analysis of this, cf. the contribution in this volume by Philip Norton.

of the situation inside the Union by providing a contrast. Second, it may say something about the possibilities of parliamentary influence not only in full-speed, but also in medium-speed Europe. This might be of interest when the Community in due time plans to include Central and Eastern Europe. Even if the idea, sometimes expressed, of using the EEA as an alternative halfway house to membership for the new democracies at the moment seems to have been abandoned, it might be revived.[3] And the EEA should anyway be seen as an experiment in multi-speed Europe, and might have some interest for other future models.

It is trite but true to point out that the EEA is a deal in which the EFTA-states keep some policy areas outside of the co-operation (*inter alia* agriculture and trade policy), in exhange for almost no influence in the areas where they do join the Community (the internal market). Norway can only have very limited influence on what is happening at the European level, and the Storting therefore even less. This point will not be elaborated.

Rather I will take as a starting point the limited powers that exist: to influence the EU, to influence the development of the EEA; or to adopt a separate national policy. I will then ask to what extent the Storting can control these powers, constitutionally and politically.

My underlying assumption is that compared to full membership the EEA medium-speed alternative creates less favourable conditions for re-parliamentarisation, at least in everyday politics. One reason is that the formal status of the Agreement camouflages the real transfer of power, and so keeps the Storting from introducing necessary reform. This includes better access to information and internal organisation. Another reason is that the direct channels to the supranational level open to Member State parliaments are closed to the Storting, while at the same time the possibilities for parliament to influence executive policy on the EEA are just as restricted as in the EU. Finally the scope for downstream control over implementation, legal and actual, is at least no better under the Agreement.

What the Storting has kept is the chance to opt out, to veto further development of the EEA or to deny implementation. But this right can only be exercised in extreme situations, and by paying a substantial political price.[4]

3 Cf. Steve Peers, 'An Ever Closer Waiting Room?: The Case for Eastern European Accession to the European Economic Area', *The Common Market Law Review* 1995, pp. 187–213.

4 For another (and more optimistic) analysis of the position of the Storting under the EEA Agreement, see Asbjørn Seim, *Stortinget–en fugl Føniks på maktutredningens ruiner?* (Bergen: 1995).

## Medium-Speed Europe: Main Elements of the EEA Agreement[5]

After long and tortuous negotiations, and an extended ratification process, the EEA Agreement came into force on 1 January 1994. By that time, original interest in the Agreement had fallen dramatically, as the four largest EFTA states had already applied for full membership of the EU.[6] Whereas Sweden, Finland and Austria joined the EU on 1 January 1995, Norway stayed within EFTA, trying hard to save the remains of what had once been regarded – even by the Community – as quite an important treaty. The EEA Agreement still stands, and the actual wording has not been altered, but the context it operates in has changed profoundly.

Formally, the Agreement is a traditional international treaty. Legislative power is not transferred. The Agreement does not create a supranational legal system, and EEA rules do not have *clear* direct effect *nor absolute* supremacy in national law in the EFTA countries. Since Norwegian law has a dualistic approach to international law, all EEA rules have to be implemented, either by parliament itself or by the government acting under delegated authority. The only formal transfer of power is in competition law, where the new EFTA Surveillance Authority (ESA) has been given much the same competence as the Commission enjoys.

In real terms, the EEA entails a massive transfer of legislative power from the Storting. The Agreement contains the whole *acquis* on the four freedoms and competition, as well as most of the rules on, *inter alia*, transport, social affairs, the environment, consumer protection, and company law. The Community acts are for the most part adopted without special exemptions. Through Art. 6 of the main part of the Agreement, the EFTA countries undertake to respect all the relevant case-law of the ECJ. According to the preamble administrative practice should be homogeneous with that in the Union, and much of the Community soft law is of relevance. The Agreement contains specific rules on institutional structure and on the necessary adaptations, but apart from that there is no independent 'EEA law'. All acts are copied from Community law, and the legal and institutional mechanisms of the Agreement are

5 For a thorough look at the EEA, see Nordberg, Hökborg, Johansson, Eliasson and Dedichen, *EEA Law* (Stockholm: Fritzes, 1993), or Sejersted, Arnesen, Rognstad, Foyn and Stemshaug, *EØS-rett* (Oslo: Universitetsforlaget, 1995).

6 On the process leading up to the EEA, see Helen Wallace (ed.), *The Wider Western Europe* (London: Pinter, 1991), and Thomas Pedersen, *European Union and the EFTA Countries* (London: Pinter, 1994). See especially Pedersen for an analysis of why the EEA process was so quickly overtaken by the process of seeking full membership of the EU.

designed to ensure that these rules are implemented in the EFTA countries as effectively as in the Member States.

In spite of its formal status, the EEA also contains several supranational elements. First, the Agreement is supposed to be further developed dynamically, as the underlying Community law develops. This is a political and not a legal obligation, but the structure of the Agreement makes it hard even from a legal point of view to veto new acts. Second, a separate institutional 'EFTA pillar' has been constructed through treaties between the EFTA countries, as a small scale model of the EU institutions. Most important are the ESA and the EFTA Court, which have been given some of the same powers as the Commission and the ECJ.[7] Third, the relationship between EEA law and national Norwegian law is not as clear as the formal nature of the Agreement would imply. Suffice it to say here that there are elements both of supremacy and direct effect. Though the extent of these principles is highly debatable, for most practical purposes they will serve effectively to undermine the legislative sovereignty of the Storting.[8]

The difference between the EEA and membership of the EU is, first, that the EFTA countries do not participate in the main decision-making procedures affecting them. Attempts by the Norwegian government to gain increased influence in the EU have largely been turned down. A 'political dialogue' has been established between the EFTA and the EU states, but it does not go very far. More important are Arts. 99 to 101 of the Agreement, which give the EFTA states the right to be heard on the proposals of the Commission, and to send national experts and civil servants to a vaguely defined and quite limited number of committees under the Commission (but not under the Council).[9]

In terms of substance, the difference is that the Agreement does not contain, *inter alia*, rules on agriculture, fisheries, commercial policy and tariffs, and taxation, as well as a number of other areas. The EFTA countries are not tied to the process towards economic and monetary union, nor do they take part in the second and third pillars of the Union.[10]

7 There is also an EEA Parliamentary Committee, but unlike the European Parliament it has no influence on the decision-making processes.

8 See Advocate-General van Gerven, 'The Genesis of EEA Law and the Principles of Primacy and Direct Effect', *Fordham International Law Review*, Vol. 16 1992–1993, pp. 955–989, and (then president of the EFTA Court) Leif Sevón, 'Primacy and Direct Effect in the EEA. Some Reflections', in *Liber Amicorum Ole Due* (Copenhagen, 1994).

9 Cfr Nordberg et al., op. cit. ch VIII.

10 However, as regards 'justice and home affairs' Norway is a signatory of several of the treaties now placed in this pillar. Norway is also negotiating to enter the Schengen agreement.

The possibility to opt out of obligations is formally much wider under the EEA Agreement than inside the Union. A signatory state can withdraw in 12 months under Art. 127. An EFTA country can refuse to adopt new Community acts into the Agreement under Art. 102. National parliaments are given a specific right of veto in Art. 103, to which I will return. There is a right to take protective measures under Arts. 112-114. The problem is that any opt-out gives the EU the right to take counter-measures, and since the EFTA countries are much the weaker party, the real freedom is not to be exaggerated.

Altogether, the EEA Agreement contains some 2,000 Community acts (including soft law). This came in two bundles. The original Agreement, as signed on 2 May 1992, contained the relevant *acquis* as of the last month of 1991. While the EEA waited to be ratified, the Community adopted most of the 1992 legislation on the internal market, and this was then introduced as 'EEA II' in 1994. Since then, a handful of new Community acts have also been introduced, though the process is not as fast as the Norwegian government would like. The aim of the Agreement is to catch up with legal developments in Community law, so that new acts are implemented at the same time both in EU and EFTA countries.

The future of the EEA Agreement is uncertain. What is clear, is that the substantial parts of the Agreement will continue to function in some way or another. Norway has joined the internal market, and this process is probably irrevocable. Legal integration has gone far, and will be difficult to reverse. What is less clear is whether the institutional structure can survive. The 'two-pillar' system, with separate EFTA institutions as well as a number of EEA organs, is already something of an anachronism. Still it is difficult to envisage an alternative, and certainly one that would give the Storting back legislative power.

## Constitutional and Political Adaptability of the Storting to European Integration

To what extent has the Norwegian Storting been constitutionally and politically prepared to surrender legislative sovereignty on the scale demanded by the European integration process? To what extent is it accustomed to sharing power with others, and how well suited is its tradition of operating to handle European affairs? As a lawyer, I will first consider the constitutional adaptability, and then briefly the question of practical politics.

The constitutional position of the Storting is strong. The written constitution of 1814 separates power between the legislator, the executive and the courts, but British-style parliamentarism was politically introduced after a dramatic case of impeachment in 1884, and accepted by legal theory as legally binding constitutional custom some 30 years later. Since then, the Storting has been formally sovereign in the sense that it is the single supreme state organ. It is only bound by the constitution, and this it can amend, though under Art. 112 that requires a two-thirds majority, and general elections between the proposal and the decision.

As the constitution stands, it puts two limitations on the Storting of interest to the Europeanisation process. The first is the theory of executive prerogatives. According to the written constitution, several tasks are specifically given to the government, and these have traditionally been interpreted not only as giving the executive a mandate, but also as prohibiting the Storting from interfering. Through the years, this once important theory has been gradually weakened, and it has long been recognised that the Storting can pass general legislation regulating the use of the prerogatives, and in some cases even give binding instructions. In any case it is always possible for the Storting to send political 'signals', which will usually be followed. Due to parliamentarism, legal theory has more or less abandoned the prerogatives as outdated, but the Storting itself is more conservative, and the tradition still influences standard operating procedures.

The most important of the prerogatives concerns foreign affairs under Art. 26 of the Constitution. This does not mean that the Storting is without powers in foreign policy. First, according to the second paragraph of Art. 26, the Storting has to accept all treaties of 'special importance' before they can be ratified. Second, the dualistic principle gives parliament control of the implementation of treaties into Norwegian law. Through the Committee on Foreign Affairs (and the Extended Committee on Foreign Affairs, which the government consults on questions of particular importance), the Storting participates in forming the general guidelines of Norwegian foreign policy.[11] But the more day-to-day running of foreign policy is of course done by the government.

The second formal limitation on the Storting, is the power of the courts to review the constitutionality of ordinary legislation. This unwritten principle was introduced in the last century by legal theory and by the courts themselves. Control lies with the ordinary courts, as there is no specific constitutional court. In practice the

[11] See Per Stavang, 'Den utvida utanriksnemnda', in: *Parlamentarisme og folkestyre* (Bergen: Alma Mater, 1994). For a thorough look at legal questions and parliamentary practice, cfr. Erik Colban: *Stortinget og utenrikspolitikken* (Oslo: 1961).

Norwegian Supreme Court has adopted a very careful line, and in the years from the early 1930s to the 1970s there were arguably no instances of any law by the Storting being found unconstitutional. However, the last 20 years or so have witnessed a modest revival of the old doctrine, reflecting no doubt a similar tendency in other European countries.[12]

The power of the courts over the Storting is limited by the fact that the written constitution is quite narrow, and unwritten principles of law are seldom given constitutional status. On the other hand, the European Convention on Human Rights has for the last 20 years been increasingly invoked against national legislation, with some success.[13] The introduction of the *acquis communautaire* through the EEA Agreement vastly increases the scope for judicial review of the acts of the Storting. Norwegian courts must be expected to go about this rather carefully, as the interface between law and politics under the *acquis* is quite unfamiliar to them. The point is, however, that the courts are already in a constitutional position to set aside parliamentary acts, and the Storting has long been familiar with this way of thinking.[14]

In real politics the Storting is far more used to power-sharing than its formal sovereignty might imply. As in any modern society, parliament is only one of many political actors, albeit an important one. To some extent the romantic heydays of parliamentary power in Norway were in the last century, but comparison is hard to make, also because the Storting held little power in foreign affairs under the union with Sweden.[15] In this century, there has been an ebb-and-flow of parliamentary influence.[16] Generally speaking, the different minority governments over the last decade have led to a flow, while the Europeanisation process signals an ebb.

[12] See Eivind Smith: *Høyesterett og folkestyret* (Oslo: Universitetsforlaget, 1993) and ibid., 'Judicial review of legislation in Norway – characteristics and recent trends', in *The Role of the Constitution in a Changing Society* (Oslo, The Norwegian Academy of Science and Letters, 1992) pp. 179–215.

[13] In 1994 a new art. 110c was introduced in the written constitution, giving international human rights a semi-constitutional status.

[14] Much more so than in the other Nordic countries, where the courts traditionally have been much more reluctant to set aside parliamentary acts. For a comparative study, cf. E. Smith, Pays scandinaves, in L. Favoreu & J.A. Jolowitz (eds.), *Le contrôle juridictionnel des lois. Légitimité, effectivité et développements récents* (Paris/Aix-en-Provence, Economica, 1986) pp. 223–282.

[15] This union lasted from 1814 until 1905. Even if Norway enjoyed a great deal of self-government under the union, and even if it was not at the time particularly unpopular among most people, it was still forced upon the country, and this has given the term 'union' a negative aspect, which was skilfully used before the referendum by the Eurosceptics.

[16] Cf. Johan P. Olsen, *Organized Democracy. Political Institutions in a Welfare State – the Case of Norway* (Oslo: Universitetsforlaget, 1983), ch. 2.

On the international level, Norway has for the last 700 years been a very minor actor, and is quite used to binding co-operation, both through treaties and in real politics. It has been argued that smaller states because of their very weakness are better positioned to adapt successfully to changing political environments.[17] Together with a strong tradition of the rule of law, this might go a long way to explaining the remarkable ease with which 15,000 pages of Community rules and regulations of quite foreign origin and form were adopted into Norwegian law in just a few years.

The adaptability of any parliament to European integration is closely connected to its normal function in national political life. A parliament is both a working legislature and a debating arena for political confrontation designed to influence public opinion, but the mix is different from country to country. The more a working legislature, with traditions of coalition-forming and early involvement, the better suited a national parliament is to influence European politics.[18] Traditionally, the Storting is very much a hard-working legislature. The committee system is highly developed, and work on concrete budgetary or legislative proposals easily covers most of the everyday life for the members. Plenary confrontations occur, of course, from time to time, but far more rarely than, for example, in the British Parliament. Television broadcasts from the Storting are normally a dull affair.

This, however, is the general picture. In European affairs, the opposite is very much the case. For 30 years or so, the relationship of Norway to the Community has arguably been the single most controversial question in Norwegian politics.[19] The confrontation threshold is low, and in the last years extremely so. Even the most technical and insignificant proposal can explode if it contains a European dimension.[20] From a democratic point of view this is not altogether unhealthy, especially when compared to the (formerly) sometimes repressive consensus on EU policy in some of the

17 See Johan P. Olsen, 'Europeanization and Nation-State Dynamics' (Arena working paper no. 9, Oslo 1995) p. 38, with further reference.

18 See Vernon Bogdanor, 'Britain and the European Community', in Jowell and Oliver (eds.), *The Changing Constitution* (Oxford: Clarendon Press, 1994), p.8.

19 Arguably, because the controversy has only surfaced twice, before the referendums in 1972 and 1994. From 1973 until the late 1980s the issue was buried, but it was always there waiting to be dug up again. What is certain, is that since the last war no other issue has to the same extent roused popular sentiments and mobilised the voters.

20 To some extent this can perhaps be linked to the fact that Norway has so little influence on European affairs anyway, that there is little pressure on the MPs to behave constructively. It might be that had Norway joined the EU, the way of handling and debating such questions would change. This, however, is at the present a highly hypothetical situation.

Member States. It enhances the role of parliament as a debating arena, and possible safety valve. On the other hand it probably weakens the capability to make decisions or to influence the government and the administration.

To some extent the relationship to European integration cuts through the traditional party lines in Norwegian politics. Most major parties are divided on the question of full membership of the EU, most dramatically the ruling Labour party. The EEA alternative is seen by many as a compromise solution. Here the Labour party is more united, and the government enjoys a comfortable majority in the Storting for further developing the Agreement. There is, however, an aggresive fighting minority in the Storting opposed both to full membership and to the EEA.[21] The effect is that of a truce between the ruling Labour party and the traditional main conservative opposition on questions relating to European affairs. This probably reduces the willingness as well as the political ability of parliament to strengthen its position on European policy in relationship to the government and the administration. The political bottom line is that any increase in parliamentary activity means strenghtening the voice of the Euro-sceptics.

The argument that the Storting should be more involved in European affairs to enhance the legitimacy of integration, rests on the premise that it has legitimacy to offer. It should be mentioned that both in 1972 and in 1994 such legitimacy was put under pressure, as it became obvious that a majority of the Storting was in favour of membership, while the majority of the population was against. The general and traditionally strong position of the Storting as a major source of political legitimacy is however probably not much affected by this. It also seems that a majority of the population is in favour of the EEA, though there has not been a referendum on the question.

## Organising the Storting to Handle European Affairs

A key to parliamentary influence in European affairs is organisation. Involvement requires a certain degree of strategy, confidentiality,

[21] The main Conservative party (Høyre) wants full membership, and as a second best it supports the government on all further development of the EEA. The Christian-Democrats (Kristelig Folkeparti) are opposed to membership, but support the EEA. The far-right Fremskrittspartiet also supports the EEA. The opponents of the EEA are the Radical Socialist party (SV) and the Centre Party (which is traditionally a conservative farmers' party, but which has broadened its electoral basis mainly because it is seen as the main Euro-opposition party). The tiny Communist party is also opposed to the EEA.

flexibility, and willingness to reach compromises. This is not something that can be done in a plenary meeting. One way or another, European policy has to be constructed in committee meetings. This has been recognized within the EU. Today parliaments in all the Member States have special committees on European affairs, though this took a long time to come about.[22] As shown elsewhere in this volume several models are conceivable, and both the constitutional mandate and the real influence of these committees varies greatly. The question of how such committees should best be organised has hardly been solved, and it is still rightly at the centre of the debate on the role of national parliaments in the EU.

The question of forming a special committee to deal with European policy was only recently brought up in the Storting. Up until the summer of 1994, European policy was handled for the most part by the Foreign Affairs Committee, and sometimes within the Extended Foreign Affairs Committee, which includes more members of parliament, and has a special role in consulting with the government. The Foreign Affairs Committee is one of the most important in the Storting, and by tradition the parliamentary leaders of the political parties usually have a seat there. This committee is, however, not particularly adapted to dealing with EU questions, especially not on a case-to-case basis, and the members have to share their attention with a number of other tasks. During the negotiations, first on the EEA, and later on membership of the Union, no need was obviously felt for a more specialised organ. Indeed, the participation of the Storting as such in the negotiation processes was not very strong, though it was kept continually informed. The big plenary debates for the most part took place after the results of the negotiations were clear.

While waiting for the EEA Agreement to come into force, the question was raised of forming a special organ. Though the process can hardly be said to have been one of very thorough preparation, it still took a year. In April 1994 the presidency of the Storting presented a six-page report, and in May it was decided, after a short debate, to form a special 'EEA Consultative Organ' (ECO), through a new Art. 13a of the internal instructions of the Storting.[23] The word

[22] For an early overview of the organisation of the various national parliaments, cf. Cristoph Sasse, 'The Control of the National Parliaments of the Nine over European Affairs' in Cassese (ed.), ***Parliamentary Control over Foreign Policy*** (Alphen aan den Rijn: Sijthoff & Noordhoff, 1980).

[23] See Innst. S. nr. 112 (1993–94), og St.tid. 1994 pp. 3321–3329. These instructions are adopted by the Storting by ordinary majority voting, and do not constitute constitutional law. They are however of great importance for how the Storting operates, and they cover many aspects that in other countries are regulated in the constitution. There is at the moment (September 1995) plans to revise Art. 13a, but the substance will probably not be much altered.

'committee' was deliberatly omitted, in order to distinguish this organ from the ordinary committees. The ECO consists of the members of the Foreign Affairs Committee, supplemented by the six Norwegian representatives to the EEA Parliamentary Committee.

The powers of the ECO are quite limited, both compared to other committees of the Storting, and (especially) when compared with, for example, the European Union Committee of the Danish parliament. It is a consultative organ only, to be used by the government to inform parliament on the case-to-case developments in the EEA. Under Art. 13a it does not vote or take formal decisions, nor does it supply the rest of the Storting with written reports. It can be called together by the chairman of the Foreign Affairs Committee, or by a third of the members of the same committee, or at the government's request. It usually meets once a month, a few days in advance of the monthly meetings of the EEA Committee. It is shown the negotiation mandate of the Norwegian government, and the representatives of the various political parties will then indicate whether this is acceptable to them. However, since the main task of the EEA Committee is to say yes or no to including new Community acts into the Agreement, there is not much else to say for the ECO either. It has little chance of influencing the actual contents of the various acts.

This deficency in decision-making could have been countered by bringing the ECO into European policy at a much earlier stage, when Norwegian civil servants meet in Commission committees, or when the government receives the formal Commission proposals for new acts under Art. 99 of the EEA. However, there are no routines for the ECO to be involved at this stage, and anyway it is also, as I will later show, probably too poorly informed to have much basis for a reasoned opinion.

When the ECO was formed, there was debate on two questions. One was on the number of representatives. There are at the moment two small parties in the Storting, the liberals and the communists, with one MP each. A suggestion was made to give them each a seat, but this was turned down by the majority. The result is that not all the parties have a seat on the ECO, so it cannot be said to be a mini-Storting (like the Danish committee). The other question was on the number of votes needed to bring cases from the ECO before a plenary meeting.[24] There was a suggestion that four votes should be enough, which would have given the parties who oppose both the EEA and EU membership a chance to bring any case into the limelight of the plenary, but this was turned down. Instead, there has to be a majority decision in the Foreign Affairs Committee. Since

[24] See Innst. S. nr. 205 (1993–94), and St.tid. (1993–94) pp. 4569–4572.

the present majority stands firmly behind the government on EEA-policy, so far no cases have been brought before the whole Storting.

When the ECO meets, the government is always represented, usually by the Minister of Foreign Affairs, or the Minister of Trade. The minister may bring his civil servants, who have to be accepted by the ECO, but they are not given the floor, only the minister speaks. The ECO can be supplemented by other committees of the Storting, when debating questions that call for special expertise. In the course of the first year this only happened a couple of times. Once the Transport Committee was called in to discuss a question of telecommunications, and on another occasion the Committee on Energy and the Environment was consulted on whether to accept Council directive 94/22 on oil and gas activity.[25]

After a year in existence, the work of the ECO is said to have found its form. It focuses on concrete cases. Debates on general questions of EEA or EU policy are left to the Foreign Affairs Committee itself, to the limited extent that such debates take place at all. In practice, the ECO is an extended branch of the Foreign Affairs Committee, with the function of keeping the six special members of the EEA Parliamentary Committee informed, and drawing on whatever expertise they might possess.

The ECO is probably not regarded as very important, as indicated by the fact that it only meets once a month, as well as by what is rumoured in the media. It is not organised to have a very strong position, and it can only be guessed why this is so. Why is there not a more specialised, fully mandated committee on European affairs? The one reason given in the plenary debate leading up to the formation of the ECO is that such a committee would overlap with the work of the Foreign Affairs Committee. Another supplementary reason might be that the parliamentary leaders of the parties, sitting on the Foreign Affairs Committee wanted to keep their eye on EEA policy. Dual committee membership is not practised in the Storting. A third part of the explanation is probably that the total influence of the Storting is so small that there did not seem to be any need for a special committee. Institutional adjustment to European integration is a learning process,[26] and a weak consultative organ could be seen as a tentative first step, to be further developed if necessary.

A final reason for the weakness of the ECO is probably the aforementioned confrontation threshold on European affairs, and the truce between the government and parts of the opposition.

[25] Cf. Council Directive on the conditions for granting and using authorisations for the prospection, exploration and production of hydrocarbons, OJ 1994 L 164/3.

[26] Cf. Johan P. Olsen: European Challenges of the Nation State (Arena working paper no. 14, Oslo 1995).

Usually in the Storting, cases that are controversial and hotly debated in the plenary are dealt with in a much more congenial and constructive manner inside confidential committee meetings (all committee meetings are confidential), but this is rumoured not to be so in the ECO, where the fighting spirit of the battle for membership is kept alive. This also hinders effective co-operation between the government and the ECO, as ministers and officials know that there are MPs waiting there to attack them on all points of potential political interest.

A weak special committee on European affairs could have been countered by extended involvement of the ordinary, specialised committees of the Storting. However, this seems not to have been done. In some instances there is probably co-operation between the committees and the corresponding ministries, under which the parliamentarians are kept continuously informed on European development in their fields, and given the chance to influence government policy. The overall picture seems, however, to be that such co-operation only takes place to a limited degree.[27] Normally, the committees are first brought into the picture after a decision has been made in the EEA Committee.

Weak committees can also to some degree be made stronger if a parliament possesses strong support staff, including in this case specialists in EU law and policy, that can serve as a source of information, analysis and initiative independently of the government. Yet again, this is not so in the Storting. The support staff of the Storting has always been weak, in all fields, when compared to many other parliaments in Western Europe. The political line seems to have been specifically that of not creating an expertise to counter that of the administration. In a small country like Norway, this might be a wise use of national resources (though I for one do not think so), but it clearly limits the possibilities of the Storting to take independent initiatives on European policy. The international secretariat of the Storting consists of nine persons, and there is no department of research. For some political reason, the Storting seems unwilling to strengthen its own hand by hiring extra staff. Instead, it has recently allocated money for the various party caucuses to improve their secretariats, but even this only to a limited degree.

Finally, it should be mentioned that before the last referendum there were plans to form a special European Union Committee, should Norway become a member. Progress, however, was surprisingly slow, especially when compared to Sweden and Finland,

[27] Such co-operation is quite normal in Norwegian political life, but I lack the empirical data to assess whether it extends to questions of European policy.

where the full blueprints were ready before the referendums. There was no parliamentary debate on the subject, and the only document produced was a 50-page internal report from the secretariat.[28] This report by no means stands comparison with the thorough political and constitutional preparations made in Sweden and Finland. The suggestion of the report was however that the Storting should create something much like the European Union Committee of the Danish Parliament, and probably this would have been done.

## Access to Information on European Affairs

Another key to parliamentary influence is information. Given the complexity and general lack of transparency in European politics, information is a necessary precondition for any kind of participation.[29] Information-gathering is mainly a practical challenge, but there are also legal implications. First, information is most effectively given when there are norms regulating what a parliament should always get. Second, there are rules on confidentiality, both in Community and national law, restricting parliamentary access. In the following, both aspects will be considered. I will start by looking at the *sources* from which the Storting receives information, and then go on to consider to what extent this information is *analysed*, and by whom.

The primary source of information on European affairs for the Storting is the government. Here the first problem arises, because the Norwegian government is not nearly so well informed as are the governments of the Member States. The extent of the problem was not fully comprehended until recently. In the course of 1994, when Norway had the status of an applicant for membership, the government was given access to the internal information networks of the Union. By all reports, the extent of information surprised Norwegian officials, and made them consider many aspects of European policy in a new light.[30] After the referendum, the

[28] Cf. Utredning vedrørende konsultasjonsordninger i EU saker (Stortingets kontor, November 1994).

[29] For a thorough look at parliamentary information-gathering on European affairs, cf. Klaus Pöhle, 'Analysis and use of information necessary for decision making in the area of Community affairs', and Francis Wattiau, 'Data processing of legisla-tive information in the European Parliament', both papers presented at a conference in Berlin at the Reichstag on March 3rd and 4th 1994 on 'The Role of Parliaments in Shaping Community Law and Transposing it into National Law'.

[30] One example that has been mentioned is that Norwegian authorities had not fully realised the extent to which the Council secretariat and the Member States are involved in the drafting of new legislative proposals. During the EEA

pipelines were shut immediately. In some cases, a few documents continued to trickle through for a few days, but then it was over. Frantic efforts by Norwegian politicians and officials in the course of December 1994 to reopen access to the networks were mostly turned down. Today, the government relies on what it can get from open sources, or by way of diplomatic channels. This is of relevance for what is passed on to the Storting in two ways. First, what the government does not have it cannot share. Second, it puts a limit on what the government is willing to share. If information is given as a right which cannot be taken away, the threshold for passing it on is lower than when it is given out of charity, and on the (express or implied) condition that any leak will have future implications. Giving information to parliamentarians, even in closed committee meetings, always entails the danger of leaks.

Another obstacle is yet again the confrontation level in the Storting. As long as some MPs are regarded as fundamental adversaries, the government will (legitimately or not) not be in a mood to supply the committees with controversial information. Recently, an official of the Foreign Ministry expressed dissatisfaction that information given to the ECO was often leaked to the press. Under such circumstances a real exhange of information is difficult.

So what does the Storting get from the Norwegian government, and when does it get it? There are of course many official channels of information. From time to time, the government presents official reports (*Stortingsmeldinger*), either on general European policy, or on specific questions. Such reports are always made when proposals are put forward in the EEA Committee on questions that will need parliamentary approval to be ratified. Later, when the acts are adopted, the Storting will get a proposition with the information needed for the implementation. Such open reports and propositions tend to come late in the decision-making process. Earlier, more confidential information on European affairs is usually given in committee meetings, mostly in the Foreign Affairs Committee. As indicated, the extent and quality varies. There is general constitutional theory on the question of what information the government on its own initiative is obliged to provide,[31] but the extent of this duty is far from clear, and it has not really been debated in constitutional terms in relation to the EU or the EEA.

*cont.*

negotiations the EFTA states stressed the importance of formal channels to the Commission, while they perhaps should have been just as keen on channels to the Council and its secretariat.

[31] Cf. Eivind Smith, 'Om Regjeringens opplysningsplikt overfor Stortinget', Dok. nr. 7 (1987–88), Vedlegg 50 (pp. 213–274).

Another question is what right the Storting has to *demand* information from the government. According to constitutional practice, the Storting can as a general rule demand any information it wants. To be legally binding, such requests have to be in the form of a law, or a plenary decision. The committees have no formally binding power to demand information. In practice formal requests are seldom put forward. Instead, the committees ask for what they want, and usually it is given to them, the limitations being political, rather than legal.

There are however two legal limits to what the Storting can ask for, and these can also be invoked against committee requests. Both are of interest to European policy. First, there are internal documents of the government and administration that the Storting cannot as a general rule demand to see, and these are seldom given out freely. On European affairs, the practice is said to be that the Foreign Affairs Committee is usually given the routine reports sent to the Foreign Ministry from the diplomatic missions abroad, including that in Brussels but not the internal PMs written in Oslo. As earlier stated, the ECO is also presented with the Norwegian negotiation mandate before meetings in the EEA Committee. It seems that the reports made by Norwegian officials meeting in Commission sub-committees are seldom or never shared with the Storting.

The second legal limitation concerns documents that are confidential by law. As a main rule, ordinary Norwegian rules of administrative confidentiality do not limit the access of the Storting. However, if the documents are classified, they are given out on a need-to-know basis, and this is normally accepted by the Storting. More difficult is the situation when the government receives documents from abroad that are classified by the sender country, or restricted under Community law. In such cases, the government might be under an international obligation not to share the information with the Storting, especially if there is risk of leaks.[32] In general, this also seems to be accepted by the Storting, though the legal position is far from clear.

In recent times, this has to my knowledge caused controversy in two cases (there are probably more). The first concerns a confidential reasoned opinion delivered by the ESA to the

[32] Norwegian officials can also be bound by Art. 122 of the Agreement, which corresponds to Art. 214 of the EC Treaty. Other Community rules on confidentiality, such as Council regulation 354/83 on the historical archives, are for the most part not included in the EEA, but this is probably of little practical significance.

government in December 1994,[33] stating that the monopoly on the importation of alcohol was contrary to the Agreement. At first the government refused to share this document with the Storting. Then political pressure was brought to bear, and it was soon handed over, as, of course, it had to be. The second instance concerned information gathered by the administration at the request of the ESA, on Norwegian state aid. This included a number of documents showing, *inter alia*, the business secrets of many Norwegian companies. Under Community (and EEA) law, such information is confidential, and it cannot be used for other purposes either. This led to a row when members of parliament demanded to see the whole file. The legal situation was far from clear, but in the end at least most of the documents were handed over.

The members of the Storting also have the right, as in most parliaments, to address questions to the government, which are answered once a week. During the struggle on the EEA and on membership, this institution was frequently used, especially by the Eurosceptics.[34] Though the line is hard to draw, most of these questions had not so much the purpose of obtaining fresh information, but rather they were used to focus on controversial political issues. It can hardly be said that such parliamentary questions in general add much to the information-gathering of the Storting, though of course they might be of informative value in specific cases.

The conclusion so far is that if the Storting wants to be well informed at an early stage, it cannot rely on information from the government only, it needs other channels. In any modern society, the mass media are a principal source of information, and over the last few years the Norwegian media have increased the extent and quality of their coverage of European affairs.[35] Contacts with organised interests provide another channel of information, and many of the major Norwegian interest organisations are linked to European networks that give them access to high-quality

[33] This was done under Art. 31 of the EFTA Agreement on the Establishment of a Surveillance Authority and a Court, which corresponds to Art. 169 of the EC Treaty.

[34] Between October 1990 and June 1994 there were a total of 112 questions on EEA and EU affairs. This includes 28 questions in the session of 1990–91, 21 in 1991–92, 12 in 1992–93, and a peak of 51 in 1993–94. (Source: Saksregisteret til St.tid.). On the function of parliamentary questions in Norwegian political life, cf. Blichner and Olsen: *Spørsmål i Stortinget. Sikkerhetsventil i petroleumspolitikken* (Oslo: Universitetsforlaget, 1986).

[35] Whether the really well informed foreign newspapers and newsletters, like the *Financial Times* or the *Agence Europe*, are read by Norwegian parliamentarians, is probably more doubtful.

information.[36] A third source is the different party apparatuses. These are to a varying degree informed on European affairs, and the struggle over the EEA and membership has led to what is probably a highly-informed class of cadres. What most of them lack, however, is the practical knowledge and political contacts which can only be obtained within the Community system. I will later return briefly to the question of how Norwegian parties are co-operating with other parties on a European level.

As a last source, the question is what information the Storting receives direct from the EU. The answer is that it does not get very much. Open information is, of course, available, and the library of the Storting, like any large library, receives masses of official publications. It also receives information from the European Parliament (EP), but it is not connected to the internal networks of the EP, for example the 'legislative backbone'-system.[37] Apart from what is published as COM-documents, it does not receive internal information directly from the Commission, nor from the secretariat of the Council.

Gathering information is one thing, analysing and understanding it quite another. Even with limited access, the mass of information sent to the Storting on European affairs is huge, and it requires professional and objective analysis to be of constructive value.[38] This is not always fully understood. One Norwegian MP commented on the information supplied to him concerning the EEA II package (which included most of the legislation on the single internal market) by saying (in my translation): 'During the last weeks we have received several metres of documents about the directives included in the EEA II. The library of the Storting deserves praise for its endeavours to supply the members with the accessible information'.[39] Ironic or not (it seems not), the statement is probably symptomatic of the situation in the Storting. Parliamentarians are often given raw material instead of compiled analysis. As stated earlier, the support staff is very limited, and it does not carry out much independent research on European affairs.

Instead, the Storting seems to rely on three sources for analysis. First, and most important, are the government and the administration. Usually such analysis is included in the open reports and

[36] The Norwegian confederation of employers (NHO) is, for example, a member of UNICE, and uses this channel actively to gain information and influence on European affairs.

[37] Cf. the paper by Francis Wattiau, cited above.

[38] To be of political value to the different MPs, information of course does not have to be objectively analysed.

[39] The member Lars Sponheim, St.forh. 1993–94, p. 3327.

propositions to the Storting, but sometimes the government also supplies internal analysis to the committees. This is done, for example, when the negotiation mandates are presented to the ECO before meetings in the EEA Committee. The problem with government analysis is, of course, that it does not enable parliament to adopt independent opinions and carry out necessary control. There is also an invisible boundary between information stating what is *really* going on, and presenting a formal analysis, which in itself is impeccable, but where reality has to be found between the lines, if anywhere. At least many of the open reports and propositions clearly belong in the second category. Due to political controversy, they are sometimes to be read more as arguments than as statements of fact.

A clear example is the passage concerning the Norwegian alcohol monopoly, in the main government proposition on the EEA Agreement. Here, the government seems more concerned with explaining why the monopoly should be kept, as if arguing before the ESA or the EFTA Court, than with analysing the real possibilities of this happening.[40]

The second source of analysis is the party apparatuses. The problem here is that such analysis is made to serve political ends, and that the findings of one party will have limited credibility with the others. However valuable, party analysis can in no way compensate for a lack of objective reports.

A third source to be mentioned is the academic community. The government frequently consults independent academics, but the Storting rarely does so. A traditional exception is the Faculty of Law in Oslo, where leading professors have sometimes been called upon by the Storting to give reasoned opinions on matters of constitutional law.[41] This tradition however seems to be in decline. When membership of the Community was last on the agenda, in the early seventies, the Storting asked for an opinion from three leading professors of law (Castberg, Andenæs and Opsahl) on the possible relationship between Community law and Norwegian law, and on the constitutional arrangements necessary to accede.[42] In 1994 there were proposals to do the same, but this time it was considered

[40] Cf. St.meld. nr. 100 (1991–92), pp. 116–119. The Finnish monopoly on imports of alcohol was later found by the EFTA Court to be in breach of the Agreement, and Norwegian authorities complied with this decision, cf. the ***Restamark-case***, Case E-1/94, preliminary ruling of 16 December 1994.

[41] To some extent this has served to make up for the lack of a special constitutional court.

[42] Cf. Dokument nr. 3 for 1961–62 og Dokument nr. 10 for 1966–67. Cf. also Carsten Smith, 'Legal issues in the Norwegian Common Market debate', 17 *Scandinavian Studies in Law* (1973) pp. 275 ff.

unnecessary. Looking at developments in Community law over the last 20 years, the reason for this can hardly be that the constitutional problems were less urgent.

## Parliamentary Control of the Government on European Policy

The most important channel for parliamentary influence on European affairs is through the national government. However well-informed and organised a parliament is, it cannot alter the fact that it is the government and its administration that represents the nation state at the European level, both inside the EU and in the EEA. This is something that cannot be altered.

The extent to which a parliament can control government policy on European affairs rests on many variables, both constitutional and political. Key elements are the possibility to instruct national representatives (ministers or civil servants) before they meet at the European level, to supervise their behaviour, and to hold them responsible upon their return. To a large extent this depends on the national political situation. Under a parliamentary system, government and the majority of parliament are seldom to be regarded as adversaries. The question is not so much who will prevail in case of conflict, but rather who should be the main policy-initiative maker. Minority governments are most prone to parliamentary control, but even they will normally have a wide margin of discretion due to the fact that the executive is always better adapted than parliament to handle foreign affairs.

Constitutionally, the first question is whether parliament has the right to instruct the government on European affairs before meetings in Brussels. This rests on whether such policy falls under an executive prerogative, and the actual contents of this prerogative. The second constitutional question is to what extent and by which procedures parliament can hold ministers responsible upon their return.

The prime example of how far a parliament can go in running national policy on European affairs is Denmark, where the EU Committee of the Folketing by all reports wields great influence, not only on general policy, but even sometimes on a case-to-case basis.[43]

[43] Cf. Andersen og Eliassen (eds.), *Det nye Europa* (Oslo: Tano, 1993) pp. 88 ff. On the constitutional status of the EU Committee, see Jørgen Albæk Jensen's contribution in this volume. For those who argue that increased parliamentary influence will strengthen the legitimacy of European integration, it is of course

Partly this seems to have been possible because of a long series of minority governments. Partly the reason might be that the traditional foreign affairs prerogative does not apply to ministers meeting in Brussels. Partly it results from the fact that the Folketing has been successful in organising the EU Committee into a flexible mini-parliament that can convene at short notice, and in which parliamentarians can gradually build up expertise. There is constitutional debate on whether the instructions of the Committee are legally binding, but for practical policy it does not seem to matter much whether they are.

A major difference between Norway and the Member States is that, of course, Norwegian ministers do not take part in Council meetings. They do however negotiate extensively with the EU, both under the EEA Agreement and on a more bilateral basis. The government is also allowed to respond to Commission proposals for new acts, and to send representatives to some Commission committees. Within the framework of the Agreement the government represents Norway in the EFTA and EEA organs, and co-decides on the future development of the EEA. All this activity can in theory be controlled by the Storting.

From a legal point of view it is unclear to what extent the foreign policy prerogative in Art. 26 of the Norwegian constitution bars the Storting from giving formally binding instructions on European policy. What is clear, is that the division between foreign and home affairs still stands, and that, unlike in Denmark, European affairs are seen as 'foreign'. This increasingly meaningless distinction is bolstered by the fact that the formal status of the Agreement is that of an ordinary international treaty, in which supranational elements are camouflaged. More unclear are the exact contents of the prerogative, which have long been debated in constitutional theory, though not specifically in relation to the Community.[44] Constitutionally it must be said to be unsolved whether the Storting is competent to issue binding instructions on European affairs in concrete cases.

In everyday politics, this might be of little significance. The Storting is always able to send out non-binding, but politically

*cont.*

food for thought that while the Danish parliament probably has the most influence on national policy of any parliament in the EU, the Danish population remains one of the most Eurosceptic.

44 Cf. *inter alia* Eckhoff, 'Utviklingslinjer i norsk statsstyre og forfatningsrett 1814–1964', *Tidsskrift for rettsvitenskap* 1964 p. 222; Andenæs, *Statsforfatningen i Norge* (Oslo: Tano, 7. utg. 1994) pp. 326 ff.; Stavang, 'Om "kongelege prerogativ" i norsk statsrett', in Stavang, *Parlamentarisme og folkestyre* (Bergen: Alma Mater, 1994) pp. 117 ff.

important 'signals', and these are normally followed. There are undoubted examples of parliament in reality instructing the government on foreign affairs. Still the very existence of the prerogative might matter because it is bound to influence standard operating procedures and the role parliamentarians see for themselves. It could be argued that a redefinition of the applicability of the prerogative on EU/EEA policy would be a useful, and perhaps even necessary precondition for increasing the influence of the Storting, as it would help parliamentarians to recast their own role.

Another limitation is that formal instructions can only be given by the Storting itself, in the form of a statute or a plenary decision, not by the standing committees. As for the EEA Consultative organ it does not even take votes, much less issue binding instructions. Again this might be of little practical significance, since in reality political 'signals' are always transmitted by the committees. Again, however, it could be argued that the constitutional rules influence actual procedures, and that it would be easier for the committees to increase their use of clear instructions on European affairs if they were given a legal mandate to do so.

It is difficult for an outsider to judge to what extent the Storting actually controls the government or participates as fellow policy-maker on European policy. During the negotiations, first on the EEA and later on membership, the Storting was kept relatively well informed, and the government knew the extent to which it could count on parliamentary support. However, both the aforementioned truce and the nature of the negotiations themselves gave the Storting little room for influence. Now that the membership question has been shelved and the Agreement is up and running, the possibilities of the Storting to take policy initiatives and instruct the government should be slightly better. The main problem, as compared to membership, is the vulnerability of the Agreement, and the fact that decision-making in the EEA rests even less than in the EU on formal procedures, and even more on traditional diplomacy, which is more difficult for a parliament to monitor and control.

Constitutionally, the Storting can always hold the government responsible for its European policy, and displace it through a vote of no-confidence. Such votes can be taken against an individual minister, or against the Cabinet.[45] This rather blunt instrument is seldom used in normal politics, and in European affairs it is particularly difficult to use. Again the reason is partly the truce between the Labour party and the Conservative party on European

[45] If a minister breaks a formally binding instruction, he can also be held legally responsible through the impeachment process, but this institution has not been used for a very long time.

affairs. Responsibility is also hindered by the fact that it is often difficult to check what a minister has said in Brussels, or how hard he has fought for the policy of his parliament. This is a problem common to parliaments in all Member States, but it also applies to the Byzantine decision-making procedures of the EEA.

All this, of course, does not mean that European affairs are of no importance for the question of who governs Norway. Being the single most controversial issue in Norwegian politics, the relationship of Norway to the Community is of great importance for political life, and the issue has figured prominently in the last few elections. Over the years, the issue of European integration has led to the downfall of three governments, though never through votes in parliament.[46] It could well influence the composition of future governments.

## Direct Parliamentary Access to the European Level?

As a supplement to controlling their governments, a key question in the EU today is whether national parliaments can be given more of a direct role at the European level. This can be done in different ways. Before the 1996 IGC there are proposals that national parliaments should be involved to some degree in the Community legislative processes, if only in a consultative capacity. Some have called for a second chamber in the European Parliament (EP). A less radical reform would be to try to improve and formalise existing relationships to the EP, or co-operation between the parliaments themselves. It has also been argued that national parliaments should re-think their way of operating, and start to act more as lobbyists, especially before the Commission, but maybe even before the Council.[47]

For the Storting, such access to the EU level is, of course, more difficult than for parliaments in the Member States. There are no national MEPs to consult with. The Storting was not invited to the conference of EC parliaments in 1990, and will probably not be

[46] The Conservative coalition government of Per Borten resigned in March 1971 because of internal disagreement over negotiations with the EC on membership. The Labour government of Trygve Bratteli resigned in October 1972 after failing to obtain a yes vote in the referendum. In November 1990 another Conservative coalition government, headed by Jan P. Syse, resigned because of disagreement on the course to be taken in the EEA negotiations.

[47] Cf. Vernon Bogdanor, 'Britain and the European Community', in Jowell and Oliver (eds.), *The Changing Constitution* (1994).

invited to future conferences. During the application period in 1994 the chairman of the Storting's Foreign Affairs Committee participated in meetings of COSAC between members of national EC Committees, but after the referendum this was terminated. Before the referendum there were proposals to place a representative of the Storting in Brussels as a listening-post (as the Danish parliament has), but for the moment such plans seem to have been abandoned.

There are other channels open to the Storting, though their importance should not be exaggerated. Under Art. 95 of the EEA there is a EEA Parliamentary Committee, comprising 12 representatives of the EP and 12 from the EFTA states (six from Norway, four from Iceland and two from Liechtenstein). However, this committee only meets twice a year, and has no decision-making powers. Dating back to the early 1980s there have also been yearly meetings bilaterally between representatives of the Storting and the EP. The function of both these arrangements is clearly not to exert direct influence, but rather to add to the information-gathering of the Storting.

At another level, Norwegian parliamentarians have always participated keenly in the Council of Europe, but this organ wields little influence on EU affairs. Another channel is through the Nordic Council, where Norwegian parliamentarians meet with those of the other Nordic countries. The present Norwegian prime minister seems to have been able to use the Nordic channel to promote Norwegian interests in the EU, but it is less clear if the parliamentarians have done the same. There are also problems connected to Nordic co-operation on European affairs. One is that when it comes down to real politics, the interests of the Nordic countries are often in conflict with one another. Another is that while Nordic co-operation becomes more important to Norway and Iceland, it has become less interesting for the three Nordic Member States.

Closely connected to parliamentary life is the co-operation going on between the political parties at the European level.[48] Much of this takes place inside or in connection with the EP, where Norwegian parties are not represented. Apart from that, Norwegian parties are to a varying degree involved in transnational party organisations at the European level. The Labour party has the best network, both bilaterally and through the Party of European Socialists (PES), where it is a member, but with some limitations,

48 Cf. Lars Svåsand, 'Norwegian Political Parties and European Party Cooperation', (paper presented at an ICCR Conference in Vienna, 5–9 April 1995), and Knut Heidar and Lars Svåsand, 'Politiske partier og europeiseringsprosesser' (Oslo: ARENA Working Paper no. 8, 1995).

*inter alia* that it is excluded from positions in the party secretariat. The Conservative party is second best, through membership of the European Democrat Union (EDU). The other parties have fewer international contacts. The common problem is that much of the party co-operation takes place in connection with the EU, which to a large extent excludes Norwegian participation.

On the EEA level the situation is different. Here the national parliaments of the EFTA countries are directly involved in the decision-making process through Art. 103 of the Agreement, which gives them the power of veto over the decisions of the EEA Committee. This is a stronger and more formalised version of the 'scrutiny reserve' insisted upon by the UK Parliament. The Article was put in to accommodate constitutional requirements in the EFTA states, and reflects the fact that formally the Agreement is only an ordinary international treaty.[49] Under Art. 26 of the Norwegian constitution new international obligations of particular importance must be accepted by the Storting before they can be ratified.

The problem with Art. 103 is that it is difficult to use. National parliaments are first to be consulted after a decision has been made in the EEA Committee, which means that consensus is already reached between national governments. Furthermore, a national veto would have the effect of blocking the decision for the whole EEA, and it would give the EU the right to take countermeasures. The veto has not yet been used, and it is not likely to be by the present Storting. If the Storting really wants to block a development in the Agreement, it is much more likely to do so by formally or informally instructing the government at an earlier stage, so that no decision is made at all.

## Parliamentary Control Over the Downstream Effects of EEA Law on Norwegian Society

From a legal point of view the possibilities for downstream influence are first determined by the extent to which the legislative competence of a national parliament is restricted and replaced by Community law. Second, there are different legal margins of interpretation and discretion left to the national legislator in the different fields of Community law. From a more practical viewpoint, one question is to what extent a parliament monitors the implementation, and how much it delegates to the government. Another is the political willingness and ability of a parliament to

[49] Cf. St.prp. nr. 100 (1991–92) p. 325.

challenge Community law and to pursue national policy in areas that are basically covered by the *acquis*. On these points, a brief comparison of the EEA to full membership might be of interest.

The formal legislative sovereignty of the Storting is much stronger than that of parliaments inside the EU. Formal legislative power has not been transferred. By its legal nature, EEA law cannot claim supremacy and direct effect in the same way as Community law does. On the other hand, there are *elements* of both supremacy and direct effect in the Agreement, the extent of which are debatable,[50] but which for most practical purposes make the position of the Storting much like that of other national parliaments.

The question of supremacy raised special problems during the EEA negotiations, with Community representatives insisting that supremacy was necessary to obtain a homogeneous market, and EFTA representatives arguing that it was constitutionally impossible as well as against the nature of the Agreement. The result was *ersatz supremacy*, through Protocol 35 of the Agreement, by which the EFTA countries undertake to give EEA-based rules precedence in case of conflict with ordinary national rules. This is implemented in Norwegian law in such a way that in most cases, the national courts will be obliged to set aside the statutes of the Storting if conflict arises.[51]

The dualistic aproach of Norwegian law to international law makes it impossible to give non-implemented rules direct effect to the same extent as in the Community. However, there has always been a principle of interpretation in Norwegian law that if at all possible, the law of the land should be interpreted so that it does not conflict with the external obligations of the nation. The significance

[50] On this debate, cf. *inter alia* van Gerven, 'The Genesis of EEA Law and the Principles of Primacy and Direct Effect', (*the Fordham International Law Review*, Vol. 16 1992–1993, pp. 955–989), Leif Sevón, 'Primacy and Direct Effect in the EEA. Some Reflections', in *Liber Amicorum Ole Due* (Copenhagen: 1994), and Sejersted et al., op. cit. ch. 8.4 and 8.5.

[51] Protocol 35 was interpreted differently by the different EFTA countries. In Norway it was implemented through Art. 2 of the Statute on Implementation of the Main Part of the EEA Agreement, which states that ordinary Norwegian law must yield in case of conflict. Constitutionally, this is not 'supremacy', since the formal right of the Storting to legislate cannot be limited unless the constitution itself is changed. This was never an option. What it means is that if the Storting wants to deviate from its obligations under the Agreement, it must say so expressly. If not, the courts should interpret the conflict in favour of EEA law. Of course, such open disloyalty is politically almost impossible, at least for thepresent majority of the Storting, and so for most purposes, supremacy is introduced. Note however that Protocol 35 and the Norwegian statute Art. 2 do not regulate the relationship of EEA rules to the Norwegian constitution, nor do they give non-implemented acts any direct effect.

(and possibly the reach) of this doctrine has been greatly enhanced by the EEA Agreement, and in most cases it will fill the same function as the principle of direct effect in Community law. In other words, EEA rules can have legal implications even if they are not implemented by the Norwegian legislator.[52]

When implementing the various acts, the Storting is once again much in the same position as other parliaments. One difference is that Community regulations are not directly applicable, but this matters little, as under EEA Art. 7 (1) they have to be implemented 'as such', which means without altering a single word. As for directives, Art. 7 (2) repeats the wording of EC Art. 189 and should be interpreted against the case law of the Court of Justice. Implementation in other words has to be clear, unambiguous and unconditional, and the Storting has no more discretion than what is expressed in the directive itself, or recognised by Community law.[53]

The implementation rate of Norway so far is good. In only a few years, Norwegian authorities have implemented 94% of the relevant *acquis*, a figure that stands comparison with the most loyal of the Member States. To some extent this might be due to Protestant discipline and a strong Nordic tradition for the rule of law. The main reason is, however, that most of the implementation was delegated to the executive. Few parliamentary statutes were passed, and the vast mass of the Agreement was introduced as government regulations. By and large this is, of course, sensible, and enables the Storting to concentrate on the more important issues.[54] There

[52] Less clear is whether the *Francovich* principle of awarding compensation to individuals who suffer from non-implementation is part of the EEA Agreement. Legally, this can be argued both ways, but the answer probably depends just as much on the more political courage of the courts (the EFTA Court or the national courts) to put such a limitation on the real discretion of the Norwegian legislator.

[53] This can also be read from EEA Art. 3, which repeats the principle of loyalty expressed in EC Art. 5. The Community criteria for loyal implementation have necessitated some changes in the way in which laws are usually issued in Norway. To a large extent, the Storting adopts statutes with a quite general wording, but then supplements this with extensive *travaux préparatoires*, explaining in a more detailed way how the provisions should be interpreted. Such statements are taken seriously by the courts, and form an important legal source in Norwegian method. This technique is, however, unacceptable under ECJ case law, and in some instances this has forced the Storting to pass more detailed legislation than it usually does. It is also new to the Storting that it cannot use the *travaux* to instruct the interpretation of the various acts.

[54] What is politically important to the various parliamentarians is, of course, not necessarily the same as what is of substantial importance to the nation. Though highly important, much of the *acquis* is of little political interest, the more so since it cannot be altered. Some Norwegian parliamentarians are said to have expressed disappointment when instead of receiving the anticipated exciting foreign legislation, they were handed masses of technical standards.

are however clear limits to the virtues of delegation. First, too much delegation reduces the ability of the Storting to see the overall picture.[55] One cannot understand the nature of Community law without knowing some of the details. Second, the way delegation is practised in Norway, it is in reality the executive that for the most part determines what acts should be brought before the Storting, and this leaves some room to cover questions of potential controversy. Third, when dividing implementation between itself and the Storting, the government has used the same standard as in ordinary national legislative work.[56] To my mind, it can be argued that the need for parliamentary supervision is more acute when it comes to legislation of foreign origin, and the Storting should consider doing more of the work itself. Again, the control function of parliament should be more emphasised.

Finally it can be asked to what extent the Storting has the political will and ability to pursue national policy, even if this is in potential conflict with EEA rules. It is well known from the debate on the effectiveness of Community law that national governments and parliaments often try to make as wide margins of appreciation for themselves as possible.[57] To a certain extent this is legitimate. Community law is, for the most part, to be administered nationally, and this always entails a certain discretion. It is also legitimate for national authorities to adopt an independent interpretation of Community obligations, as only the courts are obliged to ask for an authoritative interpretation from the ECJ (Art. 177). However, there is a grey zone between independent interpretation and disloyal behaviour. This is often exploited by national authorities, either in the hope that they will not be caught, or because they are willing to bear the legal and political burden of judgement against them in the ECJ. For an inventive national parliament, the possibilities are legion.

> Normally, such a disloyal stance is driven forth by pure national interest, but it can in some instances have more laudable aims, for example if a parliament breaks rules on the freedom of goods in order to protect the environment (beyond what is accepted under Art. 36), or induces the government to break Community rules on

55 This is especially true for the one-time implementation of the original Agreement. As the EEA is further developed through inclusion of new Community acts, the Storting has more control, since under the decision-making procedures it is often asked to ratify acts that will later be implemented by the executive.

56 Cf. Henrik Bull, 'EØS-avtalen - litt om avtalens struktur og om prinsippene for gjennomføring i nasjonal rett', *Lov og Rett* 1992, p. 597.

57 Cf. Francis Snyder, 'The Effectiveness of European Community Law: Institutions, Processes, Tools and Techniques' (1993) *Modern Law Review*, pp. 19 ff.

> confidentiality in order to preserve a national principle of open administration.[58] Such twisting and bending is something that requires a clear strategy and consensus, as well as the ability to play an underhand game. This is easier to do for a national government and administration than for a parliament. On the other hand, the position of a national parliament is more independent, and parliamentarians have the advantage of not having to stand trial before their colleagues at regular Brussels meetings. There are many examples from the history of the Community of national parliaments adopting legislation that the majority must have known was in clear conflict with Community law.[59]

At least two aspects determine to what extent a national parliament (or government) will try to squeeze Community law to gain national room for manoeuvre. The first is the risk of getting caught, and rests on the effectiveness of the supranational authorities. The second is the willingness to accept the political burden of getting caught. Both may be different under the EEA as compared with the EU. The control apparatus designed in the separate EFTA pillar is weaker and less experienced than the Commission and the ECJ. The EFTA organs are also more easily subject to political pressure from home, especially now that they mostly consist of Norwegians controlling other Norwegians, most of them former employees (or even on

[58] A good example of this is the strategy formulated by a leading Swedish lawyer and politician just a few months before he became Minister of Industry in the autumn of 1994, in order to preserve the principle of open administration protected by the Swedish constitution. To some extent, this rule of openness is bound to conflict with Community rules on confidentiality, *inter alia* Art. 214 of the Treaty of Rome and Regulation 354/83 on the historical archives of the Community. The strategy implies breaking Community rules, for the sake of a good cause, and in the hope that the Commission will not have the courage to take action, nor the ECJ the willingness to strike down on behaviour that so clearly furthers the politically correct aim of increasing transparency. Cf. Sten Heckscher and Ola Wiklund, 'Offentlighetsprincipen vid et svensk medlemskap i EU', report given to the Association of Swedish Publishers, September 1994.

[59] A good example from a neighbouring country was when the Danish Parliament in the late 1980s adopted a law imposing a certain tax on employers. The majority must have been aware that this was almost certainly in breach of a Community directive on taxation, but there was almost no parliamentary debate on this. The law soon came before a national court, and was sent to the ECJ under Art. 177, where it was found clearly to be unacceptable. Though the ruling was not given prospective effect as the Danes advocated, the Parliament still managed to avoid paying back most of the 50 billion Danish krone it had collected, by passing another law stating that companies had to show real losses in order to be repaid. As most companies had already passed the cost on to the consumers, this was something few could do. So the parliament kept its treasure, and nobody probably felt very much ashamed. Cf. case C-200/90, Dansk Denkavit and others versus Skatteministeriet, preliminary ruling of 31 March 1992.

leave) from national ministries. On the other hand, there is great pressure on the ESA and EFTA Court to show independence. At the moment it is improbable that the Norwegian authorities will dare to pressure the EFTA organs, at least openly. In the most controversial case so far, on the monopoly of imports and exports of alcohol, the Norwegian government and the majority of the Storting accepted the judgment of the ESA and the EFTA Court.[60]

This also illustrates the more general point, that since Sweden, Finland and Austria left EFTA, the vulnerability of the EEA Agreement has greatly increased. Inside the EU, there are few sanctions against a state that breaks Community law. It cannot be excluded either from the Union or from specific policy areas, and the other Member States cannot bilaterally adopt countermeasures. Under EC Art. 171(2) it can, in theory, be fined, but this instrument has so far never been used. For Norway as a member of the EEA the situation is different. Non-compliance can easily lead the EU or the specific Member States to take countermeasures, or to demand a full renegotiation. Operating an anachronism is a risky business, especially when Norway as the weaker part has the most to lose. This has led the government and the majority of the Storting to adopt a policy by which Norway has to be at least as loyal to the *acquis* as are the Member States. Combined with a lack of information, experience and effective internal organisation, this probably makes the actual room for independent parliamentary manoeuvres even smaller for the Storting than for many national parliaments inside the Union.

## Reflections from Medium-Speed Europe

So, as a conclusion, what are the differences between the position of a national parliament in medium-speed Europe and full-speed Europe? What did the Norwegian Storting gain, and what did it lose, when the people decided against membership?

The biggest gain is, of course, that the Storting has kept its powers (such as they may be) in the many areas of political and practical importance included in the EU but not in the EEA. Second, it has kept its formal powers almost intact under the Agreement, and

[60] There was no express decision against Norway on this subject. In December 1994 the EFTA Court gave a preliminary ruling stating that the Finnish monopoly on the import of alcohol was contrary to the Agreement. Two weeks later the ESA sent a reasoned opinion to the Norwegian authorities stating that it would take legal action unless the Norwegian monopoly was abandoned. After this, the authorities gave in, and changed national rules.

though this is of little practical value in everyday politics, it might come in handy if a crisis should erupt, or if the Eurosceptics should win a parliamentary majority in a future election.

When this is said, it can be argued that the EEA leaves the Storting in a poor position as compared to national parliaments inside the EU. The channels of influence open to national parliaments in the EU are, for the most, part restricted under the Agreement. Upstream, the chances of the Storting directly affecting European affairs are negligible, as it is not included in the European political processes, and the chance to influence policy through the government is also small. The ability to block further extensions of the Agreement is of limited real value. Downstream, the chances of the Storting to exploit the implementation and administration processes are at least no better than for other national parliaments, and it means little that the formal legislative sovereignty of the Storting is kept.

A clear drawback with the EEA Agreement is that its formal status to some extent covers its real nature. This might keep the Storting from making necessary reform, both as regards internal organisation and improved access to information and analysis. The status of the Agreement also keeps alive the traditional distinction between home affairs and foreign policy. In order to influence European policy a parliament must integrate it into everyday parliamentary life, and look upon it as an extension of national policy, not as an extraneous matter to be treated separately and with care. Inside the Union, this fact seems slowly to be dawning on most national parliaments. In the EEA however, the effect of the formal structure is precisely to keep European affairs as ordinary foreign policy.

What this might imply is that the medium-speed alternative could be the worst possible for national parliaments. It might have other advantages, and Norwegian national interest might very well be better served with the Agreement than with nothing at all, but it clearly hinders the chance of a national parliament to influence European affairs. At least this is so with the EEA version, which aims for market access without political and constitutional involvement. The lessons to be drawn for the EU might be that when it eventually includes the new democracies of Central and Eastern Europe, it should not choose the EEA alternative of market access only, but rather aim for political integration as the primary goal. To do otherwise could be to strangle the new democracies at birth.

The last point I will make is the possible paradox that at the same time as national parliaments inside the Union seem to be awakening a bit, and trying to regain lost power, the majority of the newly half-integrated but supposedly still sovereign Norwegian Storting seems without too much fuss to accept a certain amount of real de-parliamentarisation.

Part III

# National Parliaments and the 'Democratic Deficit'

# National Parliaments and the European Parliament - Cooperation and Conflict

*Joël Rideau*

The existence of a double democratic deficit was singled out long ago as one of the main weaknesses affecting the European Construction. The limits set to the European Parliament's powers have constantly been stressed and often used as an argument against the transfers of powers by the Member States to the European Institutions. Community law making has from the beginning been exercised by the sole Council composed by Ministers of the national governments while the European Parliament was confined to a purely advisory function. At the same time, the deprivation of the national parliaments' powers to legislate in the fields devolved to the European institutions and their lack of control of the national governments' European policy making have appeared as a recurrent theme of criticism against the European institutional system. This double statement explains the relentlessness of the battles fought by the parliaments at the European level and at the national level with the aim of changing this situation.[1]

At the European level, the necessity for an evolution of th electoral system of the European Parliament towards direct election

[1] See J. Rideau, 'Droit institutionnel de l'Union et des Communautés européennes' (Paris: LGDJ, 1994). See also T. de Berranger, 'Constitutions nationales et construction communautaire' (Paris: LGDJ, 1995).

of its Members had been perceived as unavoidable by the authors of the constitutive treaties. Though it had been established by the treaties the principle of direct election was not easily put into force. This was due to the resistance by most of the Member States, especially by France, wary of a strengthening of the democratic institution and of its federal implications. The 1976 Act concerning direct elections annexed to a Council decision, which was applied for the first time in 1979, must certainly be considered as a cornerstone in the institutional history of the Community system.

Direct elections have increased the European Parliament's will to extend its powers and weakened the obstacles raised against such an increase by the Member States.

The co-decision in the budgetary sphere, achieved in the seventies through the 1970 and 1975 treaties, was followed in the eighties by the introduction of the new cooperation procedure into the law-making procedures through the Single European Act. This procedure aimed to reinforce in certain fields the advisory power of the Parliament. The Single European Act has also granted to the Parliament a sort of limited co-decision power for the conclusion of some international agreements under the form of the assent procedure.

In the nineties, the 1992 Maastricht Treaty on European Union has allowed a few steps forward. The new part played by the European Parliament in the nomination of the Commissionners is undoubtedly a sign of the increased importance of the Assembly. The Parliament has also been granted new supervisory powers (such as: the possibility of creating temporary committees of inquiry; the establishing of the right to petition the European Parliament; the appointment of a European Ombudsman). The widening of the fields in which the cooperation procedure is used and moreover the insertion of the new co-decision procedure, though limited to a few legislative matters, bear witness to the surge of a new democratic dimension. In the same way, the right to give assent to the conclusion of international agreements has been extended to new categories of treaties and the assent procedure must also be used to carry other kinds of decisions.

Though not insignificant, those improvements have not, by far, fulfilled the European Parliament's expectations such as they were expressed by the draft treaties or constitutions drawn up by the European Parliament in 1984 (the Spinelli Draft)[2] and in 1990 (the resolution following the Colombo report[3] and the final declaration adopted by the Rome Conference of the Parliaments of the EEC).

2 Resolution of 14 February, JOCE no C 77, 19 March 1984.
3 JOCE no C 19, 28 January 1991.

These expectations were more recently reaffirmed by the draft Constitution of February 1994[4] and by the resolution adopted by the Parliament on 17 May 1995. They have been considered by the European Parliament as simple tokens of good will, given not without some reluctance by the Member States, to be followed by a major reform.

The future revision conference of 1996 provided for by the Treaty on European Union must be, according to the views developed by the Assembly, especially in its draft of a Constitution for the European Union of February 1994 and in its resolution adopted on 17 May 1995, an opportunity to achieve a major reform of the Institutions. This reform should accord to the Parliament its rightful statute as an institution embodying the democratic legitimacy at the European level not only where Community matters are concerned but also in the spheres of the Common Foreign and Security Policy and of the Cooperation in the Fields of Justice and Home Affairs.

At the national level, the European construction's development has often given to the national parliaments a feeling of frustration due to the transfer of a part of their powers to the European institutions. Partly deprived of their powers to legislate, they have considered with a certain distrust the exercise of the legislative powers by the representatives of the national governments in the Council of Ministers and often resented being called on to apply without any margin of discretion the rules laid down by the Council.

This situation explains the national parliaments' struggle for the tightening of their control on the making of the Member States' European policies by the national governments. The national parliament's fighting spirit and the results achieved differ indeed greatly from one Member State to another. However, the common trend is obvious and has been confirmed by the evolution which has shown the will of some national parliaments to maintain or strengthen their hold on the European policy making process at the national level. It has also awakened other national parliaments, anxious to exercise a sharper influence.

The conquests achieved by the European Parliament and the prospects of new democratic reforms can naturally induce some changes in the national parliaments' views and reactions. The exercise of the European legislative power according to a new scheme in which the European Parliament would fully share the legislative power with the Council could apparently soften the national parliaments' frustrations. It could make them accept more easily the loss of a part of their legislative powers in favour of a

[4] Resolution of 10 February 1994, JOCE no C 61, 28 February 1994.

system in which the European Parliament would be in charge of the legislative power on equal terms with the Council. But this result will not necessarily be achieved in all cases. One must consider that, in some Member States at least, the national parliaments would not approve such an evolution. Moreover, it could enhance their will to control the national governments. In particular, that kind of evolution could give a new strength to the dream of some parliamentary circles of a more direct part to be played by the national parliaments in European law making through a new institution representing the national parliaments which could be inserted into the European structure. Such a view is justified by the belief that the national parliaments incarnate a democratic legitimacy which is at least equal to that of the European Parliament.

The creation of a European Union with new spheres of competence devolved to the Community, especially in relation to the Economic and Monetary Union, or to the European institutions in the areas of the two other pillars with the provisions for a Common Foreign and Security Policy and for Cooperation in the Fields of Justice and Home Affairs has become a new incentive for this claim. Particularly, regarding the last two pillars, the battle has been engaged by the European Parliament which has repeatedly expressed its will in favour of an extension of the Community procedures to the decision-making process. There is no doubt that such an extension could increase the national parliaments' feeling of frustration.

At this point, one is led to consider that there does not exist a compulsory convergence between the two democratic perspectives, ie the European one and the national one, as would appear from a *prima facie* examination.

The European Parliament's approach is clearly dualist. According to its views, it is for the European Assembly to personify democracy at the European level through the exercise of a legislative power and of a supervisory power without interference from the national parliaments. This situation can involve a certain amount of cooperation between the European and the national parliaments called on to control the national governments and is supposed to preclude any conflict by the natural distinction between the parts attributed respectively to the different democratic assemblies.

It would be preposterous to present the reactions shown by the different national parliaments as uniform. Many of them, at least officially, favour for ideological reasons an approach to the European system following the guidelines drawn by the European Parliament. This statement should not, however, hide the risks of conflicts which can appear in spite of the ideological convergences or the opposition of other national parliaments to the views held by the majority of the European Parliament on the European system's evolution. The situation explains the proposals made by or in some Member States in favour of specific forms of cooperation implying an evolution of the European system along lines differing from the federal model to which the European Parliament refers.

To conclude the general views on this subject, one must consider that the duality of democratic institutions is an inescapable datum of the reality of the European system. Taking this fact into account must lead to a search for the best ways to avoid the conflicts and increase the cooperation between the European Parliament and the national parliaments. The consensus on this aim must not hide the difficulty of reaching it. The reinforcement of the two kinds of democratic centres does not offer, on the one hand, even with the support of some cooperation, a guarantee for an absence of conflicts. On the other hand, cooperation under the form of an institutionalisation of a representation of the national parliaments carries the threat of introducing the conflicts into the very heart of the European institutional system and clearly antagonises the systematisation of the federal logic. These considerations must be taken into account in the survey of the different types of possible conflicts between the European Parliament and the national parliaments and of the kind of cooperation established or to be established between them.

## The Conflicts Between the European Parliament and the National Parliaments: Transition or Stalemate for the European Union?

The possibility of conflicts between the European Parliament and the national parliaments should not be ignored. Co-existence between two kinds of democratic legitimacies clearly implies such a danger. The European electoral system, which has not yet been made uniform, leads to political discrepancies between the European Parliament's political balance and the national parliaments' political balances. It also implies very loose links in most cases between the European Parliament's members and their electors. The importance of the abstentions in the European elections is also an aggravating factor taken into account by such an analysis. The political consensus between the two main political groups in the European Parliament sharply contrasts with the distinction between a majority and a minority prevailing in most of the Member States. The political groups in the European Parliament are not the expression of real European political parties but appear as agglomerates of national forces with more or less close ideological links between them and are in fact induced by the necessities created by the European Parliament's rules regarding the creation of political groups. The over-representation of some protest or opposition groups has also often been invoked as undermining the European Parliament's democratic legitimacy.

This situation can explain the absence of homogeneity between the national parliaments and the European Parliament, which has led some national parliaments and governments to consider the European Assembly as a weaker centre of representation of the democratic will. The attachment to the national sovereignty must also be considered as in some cases it urges the Parliaments to consider themselves as the walls of that sovereignty against the extension of the European construction and as the real incarnation of democracy which could not find a full and true expression outside the Member States.

This conception is, of course, fully inconsistent with the views developed by the European Parliament which favours a federal and democratic evolution of the European system as results in particular from its draft of a Constitution for the European Union adopted in February 1994 following the main lines of the 1984 Spinelli Draft of a Treaty on European Union and from its resolution adopted on 17 May 1995. The reinforcement of this system should be linked to its democratisation including the access of the European Parliament to its full share of power in accordance with its embodiment of democracy at the European level. Following that view, the national parliaments must not interfere with the European level and are only called on to deal with national affairs and to supervise the action of the national governments related to European matters. Though elected in national frameworks, the European Parliament cannot help considering itself as a representation of a European people, whose existence is presumed, and as such of a superior democratic nature.

This situation enables the surge of conflicts. Some have already arisen but more could be brought out by the evolution of the European institutional system which could dramatically intensify the confrontation between the European Parliament and, at least, some national parliaments and affect the evolution of the European Union, the exercise of the European law making and the supervision of the institutions.

## *Conflicts concerning the evolution of the European Union*

There is in the present situation a sharp contrast between the possibilities opened up to the national parliaments and those opened up to the European Parliament regarding the evolution of the European system. The national parliaments keep a strong control on the evolution as they have to vote to authorise the ratification of the treaties amending the basic treaties (ie the Constitutive Treaties of the European Communities and the European Union Treaty). The negative vote of any national parliament can block the revision process, the only alternative being the recourse to a referendum, when such a possibility is available.

At the same time, the European Parliament is only consulted and has always sought to play a more effective part in the revision-making process to influence the content of the new texts. Its feeling of frustration during the drafting of the Single European Act and of the European Union Treaty was strongly expressed. In its resolution preceding the draft of a constitution for the European Union enacted in February 1994, the Parliament proposed the meeting of a European convention between the members of the European Parliament and the members of the national parliaments before the revision conference of 1996 in order to adopt, according to the draft of a constitution, some guidelines for a European Constitution and to entrust the Parliament with the task of adopting a final draft. The Parliament has also invited the heads of state or of government to nominate a group of independent personalities in order to examine this draft, discuss it with the Parliament and propose it to the intergovernmental conference. It has proposed to the Council and to the Commission to organise an interinstitutional conference on the same subject and invited the national parliaments to communicate their views on the system to be used for the preparation and the adoption of the final text of the constitution.

This situation explains the procedure of revision which has been provided for by the draft of a constitution. Following Article 47 of the draft, the constitution would be adopted and would come into force after being ratified by a majority of Member States representing four-fifths of the population of the Union. The Member States which would be unable to deposit their instruments of ratification would be reduced to choosing between leaving the Union or accepting their participation in the Union with the modifications adopted by the said majority. Under Article 31 of the draft, the constitutional laws revising or completing the constitution would be adopted by the European Parliament by a majority of two-thirds of its Members and by the Council unanimously for five years and at a superqualified majority after that period.

The analysis of these procedures of adoption and revision clearly shows a will to put an end to the present necessity of unanimously accepted revisions of the Basic Treaties as provided for by Article N of the European Union Treaty. Such procedures would undoubtedly limit the sovereignty of the Member States by suppressing their power to impede any unwanted change. They would at the same time suppress the veto right given to the national parliaments which they exercise through the compulsory authorisation for the ratification of treaties (which can only be avoided in some Member States by an authorisation given by a referendum).

The resolution of 17 May 1995 seems to indicate that the Parliament elected last year has taken some steps backwards as it only asks for a right of constitutional initiative and for an assent power to approve the revision, to be shared with the Council. The national parliaments would be called on to approve the ratification of the revision treaties. There is nevertheless a reference made to the organisation of a referendum or of national referendums which could be held to approve the results of the 1996 Revision Conference.

The preparation of the 1996 conference has up to now given to the European Parliament a better opportunity to be heard through its association to the working group instituted in 1994, in which two of its members are present, than had been the case in the making of the Single European Act and of the European Union Treaty. The idea of a convention of the parliaments in order to discuss the future conference is still under scrutiny.

One should also give some consideration to the conditions of entry into the third stage of the European and Monetary Union. Though the timetable established by the Treaty does not seem to leave a veto right to the Member States (the cases of Denmark and of the United Kingdom being reserved by special protocols), certain national parliaments have obtained from their governments the promise of a prior debate (The Netherlands and Germany). The weight of such debates and of the votes which could follow them cannot be ignored. The judgment given by the German Constitutional Court in October 1993 stressed the necessity of an exacting respect of the principle of democracy which could eventually be raised against any infringement which would arise from the evolution of the European Construction.

## *Conflicts concerning the exercise of the European law making or of the European policy making*

The exercise of the legislative power is actually devoted to the Council though it is partly shared with the European Parliament in the spheres where the co-decision procedure must be followed according to the EC Treaty as revised by the European Union Treaty. The national parliaments can only concur in that exercise by their influence on the national governments. This influence greatly differs from one Member State to another. Moreover, its eventual impact has on the whole been reduced by the extension given to the majority vote in the Council. As the opposition of a state can be overcome by a qualified majority, the instructions given by a national parliament to the government to vote against a proposal made by the Commission will not necessarily prevent the adoption of the text by the Council.

The proposed extension of the co-decision procedure would in fact be linked to a generalisation of the majority vote as suggested by Article 20 of the 1994 Draft Constitution. The application of the so-called Community procedures in the spheres covered by the Common Defence and Security Policy and the Cooperation in the Fields of Justice and Home Affairs would, of course, increase the feeling of frustration of their powers affecting the national parliaments as these questions are closely linked to the permanent sovereignty of the Member States. In its resolution of May 1995 the Parliament proposed to limit the use of the consultative procedure to the adoption of decisions in the sphere of the Common Defence and Security Policy, the assent procedure should only be used for a limited number of decisions (revision of the basic treaties, conclusion of international agreements, enlargments of the Union, adoption of own resources decisions), the co-decision procedure should be used for the adoption of all other kinds of decisions.

## *Conflicts concerning the exercise of the power of supervision over the European institutions*

The function of political control in the European system must also be taken into account as a theme of potential conflicts. In the present situation it is exercised over the Council and the Commission by the European Parliament at the European level. The national parliaments control the governments at the national level and through them, though indirectly, the Council which is invested with the main share of the legislative and executive powers. The effectiveness of this last control depends on national factors conditioning the type of relations between the national parliament and the government. Further, it is also related to the importance of the part played by each government in the Council. The reorganisation of the European institutional system as suggested by the Parliament's draft of a constitution would modify the present balance. Following Article 34 of the draft, the Commission would be entrusted with the power to adopt normative measures of execution of the Laws of the Union and Article 34 even provides for the possibility of delegating the legislative power to the Commission. If such a reform were adopted, it is clear that a part of the power actually exercised by the Council would then incumb to the Commission under the control of the European Parliament and would no longer be submitted to the supervision of the national parliaments. Though less clear on this point the resolution of 17 May 1995 seems to follow the same trend and it induces the same dangers.

If, according to the 1994 draft, the execution of the Union's laws would be incumbent upon the Member States, the national parliaments being accordingly called on to adopt the necessary texts when their intervention is made compulsory by the national constitutions, it is clear that their function would be of a subordinate nature as implied by the duties of the Member States to respect their obligations as Members of the Union. The exercise of this function can, as experience has shown, generate some negative reactions from the parliaments and lead them to express their antagonism through hostile votes. It should be noted that the draft has appeared to consider a reinforcement of the supervision exercised on the Member States by providing in its Article 35 for an organic law determining the means of this control.

## The Forms of Cooperation Between the European Parliament and the National Parliaments: from Empiricism to Institutionalisation?

The interest of cooperation between the European Parliament and the national parliaments has never been completely ignored by the European institutional system. The first forms of cooperation were rather empirical and limited. The evolution and the reinforcement of the European system has given birth to more intensive thinking leading to reflexions on a possible systematisation of such cooperation. The kind of cooperation to institute is, of course, closely linked to the different conceptions held on the directions to be taken by the evolution of this system.

### *The development of contacts between the European Parliament and the national parliaments*

Since the first period stretching from the beginning of the European construction in the fifties to 1979, during which the European

Parliament was composed of members of the national parliaments, the links between the European Parliament and the national parliaments have been drastically reduced. Though the plurality of mandates has not been forbidden by the new rules established by the 1976 Act, the number of members cumulating national and European mandates has strongly diminished from 100 to 30. The contacts between the assemblies have in fact been rare with very few meetings. A meeting of the presidents has convened every two years since 1983.

The direct election of 1989 has seemed to mark a turning point, probably due to the perspective opened by the negotiations of a new Treaty which has given to the European Parliament the opportunity to insist on the necessity to reinforce the relations and the talks between the European Parliament and the national parliaments in order to guarantee more efficient parliamentary control at the different levels.[5] One must also take into account the awakening of the national parliaments' interest in European Affairs due to the implementation of the European Single Act which started in 1987.

One of the main signs of this new trend has been the meeting twice a year since November 1989 of the European Affairs Committees of the national parliaments and of the Institutional Affairs Committee of the European Parliament (COSAC). These meetings have appeared as a useful forum for the exchange of ideas and the scrutiny of specific questions. They ensure better information for the parliaments and allow their members to establish useful contacts, in particular with the ministers of the country which assumes the presidency of the Union. They do not however, as has been observed, allow really concerted action of the parliaments.[6]

The resolution adopted in November 1990 by the Rome Conference of the Parliaments of the European Community has expressed the Conference's favour for reinforced cooperation between the national parliaments and the European Parliament through regular meetings of the specialised parliamentary committees and the exchange of information. It has also proposed conventions of the parliaments in order to discuss the fundamental orientations of the Community, especially when intergovernmental conferences are to be convened.

5 Resolution on the orientations of the European Parliament concerning a Draft of a Constitution for the European Union, JOCE no C 231, p. 91.

6 E. Jurgens, 'Federal option for the EC or Permanent Democracy Deficit', in C. Flinterman, A.W. Heringa, L. Waddington (eds.), *The Evolving Role of the Parliaments in Europe* (Antwerpen-Apeldoorn: Maklu Nomos, 1994) p. 87.

The question was also given some consideration by the European Council. Especially at the Council of Rome in December 1990, the chiefs of state or of government declared that it should be convenient to examine modalities which would allow the national parliaments to play their full part in the development of the Community.[7]

During the Political Union Intergovernmental Conference, a note issued by the British delegation on 6 March 1991 proposed the adoption by the Conference of a declaration by which the Member States would commit themselves to transmit to their parliaments all the legislative proposals made by the Commission, to take the necessary measures in order to allow the parliaments to survey the said proposals and to ensure that the procedures followed by the Council would make avalaible a previous examination of the final decisions at national level. The British note indicated besides some specific measures in order to intensify the contacts between the European Parliament and the national parliaments. It has been noted that the ideas developed in this note can also be found in a resolution adopted by the European Parliament on 10 October 1991.[8]

The other delegations feared that such a declaration could be interpreted as a meddling in the relations between the national governments and their parliaments and considered that it was up to the parliaments to determine the ways and means of their cooperation. This explains the careful wording of Declaration 13 by the Conference. This declaration states the importance of giving an incentive to greater participation of the national parliaments in the activities of the European Union. It has stressed the necessity of intensifying the exchange of information between the European Parliament and the national parliaments.

The declaration upholds that the governments must ensure that their parliaments receive the legislative proposals made by the Commission soon enough after their adoption to ensure their information or allow their eventual examination. More recently, the Martin report of March 1994 for the Institutional Committee of the European Parliament has insisted on the necessity for the national governments to grant further delays to examine the numerous legislative European proposals. The Conference has also insisted in its declaration on the importance of intensification of the contacts between the national parliaments and the European Parliament, especially through the granting of appropriated and reciprocal facilities and through regular meetings between members of the parliaments with an interest in the same questions.[9]

7 XXIVth General Report on the Activities of the European Communities, point 15.
8 JOCENO C280, 28 October 1991.
9 Europe Documents, no 1920, 27 January 1995.

One should note that, in 1991, the enlarged Bureau of the European Parliament adopted the Cravinho Report gathering detailed proposals for the strengthening of the links between the European Parliament and the national parliaments. Following this report, which stressed the lack of contacts between the parliamentary committees, the number of joint meetings has significantly increased. They have taken the form of Round Tables between the representatives of the National Parliamentary Committees and their European counterparts, of official contacts between European Parliamentary and the corresponding national committees and of numberless informal meetings. National parliaments have also invited the European Parliament's members to testify before them.

The links established in some Member States between the European Parliament's members elected in those countries and the members of the national parliament cannot be ignored. They have even led, in some states, to associating the European Parliament's members with the work of the specialised parliamentary committees.

The usefulness of such cooperation is obvious, though it could certainly be bettered. The exchange of information between the parliaments can certainly induce an improvement of their reciprocal understanding.

The opportunity of closer contacts between the European Parliament and the national parliaments around the annual legislative programme has been given specific consideration since this programme appears as a privileged instrument to observe the progress of the legislation proposed by the Union. It enables the European and the national parliaments to identify the proposals which the Commission will make during the year to come, to determine the time at which they are likely to be made and to check the respect of the calendar. President Hansch observed in a recent lecture given to the European Policy Forum that it was difficult up to now for the national parliaments to get interested in this programme as its writing did not involve the Council.[9] The adoption on 25 October 1993 of the Interinstitutional Declaration on Democracy, Transparency and Subsidiarity should contribute to changing things, as the Council has endeavoured to make precise its position on the programme in a declaration and promised to enforce as soon as possible the measures considered as priorities. Such an evolution should ensure to the national parliaments an opportunity to discuss those priorities with the national governments.

Some consideration has also been given to the possibility of instituting a permanent presence at the side of the European Parliament of some members of the national parliaments. Such a possibility was alluded to by one of the two declarations relating to the national parliaments which have been annexed to the European

Union Treaty. Declaration 13 refers to reciprocal and appropriated facilities. This idea has not been repealed by President Hansch who evoked in his speech to the European Policy Forum the necessity to seek a solution for carrying it out.

On the other hand, President Hansch dismissed the suggestion made by the French Minister for European Affairs, Lamassoure, of participation in the national delegations to the Council of Members of National Parliaments. The reason given was that the European Union is a union of states in which the states are represented by their governments.

## *A convention of the parliaments*

The Rome Convention of the Parliaments of December 1990 was inspired by a suggestion made by President Mitterand in a declaration before the European Parliament in October 1989 and by the Spanish Prime Minister Gonzales. This suggestion was adopted and acted upon by the European Parliament not without some prior resistance.

It should be noted that the French approach aimed at the constitution of a congress. This was repealed by both the European Parliament and the presidents of the national parliaments who preferred ad hoc meetings as is clearly shown by the declaration adopted by the Conference which refers to the organisation of Conferences of the Parliaments of the European Community when justified by the discussion about the essential orientations of the Community, especially when intergovernmental conferences convene.

The French idea was later submitted by the French delegate to the Intergovernmental Conference in an informal paper proposing the meeting of the European Parliament and of the national parliaments under the form of a conference of the parliaments three times a year.[10] The Congress would have dealt with questions related to the Common Foreign and Defence Policy and to Cooperation in the Fields of Justice and Home Affairs where the European Parliament shares the democratic legitimacy with the national parliaments. It would have been in contact with the presidents of the European Council and of the Commission. The Congress would also have been consulted on the application of the principle of subsidiarity.

[10] J. Cloos, G. Reinesch, D. Vignes, J. Weyland, *Le traité de Maastricht* (Bruxelles: Bruylant, 1993) p. 407.

The opposition of the European Parliament and of most of the national parliaments to such an institution has been upheld by the strong reserves expressed by a large majority of the Member States. It has been considered as a possible aggravating factor of the separation between the various pillars of the Union and as a threat to the powers of the European institutions. The French idea has, however, not been completely ignored by the Conference as is shown by Declaration 14 but the most controversial points of the proposal have been erased. The invitation made by the Intergovernmental Conference to the Parliaments to convene together does not refer to regular meetings but provides only for meetings when their necessity is felt. The Parliamentary Conference is to be consulted on the main orientations of the European Union and the Declaration specifies that the competences of the European Parliament and the rights of the national parliaments must not be infringed. The presidents of the European Council and of the Commission are called on to present reports on the state of the Union at each session.

The Revision Conference will have to re-examine the part that such meetings could play in the machinery of the European system. Should they be institutionalised by the future Revision Treaty and, if an affirmative answer is given to that question, on what basis? Should they meet on a regular basis? What kind of matters would they be called on to discuss?

The preparation of the 1996 Revision Conference has given a new impetus to the reflection on the changes to be brought about in the European Institutional System. One of the main trends of reflections addresses the necessity of reinforcing the role played by the parliaments in this system. Special consideration is naturally given to the extension of the European Parliament's powers but the involvement of the national parliaments must also be taken into account. Beyond the possibility of bringing some improvements to the cooperation of the national assemblies with the European Parliament and to the reinforcement of their control on the national governments, the expediency of more dramatic changes to the European institutional structure through the introduction of a new institution representing the national parliaments has been given some consideration.

## *A new European Assembly representing the national parliaments?*

It is not surprising that up to now the main proposal has come from the French Parliament as it testifies to the undoubted continuity with the proposal which was made by France during the Political Union Intergovernmental Conference of 1990 in favour of a form of representation of the national parliaments in the permanent structure of the Union. The new proposal, though a remake of old projects (upheld amongst others by Alain Poher, François Mitterand and Jacques Chirac in France) which had been rejected in particular by the European Parliament in its resolution adopted on 12 July 1990 concerning the preparation of the meeting with the European Parliaments on the future of the Community,[11] represents a new step forward beyond the idea of a Joint Conference of the Parliaments.

The French Delegations for European affairs of the National Assembly[12] and of the Senate[13] have proposed the creation of new Parliamentary bodies composed of representatives of the national parliaments. The question was also raised in an article published by the former French Prime Minister Balladur.[14]

According to the views expressed in the report established by the National Assembly's Delegation, a new body called an Interparliamentary Committee composed of two or three members of each national parliament would meet every month for short sessions. It would examine prior to the intervention of the Council or of the European Parliament whether the principle of subsidiarity had been taken into account by the proposal made by the Commission. In the event of a negative answer it could adopt an exception of subsidiarity. The Committee would also vote on the decisions related to the budget, to international agreements and to the fields of Justice and Home Affairs but would be deprived of the power to amend them.

Following the Senate delegation's views, the new body would control the decisions concerning the Common Foreign and Security Policy and the Fields of Justice and Home Affairs, two pillars which, according to the report delivered by the delegation, should keep their intergovernmental features and should not be submitted to the Community decision-making process.

These proposals were presented by the delegations during the 12th meeting of the COSAC held in Paris on 27 and 28 February 1995.[15]

It would be an understatement to say that they were not

[11] JOCE no C 231, p. 165.

[12] Délégation pour l'Union européenne, Assemblée nationale, 1994–1995, Rapport Catala, Ameline, no 1939.

[13] Délégation pour l'Union européenne, Sénat, 1994–1995, Rapport Guéna, no 104.

[14] Le Monde, 30 November 1994.

[15] Assemblée nationale, Rapport d'information no 1986 (Pandraud), XIIème conférence des organismes spécialisés dans les affaires communautaires.

welcome.[16] As could be expected, the proposal of a new chamber was refused by the European Parliament's members as it challenged their will to keep and increase the European Parliament's monopoly as an embodiment of the democratic legitimacy in the European institutions. Some members have rejected the idea as a useless complication carrying a risk of impeding the efficiency of the Community decision-making process. The proposal has also been paradoxically opposed by members of national parliaments favouring the strengthening of the national parliaments as they feared the creation of a super assembly which would further isolate the national parliaments.

Beyond the wide opposition to a new chamber, the Pandraud Report following the twelfth COSAC has clearly exposed the wide range of the positions adopted by the specialised committees of the national parliaments on the issue of the part in the European Institutional Scheme which should be devolved to the national parliaments by the Revision Conference. Besides, a lot of them had not even given consideration to the issue when the COSAC met.

The president of the French National Assembly, Philippe Seguin, has also developed an argument in favour of the introduction of a bicameral scheme with a chamber representing the national parliaments. It should also be noted that Sir Leon Brittan made a reference to bicameralism in alluding to the creation of a committee of the parliaments appearing as the highest democratic institution of the European Union.

President Hansch, in his lecture of January 1995 to the European Policy Forum, strongly objected to the creation of a representation of the national parliaments. His first argument was that it would increase the complexity of an institutional structure which is already in its present state difficult to understand even by those who actively participate in its functioning. This complexity, which has precisely been at the centre of the controversies about the Maastricht Treaty, should not be reinforced by the creation of an institution which would make the decision-making process still more difficult.

President Hansch has also raised questions about the functioning of such an institution. The use of majority votes, if it were adopted, would recreate in a parliamentary context the problems met by the governments in the Council. One can also doubt the ability of the national parliaments to authorise a certain number of their members to vote in place of the parliaments as a whole.

Finally, according to President Hansch, the creation of such a

[16] Europolitique no 2021, p. I.1, Les députés français isolés sur le rôle des Parlements dans L'UE.

chamber would generate great confusion on the respective parts of the European Parliament and of the national parliaments which should be devoted to the control of their governments rather than to the control of the institutions of the Union.

• • •

At this stage of the preparation of the Revision Conference it seems impossible to make any estimate on the reforms which could be adopted. No light has been brought by the European Council of Cannes of June 1995, things do not seem to have yet matured enough to allow major openings.

The three main institutions called on to prepare the Revision Conference seem to have followed a rather flat approach. The reports worked out by the Council and the Commission have hinted at the changes to be brought to the existing texts by establishing a balance sheet of the application of the European Union Treaty. More surprisingly, the European Parliament has not, in contradiction with its well-established habit, chosen to propose in its resolution of May 1995 a political project but has drawn a catalogue of very pragmatic claims. This document, inspired by the Martin and Bourlanges Reports, examined by the Institutional Committee, draws the position of negotiation which will be upheld by the parliament during the revision process.

It should besides be noted that the meeting of the presidents of the national parliaments held in April 1995 has decided on the creation of a think group with the aim of contributing to the Revision Conference.

The different texts adopted by the European institutions do not elaborate greatly on the relations between the national parliaments and the European Parliament and do not propose fundamental changes concerning this point. In particular, the European Parliament has suggested a partnership with the national parliaments. There should be a strengthening of the cooperation between the different parliamentary committees; the specialised parliamentary committees should also be able to discuss with the ministers the main European proposals before the meetings of the Council of the European Union. The preparation of the Revision Conference will probably allow new discussions on the subject as it should undoubtedly appear among the items put on its agenda.

There is a clear consensus on the idea of strengthening the control of the national parliaments on the national governments, especially in the sphere of the Common Foreign and Security Policy. The degree which such a control requires remains open to discussions as it is strongly dependent upon national considerations. An excessively tight control could make more difficult the adoption of decision in Community matters by the Council as it would lessen the capacity of the governments linked by Parliamentary instructions to reach compromises.

There is also a fair amount of agreement on the necessity of an extension of the cooperation between the parliaments. The need for such a cooperation could be reaffirmed in a more solemn way than has been done in the European Union Treaty and could lead to intensifying the existing links.

The creation of a chamber representing the national parliaments does not seem very likely as such a creation has met very strong opposition from the European Parliament and from most of the Member States. For that reason it does not seem worthwhile to examine more closely the pros and cons of this proposal.

More consideration should on the contrary be given to the use of conventions between the European Parliament and the national parliaments which can appear as an useful way of associating the national parliaments to the evolution of the European Union and even to the conduct of European affairs. The frequency of the meetings, the content of their agendas and the nature of their functions could contribute to reducing the separation and the conflicts between the two kinds of democratic bodies or to preventing them.

A strenghtening of the COSAC, probably with a modified composition, could also be provided for. It seems that a consensus could be reached on such an idea. This should not, however, hide the eventual discrepancies which could surge from the discussions on the nature of the strengthening and which could affect the powers and the fields concerned.

These considerations must of course take into account the framework of the general evolution of the Union which should be drawn up by the Conference. The Conference will be in charge of a very difficult task as it will be deeply divided between the representatives of the States in favour of real reforms and those who do prefer the status quo and would even perhaps enjoy a step or more backwards. It will have to consider the perspective of new enlargements of the Community in the next few years which appear as a threat to the efficiency of the European machinery.

Is federalism an answer as it is sometimes considered to be? And what kind of federalism? The reference often made to national experiences does not seem very convincing as it appears more adequate to follow the specific line of the European experience which has been its permanent feature since the fifties. However, is imagination still at the helm and is there a common political will? A positive answer seems doubtful. It would be over-optimistic to hope that the outcome of the conference could be a major reform of the institutions of the European Union. Limited changes are more likely.

The main test of success will probably be the ability of the Revision Conference to organise an institutional system allowing some Member States to go forward without being hampered by the others. A Europe with different speeds seems far less dangerous than a motionless Europe.

# Democracy Between National Government and Supranationality – A Concise Exposition

*Öyvind Österud*

## Introduction

The dominant arguments for European integration have been of a functional kind. International interdependence is supposed to have undermined public governance at the national level. A solution to common problems of an economic or environmental kind is supposed to require supranational regulation and a pooling of national sovereignties, since the problems exceed the boundaries of the nation state.

On the other hand, the number one challenge to supranational integration is popular legitimation of institutions and decision-making at this level. The ratification process of the Maastricht treaty has revealed patterns of opinion which may indicate something of a backlash to the European project in many countries.

Here, I have five major comments on the question of democracy in the context of the European Union. I will briefly discuss the dilemma of size, the connection between democracy and a national community, the contending models of a European polity, the shape of the democratic deficit, and the strengths and weaknesses of alternative solutions. The remarks on each point should be seen as mere introductions to a more thorough analysis.

## The Dilemma of Size

In a modern standard account of the implications of size for democracy, Dahl and Tufte have demonstrated the ambiguity of political influence and control.[1] There are two different dimensions of the variation of influence. One is the degree of effective citizen participation, which measures individual impact on decision-making. In this respect, there is a general argument for proximity.

The other dimension is the degree of control of significant factors, which measures the capacity of the system for effective governance. Here, there is a general argument for extension and inclusiveness.

*Ceteris paribus*, citizen influence and system capacity are inversely related with respect to the size of political units. Citizen influence decreases with increasing size, while system capacity increases. There is a trade-off between changes in the two dimensions. In principle, supranational authority at the European Union level may thus imply an augmentation of system capacity, while individual citizen influence diminishes.

One important point here is that no single unit is optimal to all types of problem-solving. Any unit, short of a single individual, is too big for handling some problems; and any unit, short of a world system, is too small for handling others. Every sovereign nation state, accordingly, is too wide in some respects and too narrow in others – too wide to accommodate every need for direct civic participation, and too narrow to shield off environmental decay, for instance. A decision-making system adapted to the full variety of types of problems would require a constantly fluctuating and flexible delineation of units.

There are various pragmatic and conventional solutions to this general challenge. The solution of the sovereign territorial state is decentralisation internally, to meet demands for proximity, and cooperation within the framework of international law externally, to approach the need for inclusiveness.

The solution of the European Union, as indicated in the Maastricht treaty, is the so-called 'principle of subsidiarity'.[2] The principle aims at striking a balance between proximity to decision-making and supranational inclusiveness. This implies that the institutions of the union decide and regulate when required to do so by the common goals of the community, while authority in other respects resides with the nation state, the region or the

1 Robert A. Dahl & Edward R. Tufte, *Size and Democracy* (Stanford: Stanford University Press, 1974).

2 See the Union Treaty, especially article 3B.

municipality. However, it is the union institutions which formulate the goals of cooperation pursuant to the regulations of the treaty, and it is the EU Court which passes judgment on interpretational disputes between the EU institutions and the individual member countries. The principle of subsidiarity does not specify where control over individual issues shall lie, but opens up the way for political argument and a legal tug-of-war with the EU Court as final arbiter. The principle does not therefore provide a sufficient basis for striking a functional balance between proximity and inclusiveness, between civic participation and system capacity.

Furthermore, it should be noted that the discussion of size and democracy as outlined above is a discussion restricted to the rather technical functionality of political units in coping with various types of problems. The questions of legitimation, national identity and political fellow feeling have so far been kept out. They have a distinct relevance as prerequisites for democratic stability.

## Nation and Democracy

Conceptually and historically there is an intimate connection between nationhood and democracy. Since the French Revolution a 'nation' is precisely a sovereign people with equal rights.[3] Even if the modern idea of nationality is ambiguous, it consistently indicates a political community, however that community is conceived and established. The notion of nation-building in political science captures the features pertinent to democratic stability, because nation-building is the process of integration which supplies the necessary degree of identification and concensus for democratic institutions to survive.

We may approach the essence of nationhood by relating it to three alternative sources of group integration.[4] The alternatives should be seen as analytical categories rather than empirically distinct types. One is the functional community, bound together by a calculation of interest and a rational estimate of joint problem-solving. This is the mode of reference in Dahl and Tufte's considerations on democracy and size, and it is, as we have noted, a prominent motive in arguments for European unification.

The second alternative is the cultural community, which is bound together by some basic collective identity, common values and

[3] Cf. the comparative investigation by Leah Greenfeld: *Nationalism. Five Roads to Modernity* (Cambridge, Mass.: Harvard University Press, 1992).

[4] See James G. March & Johan P. Olsen, *Democratic Governance*, (New York: The Free Press, 1995) esp. ch. 3.

shared purpose. The cultural community is not objectively given, since the privileged cultural token is contextually contingent. In some cases religion is predominant, while language or historical legends or institutional traditions may dominate in others.

The third alternative is a political community proper, defined as integrated by decision-making procedures, political institutions and rules of the game. In this case there is procedural rather than substantive agreement. Cultural similarities may be empirical preconditions for a viable procedural order, but they are not tied to the concept by definition.

The idea of a *nation* floats on the continuous scale between a cultural and a political community, closer to one end in some areas and countries and periods, and closer to the other end under different circumstances. Here is the key to the historical ambiguity of nationhood; its vacillation between an ethno-cultural 'German' and a civic-political 'French' meaning.[5]

The nation-*state* implies a firmer institutionalisation of the procedures and the rules of the game, and it is concomitantly – at least in principle – a functional community, supposed to be a viable framework for economic and social life. Models of nation-building tend to include public welfare policies as an expression of the more advanced stages of national integration. The nation as a political community is also a distributive concensus.

These characteristics of nationhood are directly tied up with democracy. Democracy requires agreement on procedures, rules of the game and political institutions. There is also a strong requirement for tacit understanding and trust as preconditions for political compromises and longer term stability. These preconditions are exactly what is loaded into the idea of shared nationhood. Furthermore, the shared values of national identification are expressed as a distributive concensus at the level of public policy.

The last point is validated by an argument in reverse within classical 19th century liberalism. One of Lord Acton's major arguments for a culturally multinational state was that veto groups here would block a distributive concensus and assure minimal public intervention.

## Different Models of a European Polity

European integration has been driven forward according to very different models of the aims and character of the European

[5] A nearly classical account here is Friedrich Meinecke, *Weltburgertum und Nationalstaat* (Oldenburg, München & Berlin, 1908).

Community.[6] The federalist tendency favours a constitutionally fixed separation of powers between Member States and the central institutions. The idea of democracy in a federal Europe is supranational, and requires real law-making and fiscal powers vested in the European Parliament.

In the less ambitious confederal model, sovereignty is retained within the Member States and their national parliaments. Confederalism is basically cooperation within the framework of treaties bound by international law. Democracy is undisputedly national democracy.

There is also a more ambiguous functionalist model of integration. The idea here is that cooperation in functional issue areas, to the mutual benefit of Member States in solving common problems, will proceed by spill-over to increasingly tighter integration. Democracy is expressed in national parliaments, but there is a problem with democratic control as rules of decision move from a national veto to a majority vote. When sovereignty is transferred from Member States and 'pooled' in EU institutions, there is accordingly a democratic deficit.

The European Union, as outlined in the Maastricht treaty, is a hybrid between these different models. The treaty is a compromise between political conceptions of 'Europe', and the specific character of the Union is to be decided at a later stage, starting with the 1996 intergovernmental conference.

## The Democratic Deficit

The so-called 'democratic deficit' is the gap between the powers which are transferred to the EU institutions and the popularly elected EU Parliament's control over them.[7] The EU is not a federal democracy with a parliament which has legislative and budgetary powers. The gap between the authority of the EU and parliamentary control is filled by bureaucrats and experts in the adjustment committees, by representatives of the regulating institutions, and by the tug-of-war between the delegates of the national governments

6 See a.o. Alberta M. Sbragia (ed.), *Euro-Politics* (Washington, D.C.: The Brookings Institution, 1992), and Alan S. Milward, *The European Rescue of the Nation-State* (London: Routledge, 1992). Cf. the historical overview in Derek W. Unwin, *The Community of Europe. A History of European Integration Since 1945* (London: Longman, 1991).

7 See the theoretically oriented discussion in Robert Keohane & Stanley Hoffmann (eds.), *The New European Community* (Boulder, Colorado: Westview Press, 1991).

and the organised lobby groups.

The conventional answer to the problem of democracy in the EU has been to give greater decision-making authority to the popularly elected EU Parliament. The Parliament is the institutional key to a European federal state. A strong EU Parliament will undoubtedly imply a reduction in the power of the Member States. Both through apportionment of representatives and decision-making procedures, the small states especially will experience a considerably weaker position than they do in the Union Council today.

Stronger federalisation of the EU, with greater power to the EU Parliament, will probably also reveal – or provoke – sharper antagonisms between the member countries, and might thus impede the process of integration.

Federalisation, with a determinative European Parliament, might be an inadequate institutional way of solving a deeper structural problem.[8] In terms of public debate, political identification and articulation of interests, Europe is still fragmented into national units. The mass media are still split into national segments. The multitude of languages prevent a joint discussion and a focused political debate. Geographical distance and the variety of cultural traditions are barriers to popular opinion formation and mobilization of interest across national borders. A supranational European democracy would not be based on what the Germans call a *Staatsvolk* or the French call a *nation*. Against this structural plurality, a process of federalisation at the top level would imply a deeper split between a Europeanised élite and a multitude of sub-European masses. Here is the seed of a political backlash which had already surfaced in many countries during the process of ratification of the Maastricht treaty.

There still does not exist, in short, a European *demos* which could sustain a living democracy or a viable 'republic' at the supranational level. Beyond an unspecified and contextually variable stage, European integration faces a problem of popular legitimation, in contrast to the functionalist arguments enlisted by the committed Europeans.

## The Potential Solutions

One obvious solution would be to adapt the institutional framework to the structural fragmentation of Europe; that is to freeze the con-

[8] Further in Öyvind Österud, 'Antinomies of Supra-National State-Building. Centralization, sovereignty and democracy in the EU' (Department of Political Science, University of Oslo: Working Paper 07/94, 1994).

federal model into an intergovernmental structure. This was the Gaullist spirit of the Luxembourg compromise in the 1960s, and today it is most consistently voiced from within the British government. Democratic legitimation would unambiguously be tied up with the national parliaments, and no acute democratic deficit would deligitimise the cooperative effort because the framework would be international law rather than a pool of sovereignties.

Jacques Chirac, French president since May 1995, has, among others, suggested that the European Parliament might be supplied with a second chamber of representatives from the various national assemblies, to strengthen the influence of nationally elected parlamentarians at the union level. Such a reform could, however, work both ways. It would open up a channel directly from the Member State parliaments, but it could also decouple these representatives from their constituencies. It would certainly formalise the federal structure of the union and might as well legitimise a further transfer of powers to the new two-chamber parliament.

Another solution is the quest for squaring the cultural fragmentation of Europe with some sort of *constitutional patriotism* at the supranational level.[9] This conception was developed within the democratic left of West Germany in the post-war period, in order to move German identities away from the compromised cultural-historical tribalism, towards a universalism tied up with principles of equality, democracy and human rights. At the European level, this conception involves a split between cultural and political affiliations: supranationality for functional reasons by joint problem-solving, and a 'Europe of regions and nationalities' below the overall institutional framework.

It is highly doubtful whether *Verfassungspatriotismus* became a basis for identity formation in the German Federal Republic. The precarious and problematic question of German identity resurfaced with the process of reunification from 1989, and the liberal spokesmen for constitutional patriotism felt, accordingly, uneasy about the whole project of a reunified Germany. At the European level, the whole conception is even more ethereal, as indicated not only by the notable perseverance of fragmented public spheres in Europe, but even more by the lack of popular enthusiasm for the Maastricht process.

Finally, there is an ambitious solution which envisages real European nation-building, to adapt cultural identities to the functionalist project. Identity politics are played out in the

9 Cf. the chapters on citizenship and national identity in Jürgen Habermas, *Faktizität und Geltung* (Frankfurt am Main: Suhrkamp, 1992).

construction of symbols, myth-making and moulding of historical consciousness, mediated by strategic efforts in sports, cultural events and education.

This programmatical Europeanism also faces quite high structural barriers. The fragmentation of languages, legal traditions, geopolitical forces and cultural areas make the 'European nation' a far cry from present realities. Therefore, the social preconditions for a democratic and stable federation still seem quite remote.

## Conclusion

Under present circumstances, the problems of democracy and legitimation would increase through more power to the European Parliament, rather than be reduced. The conventional institutional solution to the democratic deficit would thus be counterproductive. A strengthening of the role of national parliaments would, on the other hand, run counter to supranational trends and indications in the Maastricht treaty.

In this way, there is an inherent contradiction in the institutional development of European unification, with a *trade-off* between decision-making efficiency and democratic legitimation. Efficiency may point towards centralisation and majority voting, while legitimation is bound up with political communities and institutions at the national level.

# Index